D1564798

*Cognitive Therapy
with Schizophrenic Patients*

# Cognitive Therapy with Schizophrenic Patients

**Carlo Perris, MD**

*Umeå University
and WHO Collaborating Centre for
Research and Training in Mental Health*

**The Guilford Press**
**New York   London**

© 1989 The Guilford Press
A Division of Guilford Publications, Inc.
72 Spring Street, New York, NY 10012

Printed in the United States of America

Last digit is print number: 9 8 7 6 5 4 3 2 1

Library of Congress Cataloging-in-Publication Data

Perris, Carlo.
    Cognitive therapy with schizophrenic patients / Carlo Perris.
        p.  cm.
    Bibliography: p.
    Includes index.
    ISBN 0-89862-737-0
    1. Schizophrenia—Treatment.  2. Cognitive therapy.  I. Title.
    [DNLM: 1. Cognition.  2. Psychotherapy—methods.
    3. Schizophrenia—therapy.  WM 203 P458c]
    RC514.P44 1989
    616.89′8206—dc 19
    DNLM/DLC
    for Library of Congress                                          88-24467
                                                                          CIP

*To my wife and my children*

# *Preface*

When, in the early 1950s, I began my first appointment as a psychiatrist in a mental hospital (that is, before the introduction of neuroleptics), I was in charge of a few male wards. In one of them, which I visited every morning, there was a patient who had not left his bed for some years. He sat with the sheets drawn over his head, actively refusing any form of contact. He just accepted his bowl of food, which he ate in privacy, throwing away the bowl when he was finished. Defying the opinion of the nurses who followed me on my round, I would sit for a while on this patient's bed, trying to communicate with him despite his stubborn mutism and his opposition to letting me even lift the sheets.

One day, more than a year later, I found to my surprise that he had left his bed and was talking to the other patients. When I approached, he took my hand and said, "You are that doctor who talked to me all this time." To my even greater surprise, he then repeated some of the things I had told him during the year. His speech was still impaired, but I received a most impressive lesson that I have never forgotten: Never believe that even the most sick psychotic patient is inaccessible to human communication.

This patient later improved on psychotropic drugs and was sent home, but the lesson he taught me has remained with me for all my years in psychiatry.

Being trained in an eclectic school (at a time that neurology and psychiatry were still combined in Italy, my country of origin), I learned to take into account both the biological aspects of the mental disorders and the interpersonal approach based on the early work of Frieda Fromm-Reichmann. Later on, a too-short stay with Ludwig Binswanger strongly contributed to strengthening my opinion of the importance of the relationship between doctor and patient. During the years I have spent working in different hospitals and with all kinds of patients, I have not encountered a situation that has contradicted my original lesson.

The introduction of psychotropic drugs made the treatment of severe psychotic disorders not only possible, but also relatively easy. At the same time, I have been unable to feel attracted by a psychoanalytical approach to the patient suffering from a schizophrenic syndrome, mainly because the results claimed in psychoanalytical quarters have been difficult to evaluate in a clear-cut way. In addition, most of those results hardly concern the kind of low-socioeconomic, generally unskilled patients of whom I have been in charge.

Frequent contact with the late Silvano Arieti, with whom I taught junior residents in Italy, made me aware of the relevance of a cognitive approach to patients with schizophrenic disorders. From those occasions in the 1970s, the step to the application of the cognitive therapeutic approach developed by Aaron Beck has been very short indeed. When I began with this approach, however, virtually nothing had been written on the feasibility of cognitive psychotherapy for the long-term treatment of severely disturbed patients in a psychotic or postpsychotic condition.

This book arose from this failure to find in the available literature a comprehensive account of the applicability of cognitive psychotherapy with patients with schizophrenic disorders. It is an extension of a few short articles and conference reports, which I used as a first step in structuring my ideas and my experiences of working with this type of patient. It has grown to a chapter of some length for a handbook of cognitive psychotherapy, now in press, and later to a book that has been published in Swedish. The encouraging responses to my articles, seminars, and teaching on this subject—plus the progress I see in patients treated at the centers described in this book—have stimulated me to revise and expand the Swedish edition and prepare this present English one for a larger audience.

The present book formally treats the use of cognitive psychotherapy, both as a part of a holistic, cognitive–behavioral program implemented at small, community-based treatment centers and as individual therapy with relatively young patients suffering from a schizophrenic disorder.

Another reason for writing this book is to further the understanding of schizophrenic patients beyond the reductionistic approach (biological, psychoanalytical, or social) that all too often characterizes the polarized debates in the literature. It is my firm conviction, established during my long practice, that every attempt to treat patients with schizophrenic syndromes exclusively on the basis of faulty biochemistry, abnormal intrapsychic processes, or dysfunctional family relationships can be compared with the story of the five blind men who went "to look at an elephant." On returning, each described the elephant in terms of the particular part he was able to feel from the position where he stood. All of them were right in what they reported, but all were also wrong because they had not seen the elephant as a whole.

The diagnosis of schizophrenia is still controversial, and those who maintain that it is misused are certainly correct. On the other hand, little assistance is given to the thousands of patients suffering from this disorder by dismissing it as a myth or as a product of a conspiratorial society, as has occasionally been suggested.

To arrive at a better understanding of schizophrenic disorders and to develop a meaningful program of treatment are the primary goals of psychiatry both for the suffering that schizophrenia causes to thousands of people and to their families and for the costs to society.

Psychiatric care is now in a phase of reorganization in most of the industrialized world. It is becoming increasingly clear that a majority of the patients who earlier were admitted to mental hospitals can, in fact, remain in the community where they can be helped to attain their independence. Psychiatric care, however, has been slow to develop alternative methods to prepare the patient for a life outside the institution.

One such alternative is treated in this book. By way of introduction, a theoretical framework is presented that takes into account the interplay of cultural, social, biological, and psychological factors in the growth of psychopathological disorders. It focuses also on the route by which processes at different levels are converted into psychopathological manifestations in the individual. Further, this framework provides an overall view of the occurrence of schizophrenic disorders and their treatment while drawing attention to the various factors that cause the disorder to manifest itself differently in different patients. In accordance with this viewpoint—which is becoming generally accepted in anthropology, social psychology, clinical psychology, psychiatry, and psychoanalysis—one may identify these factors as disturbances in cognitive processes, especially in the collection and processing of information. This point of focus not only avoids reductionism, but it also indicates specific therapeutic directions by which efforts may be made to correct as many of the prevailing faults as possible.

Because of its optimistic and humanistic attributes, cognitive psychotherapy has become a well-established method of treatment in many areas. It is optimistic because it offers the patient the possibility of change by exploiting his or her own capabilities; it is humanistic because it provides the patient with hope that he or she may be able to exert at least a certain degree of control over his or her own future. These are the characteristics of cognitive psychotherapy that I particularly wish to emphasize, since it may be difficult to discover them among the more technical descriptions that follow. Among other things, it is the atmosphere of humane contact, provided by the attitudes of the therapist, that sustains the patient's motivation to work at his or her problems, even in difficult phases. At the same time, the therapist is enriched by encounters with every new patient. Also, the flexibility of cognitive therapy allows it to be used at different levels, depending on the needs and resources of the individual patient.

Although this book gives priority to the more specific therapeutic work, other aspects of a comprehensive program of treatment are also considered. This wider discussion has been included because most of the patients for whom the treatment is described have never been given the opportunity to acquire (or they have lost) many of the social skills that are self-evident for most of us. If these patients are to lead a fulfilling and independent life in the community, treatment must be holistic and multifaceted.

In the end, a book is the result of one person's endeavors. Nevertheless, during its preparation, the support that the author receives from others is immeasurable as well as invaluable. Unfortunately, I am unable to name all those who have, in one way or another, been sources of inspiration; such a list would include the numerous patients I have met over a period of many years. There are, however, a few others who deserve special thanks. My wife, Hjördis, an Associate Professor of medical psychology and herself responsible for one of our cognitive treatment centers for several years, has read various preliminary drafts of the manuscript and, through our discussions, has given me the opportunity to structure the material. My supervision of the staff at the two centers described in the book has provided me with invaluable feedback, which has been continuously refueled by contact with the patients at the centers. Paul Matussek MD, PhD, Professor of Psychotherapy in Munich, and my friend Lars-Gunnar Lundh, PhD, have willingly read preliminary versions of the manuscript and have given me invaluable encouragement and support. Michael Sharp, PhD, has skillfully translated into English the Swedish version of the book, which has served for this expanded and revised edition. Doris Cedergren has, as always, been invaluable in getting me copies of most of the articles needed for the preparation of the manuscript and in the final preparation of the list of references. The production of the book has depended on the skill of many people among the staff at Guilford Press, to whom I am most grateful; to collaborate with Seymour Weingarten, Editor-in-Chief, and with Pearl Weisinger, Production Editor, has been for me one of the most pleasurable publishing experiences.

# Contents

# I

# *Theoretical Issues*

# 1
# *Introduction*

There can be little doubt that the treatment of patients suffering from mental disorders in general and from "schizophrenia" in particular depends not only on immediate therapeutic goals but also, and to a greater extent, on the beliefs of the psychiatrist. For example, if schizophrenia is seen, as it was occasionally during the early 1970s, as a "lifestyle," then no effort will be made to find suitable treatment. Similarly, if schizophrenic disorders are assumed to have an irrevocably progressive, deteriorating course with a malignant final outcome, then such a belief will inevitably affect the setting of goals for treatment.

## THE CONCEPT OF "SCHIZOPHRENIA"

The concept of schizophrenia is still controversial. Almost 80 years after its introduction in the psychiatric terminology by E. Bleuler (1908), few authors completely neglect to include some short historical account of schizophrenia or to discuss the difficulties in reaching unanimous consensus on its true meaning. In addition, special articles in which authors of different theoretical orientations attempt to define "schizophrenia" still frequently appear in major psychiatric journals (e.g., Andreasen, 1987; M. Bleuler, 1979; Carpenter, 1987; Meltzer & Liberman, 1982; Snyder, Kety, & Goldstein, 1982; van Praag, 1976).

It is generally acknowledged that both Kraepelin (1896) and E. Bleuler (1908) regarded their conceptions of dementia praecox and of schizophrenic psychoses, respectively, as preliminary attempts to summarize clinical experiences without any pretense of describing a single disease with some consistent etiology. However, although Bleuler was quite explicit about the heterogeneity of schizophrenia, a tendency to regard schizophrenia as a unitary disease has been dominant in the psychiatric literature for a long time, side by side with an all-encompassing conception of manic depressive psychosis. Consequently, attempts at identifying other disorders distinct from the two major ones have been considered with skepticism. For example, Kasanin's conception of acute schizoaffective psychosis (Kasanin, 1933) was quickly included among the subtypes of schizophrenia, whereas Leonhard's efforts at delimiting other groups of disorders besides the schizophrenic and the manic depressive have been neglected. (Leonhard, 1957, 1975).

More recently, some agreement has occurred in regarding schizophrenic disorders as a heterogeneous group of morbid conditions still in need of being identified more exactly. Put in other words, it is currently assumed that "schizophrenia" is a name that covers a multitude of diverse clinical pictures and processes. However, although most authors seem to accept this view, this insight is easily forgotten, by biologically and psychoanalytically oriented authors alike, as soon as they discuss treatment or possible causative factors. A further common practice is that, all too often, single factors are given decisive importance. Similar misconceptions arise when, as is often the case in the psychoanalytical or psychodynamic literature, the terms "psychosis" and "psychotic disturbance" are used indiscriminately to define schizophrenic disorders, although not all psychotics are schizophrenic and not all schizophrenic patients are consistently psychotic.

Naturally, there are many exceptions to these views. One example is Schulz (1975), who, in an account of his psychotherapeutic approach to schizophrenic patients, used a title similar to that of my book. Though somewhat cumbersome, this title attempts to convey several simple messages. The first is that psychiatrists, with their present knowledge, can only discuss schizophrenic *syndromes*. Not even these are homogeneous, and their causes and outcomes are highly individual. We know that some patients will not respond significantly to any treatment at all, while others show a very favorable outcome; however, we do not have safe criteria with which to distinguish beforehand those patients who will become chronic schizophrenics and deteriorate from those who will, in the main, make a full recovery. Also, the word "with" in the subtitle serves to emphasize that all psychotherapy is undertaken *with* the patient as the most important collaborator. This emphasis is particularly relevant in cognitive psychotherapy in which the patient is always regarded as a true partner in the therapeutic work rather than as an individual to be analyzed. Also implicit in any assumption about the heterogeneity of schizophrenic disorders is that therapeutic approaches and goals have to be strictly individualized.

## DIAGNOSTIC APPROACHES

Bleuler attempted to refine Kraepelin's concept of dementia praecox by emphasizing cross-sectional phenomenology as more important than course and outcome and by introducing the concept of "latent schizophrenia." An unforeseen negative consequence of Blueler's work has been the enormous broadening of the boundaries of the concept; "schizophrenia" was much more narrowly defined within the Kraepelinian system. Furthermore, as Andreasen (1987) pointed out, clinicians and researchers have concurred that the concept has often become so ill-defined that it is almost meaningless, impairing both the selection of treatment and the conduct of research (p. 12).

One major obstacle to unanimous definition of the schizophrenic syndrome(s) is the lack of pathognomonic features, easily assessed, consistently present in each patient who receives this diagnosis. Van Praag (1976) emphasized that both Kraepelin and Bleuler showed little finesse in operationalizing the diagnostic criteria for schizophrenia and underscored that several of the symptoms that they deemed characteristic cannot be diagnosed without a fair amount of subjective interpretation. One early attempt to describe symptoms pathognomonic for schizophrenia was made by Schneider (1959). He described 11 first-rank symptoms and maintained that the presence of any of them was sufficient to warrant a diagnosis of schizophrenia, unless gross organic abnormalities were present in the brain. Although Schneider's opinion has been very influential, especially in European diagnostic practice, more recent investigations have cast some doubt on the specificity of the first-rank symptoms and, more importantly, on their consistent occurrence in patients regarded as schizophrenic (Carpenter, Strauss, & Muleh, 1973; Marneros, 1984a, 1984b). Other clinicians, on the other hand, seem to have relied more on symptoms that are difficult to objectify and in particular on those reflecting the patient's inability to enter an affective relationship with another person, thus showing a lack of "affective resonance." One well-known proponent of such an approach to diagnosis has been Rumke (1967), who emphasized the importance of the feeling that the patient evokes in the diagnostician, which he called "Praecox Gefühle" (praecox feeling). Apparently, this approach has not completely lost its appeal since it has been reproposed by the psychoanalyst Pao (1975), who, apparently, was unaware of its previous use in the psychiatric literature.

With the context of increasing awareness about the low reliability of diagnoses based on routine clinical evaluation and about the complexity of diagnostic issues in general, modern efforts focused on the development of sets of operationalized diagnostic criteria that are relatively easy to apply and should greatly improve the reliability of diagnostic judgments. Eventually, several comparable sets of criteria for schizophrenia were developed, constituting the bases from which the DSM-III (American Psychiatric Association, 1980) was developed. Since studies of the comparability of these diagnostic criteria are easily accessible (e.g., Brockington, Kendell, & Leff, 1978; Fenton, Mosher, &

Matthews, 1981; Haier, 1980; Kendell, Brockington, & Leff, 1979; NcGlashan, 1984), they are not reviewed in detail here. However, it is important to discuss some of the conclusions reached by the authors of these studies. First of all, concordance among the different criteria, however statistically significant, is far from perfect, suggesting that each of them only defines partially overlapping groups and that no objective criteria could precisely map the clinical population of schizophrenia. Second, none of the systems (including those discussed in DSM-III) taken into account by Fenton *et al.* (1981) proved to have any established construct validity. Third, it seems that available criteria are more able to predict a poor than a favorable outcome. This last point is particularly relevant for DSM-III since Spitzer, Andreasen, and Endicott (1978) emphasized that one of the aims in developing the criteria of schizophrenia was to "limit the concept so that it is not applied to individuals who are likely to return to an adequate premorbid level of adjustment" (p. 490).

Despite their shortcomings, the most thoroughly investigated diagnostic criteria are undoubtedly more reliable than routine clinical diagnosis, especially when trying to clearly define the specific population of patients used for research or treatment purposes. Since I am a proponent of a clear-cut separation of cycloid psychotic disorders from schizophrenic disorders (C. Perris, 1974, 1986a), thus excluding most of the patients who might be classified as suffering from a "schizophreniform disorder" or "atypical psychosis" according to DSM-III, the patients to which the treatment described in this book refers largely correspond to the definition given originally in DSM-III and presently refined in DSM-III-R (American Psychiatric Association, 1987).

## THE OUTCOME OF
## SCHIZOPHRENIC DISORDERS

One fundamental prerequisite of any evaluation of treatment results is a thorough knowledge of the natural course and outcome of the disorder to be treated. However, as already mentioned, we have not yet been able to identify any factor or group of factors that safely predict whether the schizophrenic syndrome shown by a particular patient will completely respond to treatment or will take a chronic course. Thus, in evaluating the scope of treatment outcome, we have to rely on what is known about the course of schizophrenic syndromes in general. I have published elsewhere (C. Perris, 1981a) a comprehensive review of studies concerned with the course of schizophrenic syndromes and I was able to reach certain important conclusions. First of all, however, it is important to clarify a commonly occurring misunderstanding, which has been already pointed out in the World Health Organization's International Pilot Study of Schizophrenia (IPSS, 1973). It is frequently believed that Kraepelin had a totally pessimistic view of the outcome of dementia praecox while Bleuler is credited with an emphasis on possible favorable outcomes. Actually, Kraepelin himself found that a certain number of his cases (about 15%) recovered. Bleuler did stress that "restitutium ad integrum" is probably never reached; however, this statement should be understood to mean that the experience of having gone through a psychotic disorder becomes an integral part of the patient's world of experiences. Thus, the person who has suffered from such a disorder can never return to exactly the same condition as prior to its occurrence.

Follow-up studies covered in my review (C. Perris, 1981a) show a wide disparity of results. However, three major long-term studies (M. Bleuler, 1972; Ciompi & Müller, 1976; Huber, Gross, & Schüttler, 1975) concur in finding that about 25% of patients made a complete recovery in the long run.

Particularly important is the possible occurrence of a spontaneous recovery late in the course of the disorder, a fact emphasized by both Huber and colleagues and by Bleuler. Huber *et al.* wrote of a "second positive break" ("zweiter positiver Knick") and specified that it occurs without any direct relation to pharmacological treatment. Another finding of interest, reported by Bleuler, who compared the results of his study with those obtained in an earlier one, is the almost complete disappearance of cases progressing very rapidly toward deterioration by the time of the first acute episode. These two findings are undoubtedly relevant for a correct evaluation of the effects of long-term psychotherapy and especially psychoanalysis, which may stretch over several years.

There is no doubt that the findings of these studies convey a feeling of hope, which is of paramount importance to patients and their families. However, the results should still be taken cautiously. Neither Bleuler nor the Bonn Group distinguished cycloid psychotic disorders from the schizophrenic disorders, and in the study by Ciompi and Müller, the 25% of patients who had made a recovery had shown a recurrent course and, thus, may have been cycloids. More recently, Armbruster, Gross, and Huber (1983) reclassified 107 of their original 449 schizophrenics as cycloid psychotics according to Perris's definition (C. Perris, 1984) and pointed out that 45% of them made a complete recovery. Also, none of the studies just reported distinguished schizophreniform disorders from other types of schizophrenic disorders. Ciompi (1980) reported that 10% of his patients had suffered from only one episode. However, he did not state whether this finding included only patients who made a complete recovery or if it also included patients who showed a chronic course. Finally, it should be pointed out that the findings by Ciompi and Müller and those by Bleuler have been criticized on methodological grounds by Shepherd and his coworkers (Watt, Katz, & Shepherd, 1983).

An important variable to take into account when evaluating recovery rates is the possible occurrence of a premorbid deviant personality makeup not necessarily related to the schizophrenic syndrome. M. Bleuler (1972), for example, made a distinction between a premorbid personality, "pronounced schizoid but within the norm" (observed in 28% of his patients), and "morbid schizoid" (24%). It is unclear to what extent deviant personality characteristics correspond to those of "schizotypal personality disorder" in DSM-III and to what extent they are associated with the manifest psychotic disorder. If personality characteristics of this type are preexistent and independent of the schizophrenic disorder, a complete recovery from the latter can be easily misinterpreted and regarded as only partial.

# 2

# *A Heuristic Frame of Reference for Psychopathology*

A discussion of the causes of mental disease is of crucial importance in a book devoted to a special type of treatment because the stance that one takes on this issue is likely to influence one's choice and conduct of treatment. Thus, a general frame of reference for the study of psychopathological conditions is provided here. The presentation of this frame of reference, upon which general attitudes to both patients and research work have been based for many years, is also intended to provide the reader with a better understanding of the method of treatment that is described in detail in this book.

## A DYNAMIC INTERACTIONAL FRAMEWORK

For several years, my coworkers and I have adopted a critical attitude to all reductionistic attempts to explain the occurrence of most mental disorders—especially the major psychotic ones—in terms of simple, linear, causative relationships (Perris, 1981b; C. Perris & H. Perris, 1985). We have instead recommended that a more holistic approach to the understanding of mental disturbances and to the choice of treatment be used. This approach is based on a comprehensive framework that takes into account not only the interactions among biological, psychological, social, and cultural factors that affect the susceptibility of an individual to psychopathological disorders but also the continuous interplay between the vulnerable individual and the environment (Eisemann, 1985; C. Perris, 1981b, 1985a; H. Perris, 1982a). Of course, this proposal is by no means unique. On the contrary, it accords well with opinions that are becoming increasingly accepted in psychiatry, especially in studies of schizophrenic syndromes (e.g., M. Bleuler, 1979; Gottesman & Shields, 1971; Zubin & Spring, 1977), but not limited to these disorders (e.g., Marsella, 1987). These opinions can be traced back to the thesis defended by Meyer (1958).

A schematic diagram of the model on which our opinions are based is shown in Figure 2-1. As can be seen in this figure, the emphasis is no longer the clinical syndrome itself, but on the concept of

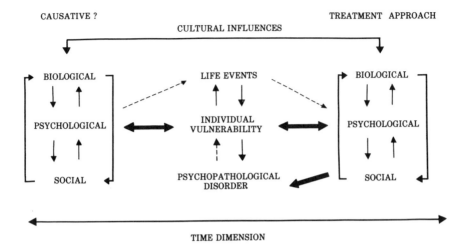

FIGURE 2-1. This interactional framework for the study of psychopathological manifestations and their treatment focuses on "individual vulnerability." The possible impact of stressful as well as buffering life events is shown in its proper context. The indication of a time course implies that individual vulnerability is not a static condition.

individual susceptibility or individual vulnerability, which is more decisive and the real nucleus of all psychopathology.

The arrows shown in Figure 2-1 indicate that interactions are assumed to exist both between those variables on the left-hand side of the diagram and between those on the right-hand side. Such interactions are of decisive importance for both the occurrence and the treatment of mental disorders. With regard to possible etiological factors, for example, it is important to emphasize that the concept of interaction implies something completely different from a simple addition of potentially causative factors. In fact, it is well known from other research fields, for instance, pharmacology, that the interaction between two or more drugs often produces effects that are completely different from those expected when only straightforward additions are assumed. Known instances of pharmacological interactions include potentialization and neutralization of specific effects. Obviously, both possible potentialization and possible neutralization of noxious effects can be taken into account in this model.

It should further be emphasized that the importance of interactive processes is not limited to the interplay between the factors belonging to the different realms indicated in the figure. The interaction encompasses, to an exceptionally high degree, the continuing dialectical transactions between the (vulnerable) person on the one hand and the (immediate and larger) environment—especially the situation in which the individual presents—on the other. A time dimension is also represented in the diagram. In fact, because of the assumed dialectical intercourse taken into account in the situation, "vulnerability" cannot be regarded as a static, unaltering condition; rather, it changes continuously throughout a person's lifetime. This change has been particularly stressed by developmental psychologists (e.g., Magnusson, 1983; Magnusson & Allen, 1982; Sameroff, 1975) and in the field of psychopathology (Erlenmeyer-Kimling, 1979) with particular reference to the interaction of hereditary and environmental factors for the occurrence of depressive disorders. In particular, Erlenmeyer-Kimling maintains that vulnerability at each specific point of time in a person's life reflects an accumulated feedback relationship that has developed between the individual's genetic predisposition and his or her complete life history. Results obtained in depressed patients (C. Perris, H. Perris, & Eisemann, 1987), which will be summarized presently, are consistent with Erlenmeyer-Kimling's assumption.

Gottesman and Shields (1971) pointed out that a diathesis–stressor model fills the chasm between geneticism and environmentalism and stressed the importance of feedback loops and chance. In particular, Gottesman and Shields maintained that their assumption may help clarify "how psychotherapy or phenothiazines or a good mother may each contribute to symptom amelioration without necessarily casting light on etiological questions" (p. 521). Brody (1981) considered vulnerability in persons who develop schizophrenic syndromes to be the result of transactions between the individuals and their environments during their entire lives but particularly during their childhoods and early teens.

Another important point is that relevant interactions may have occurred long before the actual mental disorder manifests itself. Since vital complex interactions may not be immediately connected with the onset of the disturbance, they may be difficult to discover. Consequently, interactive processes must always be conceived in a time perspective and as an essential part of the development of the individual. An example taken from studies of depressive disorders serves to illustrate this last point.

In a series of investigations, my coworkers and I have observed, in agreement with many others, a higher risk for depressive disorders among the first-degree relatives of depressed patients than in the general population (C. Perris, 1966; C. Perris, H. Perris, Ericsson, & von Knorring, 1982). This finding is normally interpreted as supporting the assumption that hereditary factors are of importance for the occurrence of depressive disorders; however, other factors cannot be excluded and may be at least as important. Among these factors is the relationship that the patient had with his or her parents during childhood and adolescence. Several investigations that my coworkers and I completed as part of a larger international project support the assumption that the depressed patient has experienced his or her parents as lacking in emotional warmth and even as being rejecting (C. Perris, Maj, H. Perris, & Eisemann, 1985; C. Perris, Arrindell, H. Perris, Eisemann, van der Ende, & von Knorring, 1986). What is of interest in this context is that this feeling of an emotionally cold parental attitude has been observed significantly more often in patients with one sick parent than in those whose parents were both in good mental health. It is thus reasonable to assume that mental disorders in a parent may also play an important part in determining the kind of relationship this parent establishes with a child. Hence, both factors—heredity and environment—interact in the development of vulnerability.

An indirect measure of increased vulnerability is obtained by considering the age at which a disorder first occurs. It has long been recognized that depressive disorders arise earlier in patients with a more pronounced hereditary trait, and this finding has commonly been interpreted as reflecting the strength of the hereditary component. Our studies have shown, however, that the age at which a depressive syndrome occurs is significantly lower in patients who present a family loading with affective disorders and who have been exposed to dysfunctional parental rearing attitudes than in those who only present a family loading (C. Perris *et al.*, 1987).

Hence, the concept of interaction together with recognition of individual vulnerability allows the significance of "life events" to be brought into proper perspective. It is a common finding that similar life events do not affect all people to the same extent, and it can be easily assumed that many stressful situations do not occur by chance but result from the interplay between a certain individual and the environment. A person who has developed an aggressive attitude comes much more easily into destructive conflicts than does a person with a different type of personality makeup (H. Perris, 1984). Again, according to Erlenmeyer-Kimling (1979), one may assent that different people deal differently with different situations. However, even in this context, both a time perspective and the individual's situation should always be taken into account.

The concept of interaction is of especially great importance with regard to treatment and cannot be reduced to the possible result of simultaneous administration of different medicines. A number of investigations have shown the occurrence of both positive and negative interactions between psychotropic drugs and psychotherapy (Beitman

& Klerman, 1984; Karasu, 1982) as well as interactions between those factors and social factors, which have been extensively reported for patients suffering from schizophrenia (Falloon & Liberman, 1983; Hogarty & Goldberg, 1973/1974; Leff & Vaughn, 1981; Leff *et al.*, 1982; Wing, 1978). However, this possible occurrence of positive or negative interactive effects is not restricted to the different methods of treatment, which are considered in the right-hand side of Figure 2-1; there is also a possible interaction between treatments and the specific vulnerability of the individual. For example, such highly individual or idiosyncratic reactions to drug treatment as oversensitivity or late side effects (e.g., McCreadie, Crorie, Barron, & Winslow, 1982) may arise to a certain extent. An individual tendency to temporarily respond favorably to a culturally accepted type of treatment should also be included in this context.

In many respects, our frame of reference can be considered to be "holistic," that is, focused on a global approach, in the sense in which this term is used in Karen Horney's school of psychoanalysis. According to the holistic principle, the individual is considered to be an integrated entity who acts, interacts, and is affected by the environment as well as his or her internal processes (Rubins, 1969).

The distinguishing feature of our frame of reference, as compared with other traditional models in psychiatry, is clearly seen by comparing the diagram shown in Figure 2-1 with those in Figure 2-2. Apart from those that consider only simple causal relations or those that regard schizophrenia to be precisely defined, it can be seen that even the relationship shown at the bottom of Figure 2-2 (which many readers are probably conscious of in their daily clinical work) is unidirectional. It takes into account the possible heterogeneity of schizophrenia and points to the possible relevance of different causative factors, but it clearly omits the role of the individual in determining the nature of his or her own experiences.

## THE CONCEPT OF
## INDIVIDUAL VULNERABILITY

It is important to define "individual vulnerability" more precisely. This idea is not new in the psychiatric literature; it can be regarded as a modern reformulation of the older term "diathesis" (predisposition toward disease or abnormality), which was employed in medicine by Greek and Roman doctors.

The term "vulnerability" has been widely known in the psychoanalytical literature ever since Sigmund Freud (1905a) used the word "Ergänzungsreihe" (complementary lines) to explain the con-

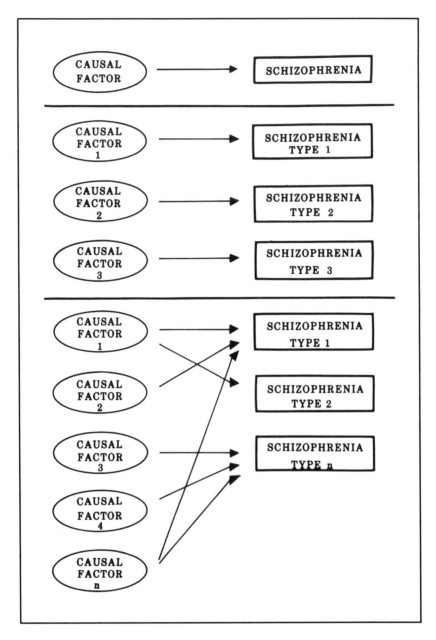

FIGURE 2-2. These different etiological models of "schizophrenia" range from one that takes into account a single causal factor responsible for a "unitary" disorder to a more current model that considers the relevance of different necessary and sufficient causal factors for the development of different schizophrenic syndromes.

nection between constitutional and temporary coincidental factors in the development of neuroses; it has also been extensively used in biological psychiatry in the studies of high-risk groups that are in progress in many centers (for a recent survey, see *Schizophrenia Bulletin, 13*, 3, 1987).

To a certain extent our concept of vulnerability is related to the concept of "Anlage" (predisposition) as used by Jaspers (1913), who stressed that all psychopathological phenomena results from hereditary Anlage and environmental influence. Jaspers drew two important conclusions from his assertion. First, even disorders that depend on hereditary factors require certain environmental conditions for their manifestation, and, on the other hand, all environmental influences require a certain Anlage to be effective. Jaspers also felt that, even in the case of unequivocal hereditary disturbances, the hereditary Anlage manifests itself within certain limits that differ in different individuals, and do not, therefore, constitute an inescapable fate. A conception similar to that of Jaspers has more recently been expressed by Anastasi (1958) in the context of human development. Anastasi maintained that there would be no one in an environment without heredity, and, in turn, there would be no place to see the effects of heredity without an environment.

While a number of modern researchers focus exclusively on heredity in their definition of individual vulnerability, and while psychoanalytical authors attempt to define vulnerability mainly in psychological terms, the approach my coworkers and I use expressly draws attention to a continuing interaction between the individual and various factors during the development of the "individual vulnerability."

To the extent that genetic factors are judged to be of importance for the occurrence of schizophrenic disorders (and there is sufficient evidence to assume that this is the case, at least for subgroups of patients), our conception of vulnerability (Figure 2-2) comes close to that proposed by Cancro (1979) in a recently published review of genetic studies of the schizophrenic syndrome. Cancro pointed out, quite correctly, that such a complex phenotype as a schizophrenic syndrome can hardly be considered to be transferred directly from generation to generation. At present, it is widely believed that what is transmitted may be a vulnerability or weakness in some particular, not yet identified, biological system, which comprises a genetic abnormality.

However, Cancro suggested that an alternative conception of vulnerability should be taken into consideration. In this conception, the transmitted trait need not be seen as anything other than a factor that determines the *type* of schizophrenic syndrome that results when an individual succumbs to the illness. Cancro's discussion of vulnerability is particularly interesting because of the conclusions that may be drawn from it. He terminates his review by emphasizing that different gene–environment combinations can lead to the phenotype or pheno- types that are necessary, but not sufficient, for the occurrence of the schizophrenic syndrome; this implies that different etiological routes are available by which the syndrome can develop. If this argument is accepted (as it is by many contemporary researchers), the search for a unitary etiology can hardly be productive since there is neither a specific environment nor a specific genetic constitution that leads definitely to schizophrenia. A similar conclusion has been reached by Kety (1980), who stressed that "the belief that the syndrome represents a single disease with a single etiology is supported by neither authority nor empirical evidence, and much of the latter argues against it" (p. 429). I agree with Cancro's and Kety's viewpoint concerning the schizophrenic syndrome, and I also maintain that their conclusions can be generalized to include other psychopathological disorders for which genetic factors have been assigned importance, for instance, depression, as well (C. Perris, 1983).

Ever since our early theoretical formulation, my coworkers and I have continued to extend the schema we used in our attempts to identify some of the different etiological components connected with depressive disorders and to examine how they interact (Eisemann, 1985; C. Perris & H. Perris, 1985; C. Perris *et al.*, 1987). Gradually, our efforts resulted in a development of an initial model (C. Perris, 1985a), which represents a proposal of criteria for an integrated theory of depression but which can be easily generalized to include other dis- orders—in particular, the schizophrenic syndromes.

This more comprehensive theoretical frame of reference is sum- marized in Figure 2-3, where it can be seen that we have progressed in our attempts to define individual vulnerability by emphasizing cogni- tive processes. We thus assume that the gathering and processing of information represents a decisive link in the chain of events that finally leads to the occurrence of psychopathological disorders. This cognitive frame of reference avoids the dichotomy between mind and body without becoming reductionistic (as opposed to classical psycho- analysis, which clearly separates the mind from the body [S. Freud, 1915; Peterfreund, 1971] and radical behaviorism, which completely neglects mental processes). Also to be emphasized is that this frame- work is neither based on the assumption of simple determinism (either biological, psychological, or environmental) nor exclusively humanis- tic existentialism. The individual is not totally free from biological and sociopsychological limitations, but we believe in the freedom of choice. As indicated by the arrows in Figure 2-1, this view is consistent with the conception of reciprocal determinism proposed by Bandura (1978) who maintained that "it is true that behavior is influenced by

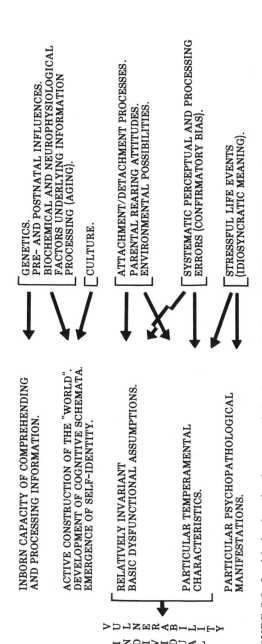

FIGURE 2-3. In this further development of the framework shown in Figure 2-1, factors that may contribute to the development of individual vulnerability are spelled out. To simplify the figure, arrows are drawn unidirectionally. Reference to Figure 2-1 emphasizes, however, the interactive nature of the influences. This framework should not be understood as a theory, but rather as a set of criteria for deriving testable hypotheses.

the environment, but the environment is partly of a person's own making" (p. 345) (see also the concept of "dynamic interaction" suggested by Magnusson & Endler, 1977).

It should be clearly stated that the schema depicted in Figure 2-3 is nothing more than a set of criteria that need to be supported by empirical data. This scheme should be regarded as heuristic, that is, as a signpost that may allow us to discover and investigate the various factors that contribute to the occurrence of mental disorders and that can affect the choice of a rational treatment strategy.

The emphasis on the importance of cognitive processes is very near the viewpoint held by Cancro. Cancro (1979) underscored the significance of "attention regulation" in the processing of information and assumed, on satisfactory grounds, that this activity, which is of particular importance in susceptibility to schizophrenic syndromes, is genetically controlled. A more detailed analysis of some of the elements shown in Figure 2-3 is given in a later section.

While the model in Figure 2-3 originated as a more comprehensive frame of reference for studying depressive syndromes and only later was extended to include other disorders, two additional models, both markedly similar to this one, have recently been proposed by authors primarily interested in the study of schizophrenic syndromes. The first of these models was presented by Ciompi (1985) in Switzerland. In his approach, Ciompi considered the influence of genetic and somatic factors (constitutional, prenatal and perinatal lesions, etc.) as well as psychosocial effects (mental trauma during infancy, the breakdown of communication within the family, poor adaptability, etc.) on the development of "premorbid vulnerability." According to Ciompi, such vulnerability, which is characterized by a reduced ability to cope with complex emotional and cognitive stimuli (i.e., which comprises a defect in the processing of information), leads to an acute psychotic breakdown when it interacts with nonspecific, stressful events and contributes later to the further course of the syndrome.

Another interactive "vulnerability/stress" model for studying the development of schizophrenic episodes has been presented by Nuechterlein and Dawson (1984a). Here again, the authors took account of enduring vulnerability characteristics (a conception related to that of the "vulnerability trait" proposed by Zubin & Spring, 1977) that interact with stress stimuli in the environment. They defined these enduring characteristics in terms of a reduction in available processing capacity, autonomous hyperreactivity to stress stimuli, and faults in social competence and adaptability. These three factors in turn are assumed to represent the product of specific and nonspecific genetic factors that interact with early environmental factors. In an early comprehensive survey of the literature concerning information processing and attentional functioning in the development and course of schizophrenic disorders, Nuechterlein and Dawson (1984b) found that many types of deficits in recognizing and processing information occur with almost equal frequency in subjects belonging to a high-risk group for schizophrenic syndromes and in patients acutely ill or who have recovered from psychotic schizophrenic disorders. These findings together imply that the disturbances described by Nuechterlein and Dawson are not directly caused by the schizophrenic psychotic disorder but represent a vulnerability that exists independently of the actual mental condition. It is important to also point out that Nuechterlein and Dawson fully recognize that some vulnerability factors may be specific for the onset of schizophrenic syndromes, while others may be related to an increased risk for the occurrence of many, varied disorders. The conception in this book is in complete agreement with Nuechterlein and Dawson's statement.

A certain degree of agreement seems to be emerging internationally that supports the relevance of a defect in cognitive processes to a closer definition of the individual vulnerability of persons who are at risk for the development of schizophrenic syndromes. If this assumption is valid (and there are many scientific observations, experimental data, and related theories that support it), then therapeutic interventions aimed particularly at a restructuring of dysfunctional cognitive processes are rational.

In this connection, it is of interest to point out that two other American authors, George and Neufeld (1985), completed a recently published appraisal of the results of research on cognitive processes and schizophrenic symptomatology and concluded that a cognitive perspective on schizophrenic symptomatology appears to be valid for an integrated, empirically based interpretation of the schizophrenic process. They felt that this would provide a basis for cognitively oriented attempts to treat schizophrenic disorders. The contents of the present volume support the view maintained by George and Neufeld.

# 3

# *The Basic Principles of Cognitive Psychotherapy*

Interest in cognitive processes is not limited to investigations of their role in the development of various psychopathological conditions. Cognitive processes are attracting increasing attention in almost all schools of psychotherapy, from the psychoanalytic to the behavior therapeutic. A comprehensive psychotherapeutic system focused primarily on cognitions has been developed during the last decades (for a recent review, see C. Perris, 1988c) and has already been shown to be particularly effective in the treatment of different types of mental disorders, including those that usually require long-term treatment. Originally introduced by Beck and Ellis in the early 1960s in the United States, cognitive psychotherapy has become a well-established method of treatment even in many European countries where active training and research centers contribute to its further refinement and diffusion. National societies of cognitive psychotherapy have been established, meetings and symposia occur frequently, and a few specialized journals are regularly issued. Since textbooks and treatment manuals are presently available in English (e.g., Beck, 1976; Beck & Emery, 1985; Beck, Rush, Shaw, & Emery, 1979; Dryden & Golden, 1986; Ellis, 1962, 1973; A. Freeman, 1983; Guidano & Liotti, 1983; Mahoney & Freeman, 1985; McMullin, 1986; R. A. Wessler & R. L. Wessler, 1980), in German (e.g., Hoffmann, 1978), in Italian (e.g., Guidano & Reda, 1981; Reda, 1986), in French (e.g., Blackburn & Cottraux, 1988) and in Swedish (e.g., Jansson, 1986; C. Perris, 1986b), the following review of the basic principles on which cognitive psychotherapy is based is brief.

The cognitive psychotherapy that forms the basis of this book was originally developed by Beck for the treatment of emotional disorders. However, modifications have been necessary (for example, concerning emphasis on the therapist–patient relationship, the length of treatment, and a cognitive reconstruction of past events) to suit patients suffering from severe schizophrenic syndromes.

It is well known that cognitive psychotherapy has deep philosophical roots, which stretch into the philosophy of the Greek and

Roman stoics (see C. Perris, 1988c, for a review), as well as roots in Sullivan's interpersonal theory (Crowley, 1980, 1985), in Adler's individual psychology (Shulman, 1985), in Horney's school of psychoanalysis (Rendon, 1985), and in Arieti's cognitive–volitional psychoanalysis (Arieti, 1974b). Cognitive psychotherapy's relationship with Arieti's cognitive–volitional school is especially relevant with patients suffering from schizophrenic disorders.

One most basic principle of cognitive psychotherapy is that the contents of a person's thoughts affect his or her feelings and lead to a definite behavioral response. The term "behavioral" in this context includes a patient's psychopathological manifestations. Two specifications of this principle are of paramount importance to avoid some common misunderstandings.

1. The term "thoughts" does not exclusively refer to thinking of which one is subjectively aware; it also includes determinants of thinking and actions resulting from influences that have been perceived without being noticed (Bowers, 1984) and, thus, are "unconscious." In other words, unconscious psychological processes are a "conceptual" (Shevrin & Dickman, 1980) or "logical" (Bowers, 1984) necessity. However, I regard unconscious cognitive processes from the vantage point of neuropsychology rather than psychoanalytic formulations (for a recent review of theories of unconscious cognitive processes, see Bowers & Meichenbaum, 1984).

2. It should also be pointed out that the connections among thoughts, emotions, and behavior are not exclusively unidirectional; they are controlled by feedback mechanisms, thus forming an interactional circuit (Figure 3-1). In this sense, this conception of the relationships among cognition, emotion, and behavior comes close to those maintained by Bandura (1978), Candland (1977), and Wachtel (1977).

## COGNITIONS IN COGNITIVE PSYCHOTHERAPY

The term "cognitions," as conceptualized in cognitive psychotherapy embraces three distinct elements: cognitive events, cognitive processes, and cognitive structures (Marzillier, 1980).

"Cognitive events" comprise thoughts, images, daydreams, and dreams. Of particular importance in the present context is the concept of "automatic thoughts" described by Beck (1976) in his theory of emotional disorders. These thoughts occur automatically and involuntarily, and they are repetitive. Beck emphasized that these thoughts are autonomous in the sense both that the patient makes no efforts to elicit them and that they are difficult to "turn off." The possible

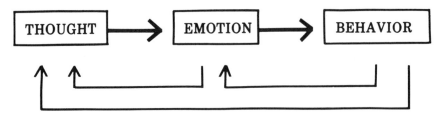

FIGURE 3-1. The assumed relationship among thoughts, emotions, and behavior is shown. The term "thoughts" does not refer exclusively to conscious thinking but includes determinants of thoughts that lie outside awareness.

automatic occurrence of dysfunctional fantasies must also be taken into account in this context.

An important distinction, recently emphasized by Richard Wessler (1986), is between evaluative cognitions or "hot cognitions," which are self-referential and negative, and nonevaluative or "cold" cognitions." Obviously, only the former are relevant in psychotherapy. It should also be stressed that both Beck (1976) and Ellis (1983-1984) assume that automatic thoughts occur outside of focal awareness and, thus, are largely unconscious.

The "cognitive processes" emphasized in cognitive psychotherapy mainly refer to errors in the recognition and in the processing of information and are considered by Marzillier (1980) to be "cognitive appraisals." They also include processes such as attention, encoding, retention, and recall of information. Beck described several cognitive distortions that often occur in mentally disturbed persons. These distortions might relate to the actual perception of a certain situation or to a subsequent evaluation of the event, that is, to a distorted processing of information. The most common cognitive faults are as follows:

1. Selective abstraction is the tendency to extract a detail from a much wider situation and use it to construct a peculiar understanding of the situation as a whole.
2. Arbitrary inference refers to erroneous thinking involved in drawing specific conclusions about a certain situation without the least support for them.
3. Overgeneralization implies the drawing of general conclusions from isolated events or the extension of conclusions to situations or events that are completely unrelated.

4. Magnification and exaggeration imply a serious misjudgment of the importance or extent of an apparently banal event or situation.
5. Dichotomous or polarized thinking means that all experiences of personal importance are processed in terms of "either/or" or black and white without any gradation whatsoever.
6. Mindreading implies that one behaves according to what one believes to be the opinion of others.
7. Personalization is the overestimation of the extent to which a particular event is related to one's self. The most extreme form of personalization is exemplified in delusional ideas of reference and persecution.

Dysfunctional cognitions of the type described above are by no means specific to any particular mental disorder. In fact, their occurrence has been reported in patients suffering from a wide variety of disorders. However, not only is it unlikely that they are specifically related to a given disorder, but it is also reasonable to assume that the occurrence of many of these cognitive distortions is distributed along a continuum in the general population. Support of this assumption can be found in research work by Tversky and Kahneman (1971), who maintained that people have erroneous intuitions about the laws of change and that intuitive predictions follow a judgmental heuristic–representativeness. In making judgments under uncertainty, people have great confidence in their fallible judgment and have difficulty searching for disconfirming information to test hypotheses (Einhorn & Hogarth, 1978). It seems, in practice, that ordinary people rely on a limited number of heuristics, which sometimes yield reasonable judgments and sometimes lead to severe and systematic errors (Kahneman & Tversky, 1973). Probably, what distinguishes ill people is the fact that several types of dysfunctional cognitive appraisals occur together in clusters and in a significantly higher frequency of situations than in ordinary people. In addition, it can be assumed that ill people are less able than healthy subjects to correct these errors.

The terms "cognitive structure" and "schema" (the latter traceable to Kant, 1791) are key concepts in cognitive psychotherapy, although other eponyms or related terms are also occasionally used to refer to the same or similar concepts. These include "belief system," "concept," "rule of life," "meaning structure," "basic assumption," "working model," "core construct," and "assumptive world." Kovacs and Beck (1978) defined cognitive structures or schemata as "relatively enduring aspects of a person's cognitive organization" and regard them as "systems for classifying stimuli." According to Beck and

Emery (1985), cognitive schemata are used to label, classify, interpret, evaluate, and assign meanings to objects and events. Another current definition of a cognitive structure is as follows: "A complex pattern which is considered to be assimilated by a person through experience. In combination with an object or a representation of an object it determines how the object is recognized and how a new representation is formed" (English & English, 1958). Mandler (1984) regarded schemata as the basic units of mind. However, he made a distinction between schemata and cognitive structures and suggested that the latter refer to a more general notion (e.g., including logical structures, strictly procedural mechanisms, etc.). According to Mandler, schemata are included under cognitive structures.

A common misunderstanding is the belief that a clear-cut separation exists between cognitions and emotions beyond that that may occur in experimental investigations and, consequently, that emphasis on cognitive schemata excludes taking into account emotion. In this context, it must be underscored that Piaget (1923, 1971, 1973), whose concept of schema is often referred to by cognitive psychotherapists, clearly stated that affective life and cognitive life are inseparable because all interaction with the environment involves both a structuring and an evaluation.

Lundh (1983), in Sweden, sharpened this concept and suggested that a person's schemata are not solely cognitive but contain a significant affective component. In other words, they comprise not only the individual's fundamental convictions (as in Beck *et al.*'s [1979] concept of "basic assumptions" and Ellis's [1983–1984] "belief system") but also his or her emotional capabilities and motivational dispositions. According to Lundh, every individual develops his or her own specific "meaning structures," which develop as a result of genetic dispositions and learning and which show themselves in that an individual tends to respond regularly in a certain way in a certain kind of situation. Seiler (1984) voiced a similar opinion when he maintained that "each cognitive structure has a particular affective or emotional quality" (p. 21). The most basic of these schemata determine our attitudes toward ourselves and our environments and correspond with what is usually called the "self." Naturally, not all meaning structures of an individual are continuously active, but each can be readily activated by both external and internal stimuli (thoughts, ruminations, imageries). Mandler (1984) pointed out that schemata are also processing mechanisms, that is, they are active in selecting evidence, in parsing the data provided by the environment, and in providing appropriate hypotheses. Beck and Emery (1985) referred to Polanyi's concept of the "tacit dimension" (Polanyi, 1966) and wrote of "silent" cognitive schemata (i.e., out of awareness) that become activated by stimuli that are perceived by an individual as a threat to his or her personal domain.

A thorough analysis of schema theory has been published by Rumelhart and Ortony (1977), who emphasized the functions of schemata. Among these functions, the authors included comprehension, storage and retrieval of input information, and making inferences about situations that are as yet unobserved. In this context, it is particularly important to point out that schematic storage is by no means passive, but is to be regarded, as originally emphasized by Bartlett (1932), as that process by which the active individual recreates his or her past experience in ever-evolving forms.

Within the framework of a developmental cognitive theory, it is assumed that the individual enters the world with genetically determined and highly differentiated capabilities for perception and reaction. Those capabilities might be regarded as rudimentary cognitive structures that are later developed and reformed by the individual in coming to terms with the environment. This is accomplished by the processes that Piaget (1936, 1978) named assimilation and accommodation, which tend toward a static (homeostasis) and dynamic (homeorhesis) equilibrium (Figure 3-2). Assimilation provides cognitive continuity and integration, while accommodation allows cognitive change. In this sense, the organism actively creates its personal world and is not just a passive receiver of stimuli. As a result of the continuing processes that Piaget described, our schemata continuously structure our experience and are structured by it. Neisser (1962) described three kinds of structural changes: absorption, displacement, and integration. By "absorption," he meant the development of new structures that contain all of the old structures (a process similar to assimilation). The term "displacement" was used by Neisser when the old and new structures are assumed to continue to exist side by side; the concept of "integration" refers to the development of *new* structures, at a more comprehensive level, that still contain parts of the old (that is, integration is similar to accommodation).

Since assimilation provides continuity of preexisting structures and integration of new data into them, a consequence of overassimilation is that new information is continuously and idiosyncratically distorted by the existing schemata. In contrast, accommodation implies a change of existing schemata in relation to new information; that is, accommodation is the process by which one takes the perspective of the other, thus transforming one's own structures. While lack of accommodation would imply the inability to learn from experience, thus a tendency to always repeat the same errors (as in the psychoanalytical concept of repetition compulsion), overaccommodation implies an overadjustment to the environment, thus a tendency to lose one's own identity.

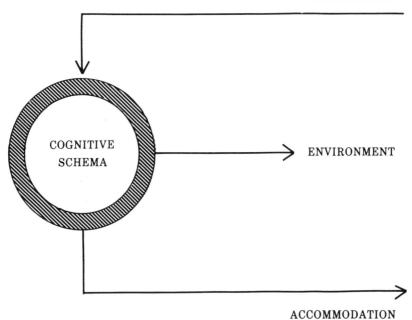

FIGURE 3-2. Schemata are continuously constructed and reconstructed through the active, bipolar processes of assimilation and accommodation, which strive toward equilibrium and adaptation.

A particular emphasis on an active construction of the world was placed not only by Piaget in his conception of action schema but also by Kelly (1955, 1970) in his related concept of "personal construct" and by Bowlby (1973a) in his concept of "working models." Bowlby, in particular, suggested that "each individual builds working models of the world and of himself in it, with the aid of which he perceives events, forecasts the future, and constructs his plans" (p. 236).

Although most cognitive structures go through a continuous process of restructuring and transformation, it is assumed that the most fundamental ones, that is, those that relate to self-concept, are relatively lasting once they are established (as in Kelly's concept of "core constructs"). The fact that we are capable of selection from a continuous flood of information supports this stability. (Recognition of this stability is necessary, as discussed in later chapters, for the correct interpretation of possible resistance during psychotherapy.) Selection means that we chose to recognize and process information that is congruent with our self-image and ignore or reject information that is

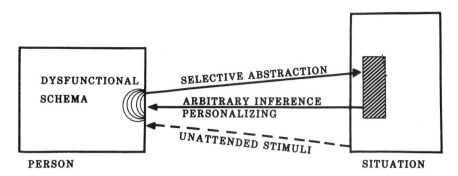

FIGURE 3-3. Some of the most frequently occurring cognitive distortions promoted by a dysfunctional schema are illustrated.

contradictory (see, for example, Markus, 1977). For example, a girl who considers herself to be particularly charming recognizes only those signals in her environment that reinforce this opinion and completely neglects all others. Similarly, a man with a negative self-image will notice and take in from his surroundings only those stimuli that confirm his dysfunctional opinion. The cognitive distortions act in this respect as a self-confirmatory bias; Figure 3-3 provides a graphic illustration of this process.

## THE GOALS OF COGNITIVE PSYCHOTHERAPY

The goals of cognitive psychotherapy are primarily to help patients to become aware of their most fundamental dysfunctional assumptions or dysfunctional life rules and to help them learn to recognize the cognitive distortions that sustain these dysfunctional self-images. When these goals have been achieved, it is then the aim of the therapy to help patients correct these cognitive distortions. Since distortions in the perception and processing of information compose the mechanism by which the most basic dysfunctional convictions are confirmed, their correction implies a severance of the feedback. Even the most basic schemata can eventually be restructured. The emphasis on long-term goals, which implies a therapeutically guided recollection of the development of dysfunctional meaning structures, along with as thorough a restructuring of an individual's self-schema as possible, means that cognitive psychotherapy must be regarded as an insight-oriented psychotherapy that aims at structural changes and not merely a supportive one.

# 4

## The Development of Dysfunctional Cognitions in Patients with Schizophrenic Syndromes

This chapter is devoted to a discussion of the development of dysfunctional cognitions at various levels in relation to psychopathology in general. Special attention is given to patients with schizophrenic disorders in order to reemphasize the rational aspects of the different therapeutic approaches considered later. The available space permits only superficial discussion of many associated complexities. However, references to appropriate literature are provided when full details of a particular problem or idea cannot be given here.

To perceive the clinical manifestations in schizophrenic patients from a perspective amenable to cognitive psychotherapy, it is necessary to return to the theoretical frame of reference shown in Figure 2-3 and to take into account several of the hypotheses that can be derived from it. Those that might be derived from cultural influences are beyond the scope of this section; however, a recent review of possible cultural determinants of schizophrenic behavior has been made available by Brody (1976). Therefore, the following concerns factors related to the individual and his or her most immediate environment.

### EARLY DEVELOPMENT

It is reasonable to assume that the individual enters the world equipped with a rudimentary set of genetically determined structures and inborn neural patterns together with associated information-processing programs that subsequently develop along a genetically controlled course. These programs allow the individual to deal in an adaptive manner with all the stimulation by information to which he or she is exposed. The psychoanalyst Peterfreund (1971) pointedly emphasized that, as a result of this stimulant information, the organism finds itself in a state of constant stress which generates nonspecific biological reactions, including manifestations of alarm and anxiety. In order to reduce stress and its associated reactions to a minimum, or even to eliminate them completely, the organism must respond in a specific adaptive manner that exerts a kind of biological control and promotes maintenance of the homeostasis and biological order. This emphasizes the notion that the infant is *not* a "blank slate" at birth. Research results from many quarters instead suggest that perceptual development, including selective perception, begins before birth. Sontag (1966), for example, has shown that the fetus *in utero* responds to loud sounds by pronounced kicking and an increased heart rate. Bower (1971, 1974) demonstrated that newborn infants are able to localize odors and to turn away from unpleasant ones prior to any experience and training. He also reported experiments that demonstrated that infants show auditory-visual coordination and adjustments to the distance of objects during the newborn period (see also Basch, 1977, for a comprehensive review of other investigations related to this topic and for a critical discussion of their relevance in a revision of psychoanalytical metapsychology). In this context, it is important to keep in mind a distinction between perception and subjective awareness. In the examples mentioned above, "perception" means that stimuli have been received, transformed, *and* encoded by the existing rudimentary structures. The infant's attentional encounters with events result in a new more developed schema (see Kagan, 1970, for an analysis of attentional processes and psychological change in infants).

Substantial evidence exists for both experimental research and clinical data indicating that higher cognitive functions are acquired in stages. However, it still is a matter of controversy whether development is cumulative and continuous or discontinuous and characterized by the emergence of new competences (Kagan, 1979). The distinction is not without important implications, for example, as concerns the deterministic importance attributed to the experiences of the first 12 months of life in psychoanalytically oriented psychotherapy; according to a "discontinuity–emergence" viewpoint, there is no good reason to give priority to the experiences of the first year of life and to regard them as more important than experiences of later years.

## Interactional Aspects

The structures of the brain that support the cognitive functions mentioned above require sensory experiences for maturation. Neuronal activity thus becomes an important factor in the reorganization of these structures. To the extent that neuronal activity is modulated by sensory signals, it is obvious that different environmental factors can affect the development of the neuronal matrix. Singer (1986) drew attention to the fact that the experience-dependent self-reorganization of the brain must be treated as an active dialogue between the brain and its surroundings. Meyersburg and Post (1979), after a review of the pertinent literature, pointed out, with a particular emphasis on the work by Yakovlev and Lecours (1967) on myelination sequences, that a parallelism between neural and behavioral developmental sequences exists in early childhood. Of particular relevance in this connection are the early interactions between the child and the caregivers that occur at a time of neural transition considered by Lipsitt (1979) to be a phase of rapid and sensitive growth rather than a period of simple neuronal immaturity. According to Brody (1981), this serves to enhance awareness that disturbances that occur at this time severely affect the sensitive development of the biological structures necessary for learning and adaptation. Also, the further development of these biological structures, assumed to occur as a result of the interaction between the growing child and the environment, may be obstructed from the very beginning if neural lesions have occurred in the prenatal stage. Weinberger (1987) recently proposed a neurodevelopmental model of "schizophrenia" that takes into account the possible interaction of a fixed "lesion" that might have occurred early in development, delaying normal brain maturational events. According to this hypothesis, the appearance of manifest symptoms is linked to the normal maturation of brain areas affected by the early developmental pathology, especially the dorsolateral prefrontal cortex.

Taking into account these assumptions about developmental discontinuities, it is worth mentioning that there is some evidence pointing to the possible occurrence of spurts in growth. H. T. Epstein (1974a, 1974b) proposed the term "phrenoblisis" for the spurts in brain and mind he has identified. According to Epstein, characteristic spurts in brain growth and intellectual development occur, roughly, at ages 6-8, 10-12, 14-17, and possibly 2-4.

An assumption can be derived from the frame of reference in Figure 2-3 stating that a disorder in the perception and/or processing of information may arise at a very early stage in the development of a person who will later suffer from a schizophrenic syndrome. The earlier such a disorder occurs, the higher the risk that its magnitude will increase in the course of the later developmental process. Evidence in the literature suggests that cognitive–emotional development may not be continuous. Thus, the possibility that important deviations from the normal course of development may occur much later than the first year of life must always be taken into account.

However, more recent research results indicate that various negative environmental influences on the brain, beyond those of an infectious, viral, toxic, or traumatic nature, can occur at the embryonal or fetus stage. Recent animal experiments on cell–matrix interactions in neural crest development (R. Perris, 1987) suggest that cell–matrix interactions are temporally and spatially crucial in initiating and supporting neural crest cell migration and that the extracellular matrix influences morphogenesis and affects regional cell type diversification during ontogeny of the neural crest. Thus, genetic and environmental factors seem to interact at a very early stage of development. Data from lower animals, however, can only very cautiously be generalized to humans.

On the other hand, Milani Comparetti (1982) maintained that the central nervous system in the fetus is, under normal conditions, already capable of dealing with problems presented to it by the environment. One example of this is fetal movement, the purpose of which is to promote balanced organic growth by avoiding the detrimental effects of a prolonged stationary position. These fetal movements are regarded as belonging to primary automatisms that are genetically determined and produced by environmental demands. These normally begin during the 10th week of pregnancy, are most manifest during infancy, and decrease during childhood. It remains largely unknown to what degree disturbances of the most early primary automatisms influence those occurring after birth and, consequently, also influence the child's reactivity to the caregivers and their attitude toward the child. However, some preliminary information exists. Sontag (1966), for example, wrote that differences in fetal activity levels appear to be predictive of restlessness and resistance to handling during the infant's first year of life.

## Early Postnatal Interactions

It has been long known that infants begin to express themselves as individuals very soon after birth. Some of them remain alert and engage the world in an affective exchange while others remain regulated or calm only by shutting out the external world. However, this fact, as underscored by Thomas, Chess, and Birch (1970), is often neglected, and early environmental influences are instead emphasized.

Recent findings by Tronick and coworkers (Tronick, Als, Adamson, Wise, & Brazelton, 1978) provide food for thought. They observed experimentally that the child turns away and retreats when he or she fails to produce an emotional response in the mother, who, in the experimental situation, had been instructed to remain indifferent to the child's approach. Basch (1977) wrote that a child's distress when the mother's face is either distorted or presented immobile indicates that the brain operates in such a way that it mistrusts incongruity. Lichtenberg (1981) recently reviewed research on the neonate and stressed its implications for psychoanalytical theory. He pointed out that, while the significance of the mother's empathic caretaking has been duly appreciated, the role of the infant in the dyadic interaction has been less well-appreciated in the psychoanalytic literature. Lichtenberg stressed that by virtue of individual differences, infants call for differing responsiveness. However, interactions initiated by the child to elicit maternal attention can go awry. Results of a follow-up study by Prechtl (1963) support this view. Prechtl studied maternal reactions to eight infants born with a variety of complications, who were irritable and prone to unpredictable state changes, and found that toward the end of their first year seven of the eight mothers expressed rejecting attitudes.

Thomas *et al.* (1970) emphasized that domineering handling by the parents may make one youngster anxious and submissive and another defiant and antagonistic. According to their observations, such differences seem to be the direct consequence of the child's own style of responding to the environment. Thomas and coworkers regarded both the "nature" and the "nurture" concepts as too simplistic and favor the hypothesis that the personality (including its deviations) is shaped by the constant interplay of temperament and environment. A similar assumption is maintained by Gaensbauer and Sands (1979). They identified a number of specific aspects of the affective "dialogue" between the infants and their caregivers that, when distorted, can elicit negative responses in the caregivers. Among those they included lack of pleasure, inconsistency and unpredictability in affective communications, shallowness of affect communication, and ambiguity/ambivalence in affect expression. Moss (1967) emphasized that fussiness and crying in the baby's first few months of life stimulate the mother to respond; however, the same behavior at 8–11 months makes the mother *less* responsive (Beckwith, 1972) and may sometimes evoke battering (R. Q. Bell, 1975). For a more detailed review of early parent–child interactions, the reader is referred to Frodi (1985) and Rutter (1979).

Recent research results (C. Perris, Jacobsson, von Knorring, Oreland, H. Perris, & Ross, 1980; H. Perris, 1982b; Schalling, Åsberg, Edman, & Oreland, 1987; von Knorring, Oreland, & Winblad, 1984; Ward, Catts, Norman, Burrows, & McConaghy, 1987) have consistently shown the occurrence of a statistically significant relationship between such personality traits as "monotony avoidance" and "sensation seeking" and the genetically controlled enzyme monoaminooxidase (MAO). Since those personality traits might be regarded as directly related to the current conception that the growing child is actively seeking information, it is reasonable to assume that inborn variations of degree in these traits make the individual particularly sensitive to environmental conditions and might influence the relation of the child to the caregivers. We can thus continue to assume the existence of important interactions that might lead to a vulnerability for later psychopathological manifestations.

In this context, studies concerned with perinatal characteristics of the offspring of schizophrenic women (e.g., McNeil & Kaij, 1976; Mednick, Mura, Schulsinger, & Mednick, 1982; Sameroff & Zax, 1973) should be taken into account. In fact, there is some evidence that schizophrenic mothers may have more delivery complications than nonschizophrenic controls. Later difficulties in motherhood due to the psychotic disorder may be assumed to negatively interact with developmental difficulties in the offspring due to perinatal complications. However, findings in the literature concerning the effects of child rearing by schizophrenic mothers (e.g., Higgins, 1976; Landau, Harth, Othnay, & Sharfhertz, 1972; Schulsinger, 1976) have been inconsistent and difficult to interpret. M. Bleuler (1974), who has followed his patients and their offspring at close quarters, emphasized that normal development can take place in the face of severe neglect, "teaching of irrationality," and parental degeneration. His conclusion was that the effect of prolonged immediate contact with an overtly psychotic parent is insufficient to explain the subsequent development of schizophrenia. On the other hand, he stressed that early childhood suffering was associated with poorer levels of adult functioning.

## Summary

It is important to emphasize that different alternatives must always be considered concerning a disturbed early relationship between the child and the caregivers. These alternatives should never be regarded as unidirectional:

1. The child, as a consequence of a disordered neural development, is unable to perceive and/or process information related to the feelings of the caregivers correctly.
2. The child, as a consequence of early neural lesions, might contribute to inhibited emotional expressions in the caregivers.
3. Negative attitudes in a child's caregivers might negatively influence the child's further neural development and thus limit the development of his or her further adaptive capabilities.

4. The occurrence of a mental disorder in the primary caregiver might contribute to the development of an insecure pattern of attachment that, in turn, will negatively influence later adaption.

According to Nuechterlein and Dawson (1984a), the documented pattern of premorbid defects in schizophrenics is consistent with the assumption of an impairment of the individual's processing capacity for goal-seeking cognitive operations. These authors wrote that several different causes must be taken into account to explain this reduced capacity in persons susceptible to schizophrenic manifestations. In their opinion (with which I agree), it is generally accepted that these defects are produced by both specific and nonspecific genetic factors, which interact with physical and environmental variables at a very early age.

It might be worthwhile here to recall Cancro's assumption (1975) that the control of attention might be a genetically governed factor that contributes to the development of a vulnerability to at least some forms of the schizophrenic syndrome. Furthermore, Cancro asserted that a disturbance in the regulation of attention might well explain the basic cognitive disorder and disorders in object relationships that characterize many schizophrenic patients. A recent critical review of studies concerning disorders of attention in patients with schizophrenic syndromes was published by Gjerde (1983), who suggested that diverse attentional deficits in schizophrenic patients might be seen to reflect a deficit of the control function that governs the mobilization and allocation of attention. Gjerde emphasized that attentional capacity is related to the state of arousal, mood, and age (see also Hasher & Zacks, 1979). In particular, the relationship between arousal and attention seems to follow the Yerkes-Dobson law: underaroused subjects function poorly because of insufficient investment of capacity, while overaroused subjects perform poorly because of noxious changes in allocation of attention (Gjerde, 1983). In this context, it is worthwhile to point out that a lowering of attention or apperceptive deterioration was regarded by Jung (1972) as a central disturbance of dementia praecox.

Cancro's hypothesis brings us closer to the identification of a possible relevant genetic factor in schizophrenia; also his last mentioned suggestion introduces an additional factor in our model, namely "attachment," in the sense defined by Bowlby (1969, 1973a, 1980) and later developed by Ainsworth (1972), Sroufe and Waters (1977), Serafica (1978), and Reite and Field (1985). This variable is of great importance both because a profitable exchange between studies of attachment and cognitive psychotherapy already exists in the literature (Beck, 1985; Bowlby, 1980, 1981; Guidano & Liotti, 1983, 1985; Liotti, 1986, 1988;

Reda, 1986) and because one assumption in our model is that disturbances of the tie of a child to the principal caregiver might contribute to the development of cognitive distortions, including a faulty regulation of attention and dysfunctional basic schemata.

## ATTACHMENT THEORY AND DEVELOPMENTAL PSYCHOPATHOLOGY

Although an extensive discussion of the relevance of attachment to cognitive psychotherapy is available in Bowlby (1985), Guidano and Liotti (1983), Liotti (1986), and Reda (1986), it is important at this point to summarize the reasons for including attachment in our theoretical frame of reference.

To begin with, Bowlby has radically separated himself, as others have also done (e.g., Lichtenberg, 1981; Mandler, 1984), from a view of human motivations centered around gratification of the primary physiological needs (i.e., secondary drive theory or "cupboard-love theory of object relations," Bowlby, 1958, 1969). Using an ethological approach, Bowlby has shown that attachment is an independent process that is a universal characteristic of primates, including humans, and that it also occurs in lower species. His attachment theory is an evolutionary object-relations theory, which considers biological structures in an attempt to explain biological order, organization, control, regulation, adaptation, and survival—concepts that are all of research interest. In this way, Bowlby's approach goes further to meet the demands of scientific theory than other object-relations theories. He also avoids usage of obsolete terms from psychoanalytical drive theory as well as the vitalistic and anthropomorphic concept of "ego" (which Peterfreund, 1971, p. 57, has called "the pre-Darwinian intelligent designer") that obstruct other object-relations theories and limit their explanatory power. According to Bowlby, attachment is a class of social behavior with a biological function specific to itself. Among other object-relations theoreticians, Balint (1937), with his concept of "primary object love," and Winnicott (1965), with his definition of "double dependence," come close to Bowlby's concept of attachment. In fact, both Balint and Winnicott seem to maintain the opinion that early object relationships may be biological givens and not solely consequences of oral instinctual needs. Also, Fairbairn's general proposition (1944, 1946) that libido is not primarily "pleasure-seeking" but, rather, is "object-seeking" might be understood as consistent with Bowlby's conception of attachment. The implications of these ideas for psychotherapy of patients with schizophrenic syndromes are discussed later in this book (see Chapters 7 and 8).

Bowlby also pointed out that the behavioral systems involved in attachment behavior develop within the infant as a result of interactions with the environment—especially with the principal figure in that environment. In most cases this is the mother, but not always. In fact, Bowlby maintained that "some infants select more than one attachment-figure almost as soon as they begin to show discrimination" (1969, p. 304).

Ethological studies (e.g., Jolly, 1972) have suggested that certain male primates show a marked ability to both care for the young and promote their socialization. In the case of humans, it has often been pointed out that when an empathic father coincides with an emotionally cool mother, he will be ranked higher in the hierarchy of attachment objects (see Ainsworth, 1972, Biller, 1974, and Hetherington, 1972, for a detailed discussion of the father's importance for the cognitive and emotional development of the child). Biller (1974) in particular asserts that genetic factors may be involved in father–child attachments in primates, including humans. In a comparison between mothers as primary caregivers and fathers as both primary and secondary caregivers, Field (1985) found that while fathers generally differ from mothers by providing more exciting stimulation, those in the role of primary caregivers functioned similarly to mothers by engaging in less excitable and subdued activities with the child. Further, an account by Freud and Dann (1951), reported by both Bowlby and Field, indicates that primary attachments to peers may also arise quite early in life.

A balanced analysis of the importance of the father during the child's earliest phase of development was presented some 20 years ago by Forrest (1966, 1967). It is strongly recommended that the reader study the original articles; however, the aspects Forrest included in his analysis that are pertinent to early infancy are discussed here. To begin with, Forrest criticized the fact that psychoanalytical theories regard the role of the father in the child's psychological development predominantly in terms of sexual competition at a relatively late stage. The author comments, somewhat ironically, that since psychoanalysis was introduced by Europeans at the turn of the century, the conventions regarding the role of mother and father prevalent at that time have been incorporated in it; consequently, the father has been expelled from both kitchen and nursery. Forrest maintained that, in this way, decisions as to when the father enters the child's world have already been made from the start. However, Forrest wrote that the presence or absence of the father as an active member of the family at birth determines whether a genuine family unit will develop. In other words, the presence or absence of the father determines whether the child is born into a group or shifts between a biological and psychological unit with the mother. All object-relation theories stress the infant's attachment to the mother as the source of both pleasure and pain, but it is seldom pointed out that the father plays an important role in the child's early experiences of security and anxiety. The father can greatly affect the relationship between the child and the mother through his attitudes to motherhood and his experience of the child. For example, a father who regards the child as a rival for the affection of the mother easily generates a tension that becomes reflected in the mother's relationship to the child. On the other hand, it is conceivable that a father who feels himself neglected, and therefore deprives the mother of a source of emotional satisfaction, contributes to an even stronger attachment between the mother and child which then emerges as the only available object of satisfaction. The father also represents one of the first "strangers" that inhabit the child's world; as such, he fulfills an important function in promoting the child's relationship with the external world and its process of identification. Even later, the father plays an important role in the child's development through the kind of activities in which he engages the child.

Whereas Forrest emphasized the role of the father *after* the birth of the child, it is important to note that the father can also exert a negative influence before the child's birth by provoking anxiety and stress in the mother. Several investigations (for a recent review of this topic, see Joffe, Vaughn, Barglow, & Benveniste, 1985) have suggested that prenatal anxiety might be related to both major morphological anomalies and minor physical anomalies as well as pregnancy and delivery complications. It has also been shown that newborn minor anomalies predict a short attention span (Magnusson & af Klinteberg, 1987; Waldrop, Bell, McLaughlin, & Halverson, 1978). Thus, should any of these complications occur, there is a high risk that mothering behavior after delivery will be disturbed from the very beginning as a result of interactive factors.

On the basis of her research results, Field (1985) concluded that different attachments probably meet different needs in the child; for instance, mothers modulate the excitement that fathers provide. Thus, differences in the quality and number of contacts of the parents with the child affect emotional arousal, which, according to Nuechterlein and Dawson (1984a), is one of the factors that contribute to the development of individual vulnerability. If we assume that engaging in exciting activities requires a great amount of accommodation of the child's cognitive emotional schema, a hypothesis concerning a higher emotional arousal, as maintained by Field, would be consistent with Mandler's assumption that both successful and unsuccessful accommodation is always accompanied by high affective arousal (Mandler,

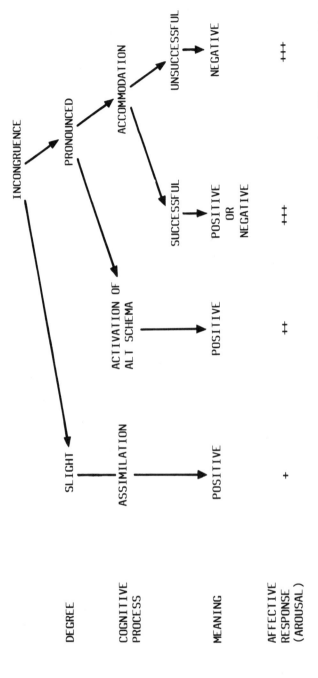

FIGURE 4-1. Various congruent schema and respectively incongruent stimuli (events) activate different cognitive processes and are accompanied by affective and arousal responses of various degrees. Adapted from Mandler, 1984.

1982, 1984; Figure 4-1). It must be kept in mind that, whereas symptoms of arousal do not occur until 1–2 seconds after the onset of a stimulus, the time course of schema activation is much faster, probably between 300 and 1,000 milliseconds (Mandler, 1984).

Recognition that attachment figures other than the mother are important is of great significance since it facilitates the avoidance of a relapse into the conception of the "schizophrenogenic mother" proposed by Fromm-Reichmann in 1948. More on the possible relevance of the parent–child relationship to the development of schizophrenic syndromes is discussed in a following section (see "From the 'Schizophrenogenic Mother' to the 'Schizophrenogenic Family' and Beyond," below).

Another reason for the adoption of Bowlby's theory of attachment rests on the fact that attachment is not regarded as restricted to childhood as in other object-relations theories, but remains important throughout the entire life cycle. Bowlby (1973a, p. 407) wrote that "confidence in the accessibility and responsiveness of attachment figures, or lack of it, is built up slowly during all the years of immaturity, and . . . once developed, expectations tend to persist relatively unchanged throughout the rest of life." Such a viewpoint is relevant not only because it allows a correct interpretation of the effects of eventual losses later in life, but also because it illuminates the problems that are often encountered in young patients who are still living with their parents and feel unable to move out on their own. In fact, when a satisfactory, secure attachment to primary caregivers has not developed, this negatively influences competence in the peer group later in childhood (Easterbrooks & Lamb, 1979; Matas, Arend, Sroufe, 1978; Pastor, 1981; Rutter, 1979; Waters, Wippman, & Sroufe, 1979), thus disturbing the process of affiliation (Bemporad, 1984). Consistent research findings (e.g., O'Neil & Robins, 1958; Watt, 1978) suggest the occurrence of early deviance in the social behavior of children who later develop a schizophrenic syndrome.

Opinions regarding the time at which early attachments are first formed differ among object-relations theorists, as Bowlby (1969) has thoroughly discussed. In this connection, it is worth pointing out that, although Bowlby wrote that orientation and signals directed toward one (or more) discriminated figure(s) occurs by 3–6 months of age, attachment behavior, defined as maintenance of proximity to a discriminated figure, does not begin before the age of 6 months. Other, more recent, investigations, however, suggest that attachment to the mother, the father, and peers can be developed even during the very first months of life, involving other sensorial modalities than the visual mode (e.g., tactile contact; see Kernberg, 1982, and Leon, 1984, for a recent discussion of this topic from a psychoanalytic perspective) and that this reflects the existence of very important and complex psychobiological interactive processes (Fox, 1985; Reite & Capitanio, 1985). Repeated animal experiments (see McKinney, 1985, for a recent review) have shown that disturbances in early attachments, in particular separation from the (biological *or* foster) mother caused marked changes in the concentration of 5-hydroxytryptamine in the hypothalamus as well as an enhanced plasma cortisol level, suggesting high arousal. Thus, if attachment theory and possible disturbances in attachment are taken into account, a bridge may be constructed between psychological environmental stress and biological variables, forming an additional link in the development of individual vulnerability.

Another extremely important reason for our interest in Bowlby's theory is that it presupposes a genetically dependent readiness to develop certain types of "behavior systems" or cognitive maps (in practice corresponding to the information-processing programs mentioned earlier), which become increasingly complex as the child grows up. One important "map" facilitates the comprehension of object permanence. Bell (1970) showed that an interaction exists between the quality of the attachment and cognitive development such that mother permanence develops earlier than object permanence under especially favorable conditions (see also Sroufe & Waters, 1977).

Bowlby's theory also includes concepts, for instance, "defensive exclusion" (which may be compared with "selective inatttention," Sullivan, 1954) that replace concepts (e.g., repression) that are more difficult to explain scientifically; furthermore, these concepts are particularly important for a closer understanding of the disturbances in information processing found in patients with schizophrenic syndromes.

In addition, Bowlby stated that psychopathology should be considered to be the result of a fault in the individual's psychological development and not the result of a fixation or regression to some definite earlier stage of development. Implicit in this idea is that the "fault" refers to the continuous processes of attachment and separation that humans go through during their whole developmental cycle. The knowledge derived from Bowlby's theory and from the research work on which it is based is particularly important for understanding the ambivalence of the schizophrenic patient when confronted with a relationship with apparently opposing characteristics. This ambivalence, which is probably (later in childhood) aggravated by communication disorders of which Bateson's "double bind" (Bateson, Jackson, Haley, & Weakland, 1956) is but one type, may result in a split self-image in the patient, laying the foundation for the growth of some strongly dysfunctional conceptions.

Finally, Bowlby's attachment theory is of particular interest because it can be related to other theories of normal and deviant human development that are especially relevant to cognitive psychotherapy.

## OTHER RELEVANT THEORIES

According to Bowlby, the set goal of the attachment system is proximity to caregiver. However, he also stressed the importance of felt security when he defined his concept of a "secure base" from which the child operates (Bowlby, 1973b). Sroufe and Waters (1977) and Ainsworth and her coworkers (Ainsworth, Blehar, Waters, & Wall, 1978) emphasized even more strongly that the set goal of the attachment system should be conceived as felt security and that the function of this system is not only to provide protection but also to foster exploration of the environment. The focus on the mother–child bond and on the concept of security as important determinants of future functioning and relationships, and the emphasis given to proximity seeking and to exploratory behavioral systems, allows for relating Bowlby's theory to the theory of human development proposed by Horney (1937, 1950), who has been a stimulating source of inspiration for cognitive therapy theorists. In particular, Horney's description of "neurotic claims" (Horney, 1950) largely overlaps with Ellis's conception of (basic) "irrational beliefs" (Ellis, 1962), and her concept of "the tyranny of the shoulds" is incorporated in both Beck's and Ellis's cognitive theories of emotional disorders. Horney suggested that the child requires a sense of inner security for a positive development toward self-realization and described three fundamental forms of relating—moving toward people, moving against people, and moving away from people—as necessary prerequisites for adaptation and good human relationships. Recently, Feiring (1983) pointed out that the attachment system of proximity seeking is related to Horney's concept of "moving toward people," whereas the exploratory system is related to the concept of "moving away from people."

Certain (dysfunctional) basic assumptions are supposed to underlie different styles of relating. For example, one assumption or fundamental belief behind the mode of moving away from people is, as Feiring (1983) put it, "if I withdraw, you can't hurt me." Horney suggested that rigidity and indiscrimination in the prevalence of any of the relating modalities were the essence of a neurotic development. However, it is my experience that such a personal rule of life, developed in contact with inconsistent and egocentric parents who showed minimal respect for individuality, may easily be detected in patients who develop a schizophrenic syndrome as well.

The complementarity of Bowlby's and Horney's theories has been stressed by H. A. Paul (1984), who again emphasized the resemblance between attachment patterns described by Ainsworth *et al.* (1978) and the interpersonal movements postulated by Horney and who pointed out that both Horney and Bowlby have voiced the deep belief that people are not victims of driving forces but are able to grow freely if growth is not obstructed by environmental conditions.

Bowlby's (1969) replacement of the orally derived theory of internal objects by a theory of "working models" of world and self, conceived as being constructed by each individual, establishes an important link between attachment theory and Piaget's constructivistic developmental psychology. In particular, an emphasis on goal-directed activity present from birth is shared by both Piaget and Bowlby. However, the concept of "structure" implicit in Bowlby's term "working models" has been recently criticized from a Piagetian perspective (Clinton, 1986). In fact, Clinton pointed out that the notion of "structure" is not thoroughly discussed by Bowlby. In particular, Piaget's characterization of structures as systems of transformation and self-regulation (Piaget, 1971) has been regrettably neglected in his conceptualization of behavior systems and working models. However, this notion, asserted Clinton, is important for the manner in which the infant monitors and resolves discrepancies between instructions and performance and has implications for how others interact with him or her.

Bowlby's emphasis on constructivism connects with another theory that has been of value in establishing the foundations of cognitive psychotherapy: Kelly's Personal Constructs Theory (Kelly, 1955; see C. Perris, 1986b, for a recent discussion of Kelly's impact on cognitive therapy theorizing). Kelly's basic postulate is, "A person's processes are channelized by the ways in which he anticipates events" (p. 9). Thus, Kelly started, like Piaget, with an emphasis on process and did not subscribe to a concept of drive without which a person would be inert. Rather than rewards and punishment or drive reduction, what governs the direction in which a person's behavior develops is the confirmation and disconfirmation of his or her predictions. The units of experience for Kelly are anticipation, confirmation or disconfirmation, and constructive revision. Constructs are a guide to living; when predictions made in this way fail, the relationships between the constructs are modified. People differ, however, in their ability to profit from experience in altering their constructs. This difference was named by Kelly "permeability."

Theoreticians working in the field of personal constructs theory (e.g., O'Reilly, 1977; Salmon, 1970; Shotter, 1970) have explored the origins of personal constructs and underlined the importance of the child's interpersonal relationships in general, and of the relationship to a significant adult in particular, for the development of the very early constructs. Salmon wrote that the mother assists the child to define the significance of different situations, especially in the early stages of development, by transmitting a construct that enables the child to deal with these situations. She pointed out that such a capacity implies the mother's readiness to adopt a nonmanipulative, empathic approach to her child, but that the approach must always be understood from an interpersonal perspective involving both the mother and the child. O'Reilly summarized his views on this issue by proposing that a child born in a humane connection wins admission into this system through his or her relationship with an adult custodian.

Hypotheses concerning schizophrenic disorders derived from Kelly's theory have been extensively investigated by Bannister (Bannister, 1960, 1977; see also Rabin, Doneson, & Jentons, 1979, for a recent review) who emphasized that thought-disordered schizophrenics lack the stable constructs necessary to predict regularities in events.

Unfortunately, it is not possible at this juncture fully to discuss alternative, possibly relevant, developmental theories that may be connected with our model, for instance, Werner's organismic developmental point of view (Werner, 1948), which has been taken into account with reference to schizophrenia by, for instance, Arieti (1955) and Goldman (1962). Werner's central notion is that development proceeds from a state of globality and lack of differentiation to a state of increasing differentiation, articulation, and hierarchic integration. He differentiated levels of mental functioning through the use of such distinctions as syncretic–discrete, diffuse–articulated, rigid–flexible, and labile–stable. As will be pointed out later, these concepts are particularly relevant for a characterization of cognitive distortions in patients suffering from schizophrenic syndromes (see "Decentering and Egocentrism," Chapter 9).

Modern research findings, which have only been summarized here, cast a new light on the development of cognitive–emotional structures in humans. I subscribe to the opinion advanced by Basch (1977) that, "When psychoanalysts speak of part object perception in infants, and of object permanence existing long before symbolic capacity is achieved . . . they are confusing progress in the complexity of transactional adaptation with a capacity for abstraction and symbol formation" (p. 249). The psychoanalytical conceptualization of infancy has been criticized (Peterfreund, 1978) from a cognitive perspective and I concur with this criticism. My main hypothesis is that different disturbing factors may interact at various stages of cognitive–emotional development, thus contributing to the development of vulnerability, and that hypotheses that connect the occurrence of all kinds of manifest schizophrenic syndromes exclusively to a disordered self-object differentiation are reductionistic.

## PARENTAL REARING ATTITUDES

The importance assigned to the concepts of attachment and communication in our model is intimately connected with the meaning ascribed to the experience by patients of their parents' (or parental substitutes') rearing attitudes. Despite a certain inconsistency in the literature, reported results seem to show that patients suffering from schizophrenic syndromes have often experienced rejection, domination, and demands by their mothers (Alanen, 1958; Heilbrun, 1960, 1973; Hirsch & Leff, 1975; Liem, 1980; Parker, 1983; Reichhard & Tillman, 1950). Regarding the patients' experiences of their fathers, results are more uncertain. The father has been traditionally described as peripheral and weak, insecure in his masculinity, with low self-esteem (Cheek, 1965; Heilbrun, 1973; Lidz, Cornelison, Fleck, & Terry, 1957). However, studies do exist where the father has been felt, especially by male patients, to be the more dominating parent (Farina & Holzberg, 1967; Piety, 1967): Parker (1983) reported that schizophrenic patients regard both parents as being less caring than do healthy persons. Biller (1974) pointed out that boys who have experienced loss of their father (either from his absence or from his weakness) tend to become uncertain in their relationships with peers and with persons of authority while at the same time becoming more attached to their mother.

Heilbrun has been a major proponent of a theory of schizophrenic development based on the experience of aversive maternal control. According to Heilbrun (1973), this experience introduces "a type of pathological circularity into the child's development" (p. 151) in the sense that maternal control and maternal rejection contribute to shape a poor self-image and to foster expectations of further rejections. These expectations act as deterrents in the initiation of new relationships that could lead to independence. Thus, the child "remains entrenched in the very relationship which instigated his problems" (p. 151). For Heilbrun, the role of the father is decidedly of a secondary importance.

Many difficulties clearly arise when attempting to correlate the fostering attitudes of parents with psychopathological disorders that occur in the child later in life. Some of the more common pitfalls, for instance, the use of patient groups that are too small to warrant generalization, faulty definitions of disorders, and the use of unreliable measuring instruments, have been extensively discussed in the literature (e.g., Parker, 1983; C. Perris, 1987c). Other more serious errors arise when schizophrenic patients are treated as a homogeneous group and, especially, when a possible simple linear relationship between deviant fostering attitudes and a poorly defined and hardly unitary disease is sought. My theoretical framework explicitly stresses interactions and focuses on the concept of vulnerability. Consequently, much more importance is attached to studies in which attempts are made to assess to what extent the development of different characteristics in children that might increase their particular vulnerability is affected by deviant fostering practices in their parents. Studies by Rosenthal, Wender, Kety, Schulsinger, Welner, and Rieder (1975) are consistent with this approach. These authors tried to tease apart the effects of heredity and rearing on the development of psychopathological disorders in the child. According to their conclusions, both quality of rearing and hereditary input affect the development of psychopathological disorders, but the amount of variance explained by rearing tends to be low.

Investigations of how rearing practices promote the development of dysfunctional personality characteristics are especially relevant in this context, and several publications are available (see C. Perris, Eisemann, Ericsson, von Knorring, & H. Perris, 1983, and C. Perris, 1987c, for updated surveys). One study of this kind was reported by Willenson (1960), who compared personality structures in persons who regarded themselves as being accepted and respected by their parents with those in persons who had experienced parental rejection. The results showed that the latter lack self-esteem, show less self-respect, and are more self-critical than the former. These observations accord well with those of Watson (1957) and Flaherty and Richman (1986), who found that the experience of a liberal and warm fostering attitude by the parents was strongly related with better socialization, an enhanced ability to cooperate, and a wider social network in the children. From our investigations (Jacobsson, Lindström, von Knorring, C. Perris, & H. Perris, 1980; C. Perris *et al.*, 1983), my coworkers and I have been able to show, as have many others, a strong relationship between the experience of a rejecting, love-depriving parental attitude and aggressive traits in the personalities of both healthy and previously depressed subjects.

Of particular interest for my theoretical framework are those studies in which possible relationships between parental fostering attitudes and cognitive development have been investigated. Research in this field has suggested that a deviant verbal ability is promoted by a close relationship to a demanding and intrusive mother (e.g., Bing, 1963) and that excessive parental control hampers the development of flexible thought (Busse, 1969). Hess and Shipman (1965) reported results consistent with those just mentioned. They found that the growth of cognitive processes, for instance, the ability to solve problems, is promoted in families with a system of control that permits a wide choice of alternative actions, while it is retarded in families where rigid, emotionally cool, and rejective fostering attitudes predominate. Heilbrun, Orr, and Harrell (1966) reported that healthy college males rating their mothers as highly controlling–low nurturant were poorer in conceptual performance than those who had rated their mothers as low controlling–highly nurturant. More recently, Litovsky and Dusek (1985) reported a positive correlation between an atmosphere of parental acceptance and self-esteem in adolescents. In particular, they found that high–self-esteem adolescents perceived their parents as more accepting and as using less psychological control. The results obtained by Litovsky and Dusek are consistent with those reported by several other authors (e.g., Coopersmith, 1967, Gecas, 1972, and Walker & Greene, 1986, to mention a few). G. R. Adams and Jones (1982) and Riley, Adams, and Nielsen (1984) reported results supporting the hypothesis that a significant relationship exists between parental rejection and control and adolescent egocentrism. On the other hand, Baron (1986) showed that egocentrism is signficantly related to the development of basic dysfunctional attitudes of the kind taken into account by Beck (1976) in his theory of emotional disorders. These last results are of particular interest because egocentrism is a variable that characterizes several of the cognitive distortions in patients with schizophrenic syndromes.

Further research has concerned possible relationships between experienced parental rearing attitudes and locus of control of reinforcement (Rotter, 1966). Locus of control is a cognitive personality variable that refers to the belief that one has control over events and actions in one's life (internal control) as contrasted with the belief that one has no control over events and actions in one's life, which are controlled, instead, by luck, chance, fate, or powerful others (external control). Assumptions concerning locus of control are included in almost all theories of cognitive psychotherapy. Repeated investigations (Austrin & Aubuchon, 1979; Davis & Phares, 1969; Levenson, 1973a, 1973b; MacDonald, 1971; Nowicki & Segal, 1974; Rohner, Chaille, & Rohner, 1980) have consistently shown that externality is significantly correlated with parental rearing characterized by protectiveness, punitiveness, and control. By contrast, internality appeared to be related to parental acceptance, parental nurturance, and trust in parents. Furthermore, other studies have shown that externality is positively correlated with measures suggesting low self-esteem (e.g., Fish & Karabenick, 1971).

Obviously, the intrafamilial transactions relevant as possible contributors to the development of vulnerability are not limited to rearing practices. Other important aspects concerning the family characteristics of the schizophrenic patients are discussed below. The purpose of this review has been to draw attention to those different factors that are relevant to the development of dysfunctional cognitions in patients with schizophrenic syndromes and to point out how these factors may interact with each other. Other important factors are discussed later (see "Recognition of Cognitive Distortions," Chapter 9).

## FROM THE "SCHIZOPHRENOGENIC MOTHER" TO THE "SCHIZOPHRENOGENIC FAMILY" AND BEYOND

Questions concerning the role of the parents and the role of the family environment in the development of the mental disorder of the patient have long been of central importance, particularly in schizophrenic patients. A critical examination of the various hypotheses that have been presented and the innumerable studies that have been carried out is beyond the scope of this book, and the reader is referred to the more specialized literature (e.g., Fontana, 1966; G. Frank, 1965; Goldstein & Rodnick, 1975; Lidz, 1972; Liem, 1980; Reiss, 1975; Wynne, 1981; Wynne, Toohey, & Doane, 1979). In the present context, however, attention must be drawn to some of these hypotheses because of their significance in psychotherapy.

Diverse opinions exist, especially in the psychoanalytical literature, about how one correctly judges the reports given by patients of their early experiences with others of importance in their environment—especially their mothers. Arieti (1955, 1959, 1968, 1974a, 1974c) is one researcher who has changed his opinion on this topic. In his early writings, Arieti (1955, 1957) adopted wholeheartedly the prevalent conception of the so-called schizophrenogenic mother, introduced into the literature by Fromm-Reichmann (1948), who wrote, "The schizophrenic is painfully distrustful and resentful of other people, due to the severe early warp and rejection he encountered in important people of his infancy and childhood, as a rule, mainly in a schizophrenogenic mother" (pp. 249-250). Arieti (1957) maintained that, "Thus schizophrenia is interpreted as a result not of increased pressure of the instinctual drives, but of the early severe interpersonal conflict. . . . The very critical and antagonistic attitude of the parent is originally introjected by the preschizophrenic child, who will acquire a critical condemnatory attitude toward himself" (p. 539). Such opinions echoed what was generally believed in psychoanalytical circles at that time, as synthetized in Searles's (1959) statement, "My clinical experience has indicated that the individual becomes schizophrenic partly by reason of a long-continued effort, a largely or wholly unconscious effort, on the part of some person or persons highly important in his upbringing to drive him crazy" (p. 1).

In his later articles, Arieti (1968, 1974a, 1974c) maintained, however, that a study of the home environments of patients he had personally treated showed that only 25% of the mothers appeared to conform to the grotesque, stereotypical picture of a "monster of motherhood" that had been previously described. It is remarkable that Arieti did not indicate the proportion of possible pathogenic fathers, although he kept "some statistics" of his cases and mentioned that in some cases the father was the dominating parent. Arieti's analysis was retrospective, and he never attempted to verify it with later case histories. Arieti's opinions were not based on extensive data, since they were derived from his own psychoanalytical work with schizophrenic patients. Also, there is no evidence suggesting that Arieti met all of the mothers who were the basis of his different opinions.

Naturally, Arieti is not the only psychoanalyst prone to speculative generalizations. Much more worthy of comment is Arieti's assertion in his later writings that psychoanalysts have been led to believe what patients tell them during analysis, so they consequently commit mistakes similar to those made by Sigmund Freud when he believed his patients' recollections of sexual abuse during childhood. Arieti's conclusion was that patients' memories of disturbing influences by parents are products of their distorted reconstructions of what had actually happened, that is, figments of their imaginations. Thus, although Arieti himself admitted that one of four of his unselected patients had had a mother who corresponded to the stereotype of the schizophrenogenic mother, and that in a few cases the father might have been pathogenic, at the end he preferred to follow the path indicated by Freud in his discussion of "Dora" and to neglect the "historical truth." It is likely that sources of confusion concerning this issue are related to the psychoanalytical tendency to view "schizophrenia" as a unitary disorder (despite claims to the contrary), to the search for reductionistic linear causal relationships, and to generalizing to the whole population of patients with schizophrenic syndromes the findings observed in a few cases.

Other investigations carried out by other psychoanalysts have given results different from those reported by Arieti. Alanen (1958) carried out a careful personal study of the mothers of 100 schizophrenic patients. He found that at least 84% of these mothers were themselves suffering from severe mental disorders. Alanen stressed that an analysis of the relationship between mother and child revealed a common occurrence (85%) of a certain type of mother, characterized by a dominating and nonunderstanding attitude to her child. Alanen's results are consistent with those obtained by Ernst (1956), who personally examined the family environments of his patients, which had been described as ordinary, and who found that in reality serious conflicts existed in almost all of them. More recently, Roeder (1986) reported on an extensive investigation of the mothers of 72 patients undergoing psychoanalytical therapy in Munich. According to Roeder, 16 of them could be described as overprotective and possessive. The majority, however, were characterized as withdrawn, emotionally cold, and reserved.

Although many shifting descriptions of the mothers of schizophrenic patients are found in the literature, it appears that analytical authors often tend to generalize from experiences with only a few patients and to use powerfully negative language that may well conceal different forms of transference and countertransference reactions. For example, Arieti (1968) wrote that the expression "monstrous human being" has been used, and Rosen (1962) described these mothers as possessing "a perverse feeling of motherhood." Other common descriptions include "coldly sadistic" and "mean and vindictive." Aside from the unexpected use of particularly strong derogatory terminology in the psychoanalytical literature, it is also surprising that so little was done, at a time when the concept of the schizophrenogenic mother prevailed, to spread information about the possible grounds for these mothers' "perverse" attitudes toward their children. Instead, suspicion of some premeditating evil pervaded the general opinion, making hundreds of mothers into scapegoats. Arieti (1968), in retracting his earlier opinion on the schizophrenogenic mother, suggested that many patients have reconstructed their image of the mother (who, of course, had at least some negative characteristics) negatively, developing an "antiparental zeal" (Arieti, 1976). He assumed that the child becomes oversensitive to the negative characteristics of the mother because those are the parts that hurt and to which he or she responds deeply, neglecting all other (positive) characteristics. Once again, however, no mention is made of the father.

Arieti's interpretation is understandable from a cognitive psychotherapeutic perspective and becomes meaningful if the concept of "vulnerability" is taken into account. It also reaffirms the doubts voiced by Fromm-Reichmann (1948), who allowed for the possibility that the schizophrenic may merely interpret rejection by the mother rather than be exposed to it. However, Arieti's formulation leaves the reader uncertain about the extent of what may have really happened and about the importance assigned to the "historical truth." A further contradiction in Arieti's writings is apparent in one of his reviews of the individual psychotherapy of schizophrenia (Arieti, 1962a). In this review, Arieti, when defining the characteristics of "relatedness" in conceptualizing the therapist–patient relationship, pointed out that relatedness should not be considered only supportive but should also be considered "nutritional" in order to give to the patient "what he did not have before in sufficient quantity" (Arieti, 1962a, p. 24); this again implies defective mothering. Similar implicit assumptions recur in the writings of almost all object-relations theoreticians, even in those of authors who emphasize a biological component in the growth of object relations (Modell, 1963).

There have been a few attempts to identify the reasons for the mothers' dysfunctional behavior toward their children. Szalita-Pemow (1951), for example, maintained that the mother of the schizophrenic patient is as she is because she "rejects and disapproves of herself rather than of the baby" (p. 296), while Searles (1958b) emphasized that such a mother fears her own "love-feelings," which she perceives to be destructive and which she therefore represses. It is as a result of this repression, wrote Searles, that the child who later becomes schizophrenic is deprived of the love needed for a sound development and that the child feels his or her own love to be rejected. Searles pointed out that these mothers in their turn have often experienced contact difficulties with their own mothers. Alanen (1958) asserted that the majority of mothers of schizophrenics are mentally disturbed (although not necessarily schizophrenic), causing the relationship with the child to become highly dysfunctional. In a later, more provocative, article, Searles (1959) regarded the effort to drive the other person crazy as a psychological equivalent of murder. Searles maintained that this effort can be dominated "by a desire to externalize, and thus get rid of, the threatening craziness in oneself" (p. 7). On the other hand, Searles (1958b, 1959) stressed that the child loves the mother so deeply that he or she sacrifices developing individually to the symbiosis necessary for the mother's personality functioning. A conception akin to that maintained by Searles is evident in a later article by Waxler (1975), who suggested that deviance (even in the form of schizophrenia) is required in all families because it serves several important functions; he maintained that "certain family members, if they do not volunteer, are induced by the family to behave in a deviant way" (p. 39).

The role of the father has often been neglected in early discussions. The father has, for the most part, been required as a passive and ineffective individual incapable of compensations for the dominance of the mother, but occasionally he has been described as tyrannical or sadistic, dominating or overtly rejective (Rubins, 1969). Only in a few reports has the father clearly been assigned the responsibility for a seriously disturbed and pathogenic relationship with the child who later becomes schizophrenic (Bowen, Dysinger, & Basamania, 1959; Cheek, 1965; Fleck, Lidz, & Cornelison, 1963; Lidz & Lidz, 1949;

Searles, 1959). In some of these cases, a hidden or open incestuous relationship has been particularly stressed. A relationship of this kind resulting in a schizophrenic disorder was described by F. Scott Fitzgerald in his famous novel *Tender Is the Night*. On the basis of similar reasoning, some investigators have attempted to find differences in paternal attitudes depending on the sex of the patient, but the results of such studies have been inconsistent.

In cognitive psychotherapy, it is evident that our recollections of past event are reconstructed and may be distorted through the same mechanisms that distort the perception and the processing of more recent information; still, it is a big step to the idea of "fantasy theory." A cognitive therapist emphasizes the patient's idiosyncratic perception of external events, but he or she does not ignore the historical truth. Exceptions are to be found, however, in psychoanalytical quarters; Miller, Bowly, Kohut, and Peterfreund are examples.

The results of many recent investigations, which reveal a frighteningly high occurrence of sexual abuse and other maltreatment of children, should provide food for thought for those who blindly cling to "fantasy theory" or "distorted reconstructions." If one accepts that these child abuse statistics represent the tip of the iceberg, widespread ill treatment does not appear at all unreasonable. In my opinion, it would be disastrous for many schizophrenic patients if, during therapy, the therapist were to suggest that "they do not know what they are expected not to know, or that they have not felt what one expects them not to have felt" (Bowlby, 1979).

Accepting the historical truth does not mean that the likely occurrence of later distorted reconstructions is rejected but emphasizes that both aspects of this interactional process must be taken into account. Also, an acceptance of the historical truth does not imply that a causal relationship between dysfunctional parenting and "schizophrenia" is also accepted.

The parent–child relationship has not, however, been the only focus for investigation. By the late 1940s, the interest of some researchers was focused on the family as a whole rather than on a single parent. Three different research groups have been instrumental in this change of interest: that of Lidz at Yale University; that of Bateson in Palo Alto; and that of Wynne, first at Bethesda and later in New York. Many others have later joined these pioneers including Alanen in Finland, Ernst in Switzerland, and Laing and Cooper in the United Kingdom, to name some of the most prominent.

Even though the aspects of familial patterns addressed by the three original groups are quite similar, some differences exist. The Lidz group emphasized narcissistic preoccupations in the parents and described specific parental relationships (marital schism and marital skew) conducive to the development of schizophrenia (Lidz *et al.*, 1957). Bateson and coworkers attached importance to ambiguities in communication, particularly the concept of double bind (Bateson *et al.*, 1956). Wynne and his colleagues concentrated on the parents' amorphous and fragmented style of communication and "pseudomutuality" (Wynne *et al.*, 1979). Unfortunately, a detailed analysis of these somewhat differing points of focus cannot be given here, and the reader is referred to the comprehensive surveys quoted at the beginning of this section. However, it is important to point out here that this change of viewpoint, from the earlier focus on the single parent, has meant that interest in the entire family in therapy has increased enormously. However, neither family theories of schizophrenia (M. J. Goldstein & Rodnick, 1975; Lancet, 1975); nor the family therapy approach to the schizophrenic patient (Massie & Beels, 1972) have resisted later criticism. Goldstein and Rodnick (1975) concluded their review by stating that evidence did not permit a clear-cut statement on the role of family factors in the development of schizophrenia, and Beels (1975) stated, a little boldly, that there was hardly anyone who would assert that family therapy constituted a high-priority method of treatment for schizophrenic patients. In their survey of 1980, L. R. Mosher and Keith pointed out that no documentation in support of the decisive importance of family therapy in the treatment of schizophrenic patients had been forthcoming.

More recently, attention has been focused on the possible impact of communication deviance (CD) in the family on thinking in schizophrenic patients (Sass, Gunderson, Thaler-Singer, & Wynne, 1984). The results of these investigations suggest that schizophrenics with pronounced formal thought disorders have parents with more pronounced speech CD than do patients with constricted forms of thinking. Thus, it seems that the chimerical aim of identifying family factors causative of schizophrenia is being abandoned; instead, the aim of identifying to what extent dysfunctional patterns of communication within the family may be related to specific clinical manifestations is being substituted. In this respect, the studies of Reiss (1967, 1971), which attempt to relate family interaction to individual thinking, are particularly relevant because they suggest a relationship between family interaction and the thought and perception of individual members; thus, they are consistent with assumptions on the development of vulnerability.

Studies of a different type were initiated at the beginning of 1960s by Brown and coworkers (Brown, Monck, Carstairs, & Wing, 1962; Brown, Birley, & Wing, 1972) in the United Kingdom and were further developed by Julian Leff and his colleagues (Kuipers, 1979; Leff & Vaughn, 1981; Leff *et al.*, 1982; Vaughn & Leff, 1976). These authors studied the extent to which a domestic environment characterized by an openly critical or overintrusive attitude toward the patient affected the course of the schizophrenic syndrome. The concept of expressed emotions (EEs) was used to assess the manifest emotional atmosphere in the family; see Kuipers (1979) for a review of the concept of EEs. The results of several independent investigations seem to confirm the assumption that a family environment with a high index of EEs may precipitate relapse in otherwise well-stabilized patients. Two factors appear to mediate this effect: the amount of face-to-face contact with relatives and medication. Low contact and regular medication appear to be the best predictors of a reduced relapse rate, while the effect of adequate medication seems to be counteracted by frequent exposition to EEs.

The results of these studies, and the problems following the overall reduction in hospital beds for schizophrenic patients, have produced still another shift of interest concerning families of schizophrenics. Although some attempts in this direction were presented a few decades ago (Evans, Bullard, & Solomon, 1961), it is only recently that the role of the family as a resource in the management of the mentally ill has been actively addressed. Supportive, psychoeducational strategies have been developed for interventions with families, especially those with a high index of EEs (Anderson, Reiss, & Hogarty, 1986; Falloon, Boyd, & McGill, 1984; Leff & Vaughn, 1981; Leff *et al.*, 1982; Strachan, 1986). The reported results concerning varied methods of intervention have demonstrated a significant decrease in relapse rate (and, to a certain extent, an improvement in social functioning) after psychosocial interventions used in combination with neuroleptic medication. Since these interventions are concrete and practical, and some of them are clearly based on cognitive–behavioral therapeutic techniques (e.g., problem-solving), they fit well with an even more holistic program than that described in this book. We already carry out, albeit unsystematically, similar interventions with the families of the patients admitted to our centers, and we plan to expand this part of the program in the near future.

Taking into account the results of most of the studies reported above that demonstrate the effects of different parental attitudes on cognitive development, the hypothesis can be derived (C. Perris, 1987c) that the link between parental rearing attitudes and dysfunctional familial interactions on the one side, and psychopathology in the developing individual on the other side, can be conceptualized in terms of the development of dysfunctional self-schemata, as illustrated in Figure 4-2, which enhance the child's vulnerability. In this context, it is worth mentioning that Parker (1983) reported that schizophrenic patients who had experienced their parents as emotionally cool

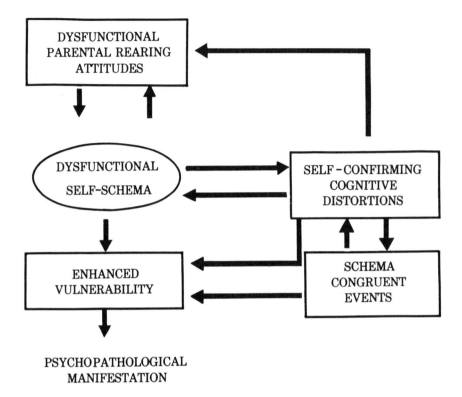

FIGURE 4-2. This represents the possible relationship between parental rearing attitudes and the occurrence of psychopathological manifestations in the offspring. The two are linked by the development of dysfunctional meaning structures in the offspring. These structures are continuously validated and reinforced by various cognitive distortions.

showed a greater frequency of readmissions. Thus, it would appear that the parental attitude experienced by the patients as children continues to be of predictive value even later in adulthood.

Before concluding this section, it is important to emphasize, once again, that the relationship between the parents (and other relatives) and the child who later becomes schizophrenic must always be considered from an interactional perspective, taking into account both the historical truth and successive reconstructions, and must not be understood in terms of linear causality. Furthermore, the development of dysfunctional self-schemata shall not be understood as occurring exclusively early in life; it is a structuring and restructuring process that continues into adulthood.

## CONCLUDING REMARKS

Space constraints have not allowed the inclusion here of a critical analysis of a large body of research concerning the neurophysiological and biochemical mechanisms assumed to be relevant to the cognitive disturbances observed in patients with schizophrenic disorders or to the structural brain changes reported to occur in subgroups of patients. It is also impossible at this juncture to deal with all relevant literature concerning the importance of life events to the occurrence of schizophrenic syndromes that has accumulated since the early studies by Brown and Birley (1968). On the other hand, a survey of the most relevant findings has been made available by Godwin-Rabkin (1980), and a critical appraisal of what has been labeled the "triggering hypothesis" has been published by R. Day (1981). However, since life events are comprised in the conceptual schema reported in Figure 2-1, and since their relevance is much debated, importance must be attributed to stressful life events not only as occasional precipitants of acute schizophrenic syndromes, but also as important contributors to the development of vulnerability. In other words, it is impossible to disentangle life events from other pathogenic influences in the past. Thus, important events might have occurred long before the onset of manifest psychopathology, contributing to making the person who has experienced them even more vulnerable. For example, the sudden loss of her father at age 11 was the event that emphasized a disturbed relationship between one of our patients and her mother. In another case, sexual abuse at age 10 was the event that strongly influenced the capacity for a patient to establish interindividual relationships, and it was the beginning of a tendency for withdrawal. In both cases, however, manifest psychotic symptoms occurred for the first time several years later.

Another assumption, clearly indicated in my model, is that the impact of life events must always be seen in relation to the vulnerability of the individual who experiences them (H. Perris, 1982a). Research work carried out by my coworkers and I suggests that both biological correlates of temperamental variables (H. Perris, von Knorring, Oreland, & C. Perris, 1984) and individual perceptual reactance (von Knorring, Jacobsson, C. Perris, & H. Perris, 1980) may be important determinants of the experience of life events.

"Schizophrenia" is a provisional collective denomination for heterogeneous disorders that only share (and only to a certain extent) some common characteristics. At the present state of our knowledge, we can only speak about "schizophrenic syndromes." It is obvious that no single factor (or group of factors) can consistently be singled out as the true ultimate cause of all schizophrenic syndromes.

The concept of "individual vulnerability" is preferred in studying schizophrenic syndromes to single causal variables, independently of whether those variables are pertinent to the biological, intrapsychic, or social domains. To take vulnerability into account is heuristic in that it allows us to try to become aware of how factors from many different domains may interact to enhance this vulnerability. Furthermore, a focus on vulnerability also allows us to take into account the important impact of protective or "buffering" factors (Rutter, 1985), which can mitigate the negative influence of stressful experiences at various periods of an individual's life and make him or her resilient in the face of adversity.

The frame of reference illustrated in Figures 2-1 and 2-3 cannot, at its present stage, be regarded as a theory of mental disorders or of schizophrenia. The framework only indicates the most important criteria for research. Its advantage is that it indicates specific hypotheses that can be derived and tested. The particular focus on cognitive processes also allows us to bridge the gap between biological and psychosocial factors.

Theoreticians who have proposed similar models focusing on vulnerability have taken into account the concept of "threshold" to explain the breakthrough of manifest episodes of illness (e.g., Zubin & Spring, 1977). Although the concept of threshold is undoubtedly pertinent, it does not represent a feasible approach with which to map the concomitant contribution of different factors to the occurrence of schizophrenic disorders and their discontinuous course.

Understanding of the necessity of looking for new approaches in order to capture the interrelationships among different variables is emerging. One such approach focuses on the "catastrophe theory" proposed by the French mathematician Thom (1975) and further developed by Zeeman (1976). Thom's theory is derived from topology, the branch of mathematics concerned with the properties of surfaces in many dimensions. Topology is relevant because the underlying forces in nature can be described by smooth surfaces of equilibrium; it is when the equilibrium breaks down that catastrophes occur (Zeeman, 1976). Catastrophe theory attempts to describe the shapes of all possible equilibrium surfaces. Thom has solved this problem for processes controlled by no more than four factors in terms of seven elementary forms, which he calls the elementary catastrophes (i.e., fold, cusp, swallowtail, hyperbolic umbilic, elliptic umbilic, butterfly, and parabolic umbilic). Even the catastrophes that cannot be drawn can be employed in modeling phenomena, and the movement of a point over the behavior surface can be studied analytically. As Zeeman pointed out, the method can be applied with particular effectiveness in those situations where gradually changing forces or motivations (as in vulnerability factors) lead to abrupt changes in behavior (e.g., the breakthrough of a schizophrenic syndrome).

While this book cannot deal with different applications of catastrophe theory (e.g., as in optics, engineering, embryology; see Stewart, 1975), it is worthwhile to point out that its use for the study of possible interactions among neurochemical and environmental influences in the control of schizophrenia has been recently discussed by MacCulloch and Waddington (1979). Zeeman (1976) described its application for the occurrence and treatment of anorexia nervosa and for the study of cathartic release from self-pity (Figure 4-3).

Since a focus on vulnerability and on a great variety of factors assumed to interact in influencing it is not reductionistic, treatment

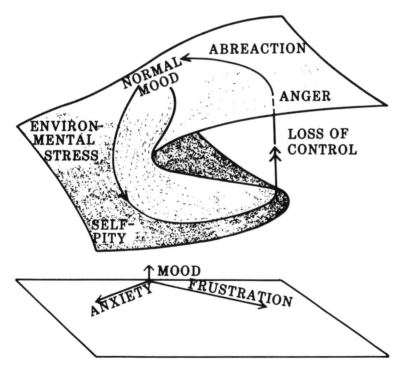

FIGURE 4-3. A cusp catastrophe, in which anxiety and frustration are the factors assumed to influence mood, illustrates the abreactive release from anger. When the control point (on the right in the figure) crosses the cusp, the mood changes catastrophically from self-pity to anger, and thereafter a release of tension follows. Adapted from *Catastrophe Theory*, by E. C. Zeeman. Copyright © 1976 by Scientific American, Inc. All rights reserved.

approaches guided by this concept will not be reductionistic either. I fully agree with Cancro and Angrist (1978) that "No single treatment can hope to achieve the range of possible therapeutic goals" (p. 202). Thus, there is no sense either to prolong psychoanalytical treatment for decades before acknowledging the limits of analysis (Freedman, 1972; Rothstein, 1982; Zimmerman, 1982) or to be disappointed if a sizeable proportion of patients with schizophrenic syndromes do not fully respond to modern psychopharmacological treatment.

However, most of our patients, irrespective of diagnostic grouping or causal considerations, have incorporated dysfunctional cognitions and, more specifically, have developed dysfunctional basic schemata or dysfunctional meaning structures. These not only determine their self-conception, but they also strongly influence their evaluation of past, present, and future relationships with the environment. The assumptions on which we base our cognitive psychotherapeutic approach are summarized as follows (C. Perris, 1988b).

1. The individual who will develop a schizophrenic syndrome has, for various reasons related to his or her particular predicament, developed a fundamentally dysfunctional self-schema comprising both a dysfunctional self-image and dysfunctional basic assumptions (or basic rules of life) concerning his or her relationship with the environment. Both the self-schema (encompassing the individual's emotional capabilities and motivational dispositions) and the dysfunctional basic assumptions are assumed to be largely unconscious.

2. The dysfunctional self-schema and the dysfunctional basic assumptions, thus incorporated, are continuously sustained by a variety of cognitive distortions in the comprehension and processing of information. These distortions might relate to the actual perception of a certain situation or to a subsequent evaluation of the event. Biochemical and neurophysiological factors contribute to the particular characteristics of some of these distortions.

3. Schema-related, automatic dysfunctional thoughts occur, involuntarily and repetitively, every time the dysfunctional self-schema is activated by either external or internal stimuli perceived by the individual as a threat to his or her personal domain. Even dysfunctional automatic thoughts are assumed to occur out of focal awareness and, thus, to be largely unconscious.

# 5

# Psychotherapy and Schizophrenic Syndromes

Before describing the way in which cognitive psychotherapy is applied with patients suffering from schizophrenic syndromes, a few general comments on psychotherapy with schizophrenic patients are presented. It is hoped that these remarks will allow the reader to assess what cognitive therapy has to offer in this field.

During recent years, a number of reviews of the psychotherapy of "schizophrenia" have appeared (e.g., Arieti, 1962a, 1974a; Day & Semrad, 1978; Gunderson, 1979; Gunderson & Mosher, 1975; Matussek, 1976; Rubins, 1972; Spotnitz, 1986; Will, 1975; to mention a few). They have provided details of the applicability of psychoanalysis and psychoanalytically oriented psychotherapy to this type of disorder. The following general remarks are based on a conservative interpretation of the message contained in the above surveys and on other relevant literature.

The first point that can be made, and with which most authors agree, is that traditional psychoanalytical technique is not directly applicable to schizophrenic patients. This opinion was originally maintained by Freud, who, according to Federn (1943, p. 136), regarded psychotics to be "a nuisance to psychoanalysis." Freud (1911–1914) warned against accepting schizophrenics for treatment on the basis of their incurability and later affirmed that "they have no capacity for transference" (Freud, 1917, p. 447). However, Freud's pessimistic opinion concerning the ability of such patients to develop a genuine transference was soon shown to be unjustified by those analysts who devoted themselves to the treatment of schizophrenic patients (e.g., Federn, 1943; Fromm-Reichmann, 1939; Sullivan, 1931). On the other hand, it should not be forgotten that Freud himself had predicted that technical modifications were perhaps needed if his method were to be applicable to this type of patient. It is interesting from a historical perspective that the term "psychoanalytically oriented psychotherapy" was coined by Fromm-Reichmann (1948) especially for the modified psychoanalysis that she conducted with her schizophrenic patients. She maintained in this context that "every psychiatrist must find his own style in his psychotherapeutic approach to schizophrenic patients" (Fromm-Reichmann, 1954, p. 418). Later authors (e.g., Bover, 1961) have frequently used the concept of "parameter," introduced by Eissler (1953), to indicate any deviation, both quantitative and qualitative, from the basic technique. In practice, it seems that most analysts have felt free to adapt their approach to the actual condition of the patient rather than to expect the patient to adapt strictly to the technical rules of their method. One of the most conservative in this respect seems to have been McLaughlin (1982) whereas one of the most deviant appears to have been Rosen (1947, 1962), with his "direct" approach.

Cognitive psychotherapy with schizophrenic patients has, as discussed in Part 3 of this book, several points of contact with the psychotherapy recommended by many analysts, especially those who are particularly active in their approach. It should not be surprising that most connections are with the work by Arieti, who was one of the first to stress the importance of a cognitive dimension in psychoanalysis (Arieti, 1948); with Shulman (1968), who was schooled in Adler's tradition and who emphasized the necessity to focus treatment on a change in the patients' erroneous preconceptions; and with Jacobs (1980, 1982), who was clearly inspired by Beck's cognitive therapy. However, as shown later, adherence to Bowlby's attachment theory establishes an important link with object-relations analysts as well, especially concerning the therapist–patient relationship.

A second point of agreement concerns the significance ascribed by almost all authors, independently of theoretical orientation, to the therapist–patient relationship, which may also include assistant therapists (Arieti & Lorraine, 1972; Cox, 1986; Day & Semrad, 1978; Federn, 1943; Rosen, 1962). The relationship between therapist and patient has been defined by Arieti (1962a) as one of "relatedness" in the sense that this term has in the interpersonal psychiatric school. In this context, "relatedness" not only implies the establishment of a good contact with the patient, but also includes the classical psychoanalytical concepts of transference and countertransference (with emphasis on the latter) and, to a certain extent, the idea of object relationship. Emphasis is thus placed on "empathy," which Searles (1958a) defined as a kind of "mutual intuition" (also see Fromm-Reichmann, 1955; Szalita-Pemow, 1955) and which Arieti (1974a) and Shulman (1968, p. 390) interpreted in terms of an I–Thou relationship in Buber's meaning— that is, "complete contact with a person who is relied upon" (Buber, 1954; also see Binswanger, 1942, for the concept of a "dual" relationship). Both Sullivan and Federn recognized the importance of a positive transference, and Arieti referred to an atmosphere of "basic trust" as the primary characteristic of the relationship that should develop between the therapist and the patient. Haugsgjerd (1985) preferred Bion's terminology (1977) and discussed the relationship in terms of the "containing" function of the therapist, to which he referred as "how we receive the patient's externalizations and how we treat them in our own psyche" (Haugsgjerd, 1983, p. 240). This conception is, to a certain extent, similar to the concept of "counteridentification with the psychotic patient" used by Benedetti (1974), who also stressed the therapist's taking on the burden of the patient's psychotic experience. Tähkä (1984) stressed the importance of the therapist as an object with potential for good object relations in the psychotic's isolated world.

Arieti (1962a, 1974a) also emphasized that "relatedness" should not be regarded exclusively as a component in a supportive therapy since it is "nutritional" in the sense that it primarily functions to provide the patient with something he or she has been deprived of earlier in life; see the concept of "restitutive experience" in Sullivan's approach (1931a); the term "corrective Ego-experience" used by Anna Freud (1951); the "facilitating environment" stressed by Winnicott (1965) and used by Eldred (1972); or "anaclitic countertransference" as used by Spotnitz (1986). Both Eissler (1943) and Wexler (1951) maintained that the love and patience shown to the patient are to be regarded as being developmentally related to earlier feelings of contempt and hostility. Karon (1963) wrote that it "is better to react inappropriately occasionally in a warm spontaneous relationship than to create a cold, distant climate during the sessions" (p. 32). In his later writings, Rosen (1962) interpreted the role of the therapist as that of a foster parent. He maintained that the environment in which the patient undergoes treatment is a foster home and that the patient will there find compensation for earlier deprivations. Within the framework of the object relations approach to therapy used by Azima and his coworkers (Azima, 1963; Azima, Wittkower, & LaTendresse, 1958), this parental attitude to the patient is employed to promote a return to child-like behavior. The term "regression" is avoided here for reasons that will later become apparent.

The type of relationship between therapist and patient fostered in cognitive psychotherapy is described in detail later (see "The Therapeutic Relationship" in Chapter 8). Issues of transference and countertransference are also discussed further from a cognitive psychotherapeutic perspective (see "Transference and Countertransference," Chapter 10). However, it can be mentioned here that the approach to the therapist–patient relationship followed by cognitive psychotherapists is in line with most of those described above.

An additional point of common agreement (except on the part of Rosen and some followers of the object-relations approach who favor the promotion of regression) concerns the emphasis given to the patient's "healthy side" in the therapeutic approach (e.g., Arieti, 1966; Benedetti, 1972; Ewalt, 1963; Fromm-Reichmann, 1954; Katan, 1954; Rosenfeld, 1965; Rubins, 1972; Spotnitz, 1986). Arieti ascribed the activity of the therapist great importance during therapy and suggested that he or she become engaged in the daily life of the patient between therapy sessions. It is for such purposes that Arieti, consistent with what Federn (1943) had suggested, often employed an assistant therapist to visit the patient at home in between therapy sessions (Arieti & Lorraine, 1972). Cox (1986), who apparently mostly treated inpatients, made frequent mention of the nurses who are part of the therapeutic team.

Finally, Arieti (1962a, 1974a) maintained, in agreement with what Sullivan (1954) had proposed that the patient wishes to be given tasks of graded difficulty, the execution of which enhances the newly acquired self-confidence, particularly toward the end of treatment. This opinion was also maintained by Jung (1972), who asserted that therapeutic intervention aims at restoring conscious awareness by inducing concentration on reality and by engaging the patient in activities that lure him or her away from the unconscious. Elsewhere, Jung (1966) stressed the individual character of psychogenic disorders and warned psychotherapists that fixed therapeutic methods cannot be applied to individual patients. As seen in later sections, the involvement of the patient in different tasks is one of the major characteristics of cognitive psychotherapy (see "Social Training" and "Homework," Chapter 7, as well as Part 3).

It is also important to mention that the controversy concerning the use of psychotropic drugs in connection with psychotherapy appears to have subsided. A sober attitude to this issue now appears to dominate. It is the prevalent opinion that an adequate and strictly individualized use of medicine is in many cases unavoidable for effective psychotherapy (Arieti, 1974a; Eldred, 1972; Gunderson, 1979; Hymowitz & Spohn, 1980; Matussek, 1981; Rubins, 1972; Rubins & Rucker, 1974). Eldred went so far as to write, "Only by eliminating critical cortical areas of mentation can a psychoanalyst today champion the exclusive efficacy of psychoanalytic treatment. Those of us who do this kind of work with schizophrenics can use any help we can get from other methods of treatment" (Eldred, 1972, p. 155). In this context, it is of interest to point out that Hymowitz and Spohn (1980) have been able to show that antipsychotic drug treatment seems to potentiate the reality attunement of patients, enhancing their capacity to benefit from verbally oriented psychotherapy. My own experience, which dates back to before the commercial availability of modern psychotropic drugs, supports this contention. I also strongly support Matussek's recommendation (1981) that when medication (or any other therapeutic measure beside psychotherapy) becomes necessary, the therapist should undertake responsibility for its administration. When a therapist has initiated treatment of a patient and has succeeded in establishing a relationship based on trust, it is essentially that he or she also assume responsibility for measures deemed necessary. This is true even if the therapist does not totally approve. However, there still are analysts, for example Spotnitz (1986), who refer patients in need of drugs to a practitioner who specializes in pharmacotherapy. Spotnitz wrote that "for analytic psychotherapists to give the drugs themselves tends to interfere with the transference situation, reducing the chances of clinical success" (p. 32).

Only when attention is diverted from the foregoing points to consider other aspects of treatment is it realized that solid ground has been relinquished. It is, for example, impossible to conceive of any set of "parameters" or variations of therapeutic technique that would be accepted by everyone. Each therapist seems to follow his or her own course with regard to both technique and choice of patients, at least as concerns the phase of illness when treatment is implemented. Conflicting technical approaches (e.g., passivity or activity of the therapist, a regression-promoting or regression-hindering attitude, emphasis on interpretations or opposition to their employment, etc.) are asserted with an equal fervor by different therapists. This lack of concordance should not be surprising, though adoption of the viewpoint of Luborsky and Spences (1971) that "psychoanalysts, like other psychotherapists, literally do not know how they achieve their results" seems too drastic.

At a time when there were fewer schools of psychotherapy than there are today, Freud himself held the decided opinion that methods of treatment were personal instruments that could differ somewhat from analyst to analyst (S. Freud, 1911–1914, p. 111). However, alternative variations should be considered beside those concerning a therapist's personal style. The most important variations concern the particular theoretical frame of reference adopted by the therapist, the actual condition of the patient when psychotherapy begins, and the question of whether psychotherapy is conducted with inpatients or outpatients. This last point is discussed more extensively later.

Among several general common denominators that link most therapists is that all five basic classical methods considered by Bibring (1954)—that is, the suggestive, the cathartic, the manipulative, the interpretive, and the explanative—are included, to different degrees, in all therapeutic work. Also, the classical emphasis on transference development and transference resolution (albeit of a different type than used in the analysis of neurotic patients) exists in most reports.

At first glance, it might be thought that the variation in methods guarantees the avoidance of what Peterfreund (1976, 1983) has called a "stereotyped approach to therapy." However, while there certainly are therapists who can entertain different theoretical models with ease, as Kohut (1977), for example, has reported in some of his case studies, this is probably not a widespread phenomenon; also, few of the different models used by one person are likely to be radical departures from the theory in which he or she has been trained. Several examples reported by Peterfreund support this viewpoint. Other problems related to variations in theoretical understanding and the differences in treatment methods that have appeared in the literature are discussed in the "Conclusions" section of this chapter. It is suggested that overadherence to a certain theoretical approach may be one reason why some individuals' therapies last over a decade.

One remarkable example frequently occurs in the psychoanalytic literature. On the one side, the occurrence of spontaneous recovery is strongly emphasized to criticize both biological conceptions of schizophrenia and opinions concerning a chronic deteriorating course. In particular, the opinions of M. Bleuler (1972, 1979) and Cancro (1982) that schizophrenic patients in the long run do tend to recover are frequently mentioned. On the other hand, improvements of various degrees, often achieved after more than a decade of psychoanalytical treatment, are attributed without reservation to the psychotherapeutic treatment.

The question of the length of treatment is especially troublesome when one considers that many reported therapies have been performed with inpatients. Even if one is critical of extremely short hospital admissions, especially when these are not combined with a purposeful follow-up after discharge, it remains to be demonstrated that years of therapy, even in units with a pronounced milieu-therapeutic character, are not associated with any disadvantages. Haugsgjerd (1983) in Norway advocated lengthy hospital treatment, while Salokangas (1986) in Finland reported poorer results with patients who had remained a longer time in a milieu-therapeutic unit. The latter were, however, more satisfied with their treatment than members of a control group who received care in a more traditional setting.

## EFFICACY OF PSYCHOANALYTICAL PSYCHOTHERAPY

The evaluation of the specific effects of psychoanalytical psychotherapy on schizophrenic patients constitutes an extremely controversial question that, for several reasons, requires the taking up of a position.

While the adoption of any position whatsoever will produce an out-cry—at least in some quarters—this issue must be discussed.

I am completely convinced that every psychotherapy conducted for an extended period implies a unique emotional investment in a human relationship between the therapist and his or her patient; therefore, it would be inconceivable that the therapy could not have a profound influence. In addition, I accept that a few especially devoted therapists (and all those who have worked for a long time with schizophrenic patients must be devoted) have been able to achieve excellent results with isolated patients. However, neither these results nor the value of psychotherapy in general for schizophrenic patients is in question. What must be answered, instead, are questions concerning whether psychoanalytical psychotherapy offers the most appropriate alternative for schizophrenic patients, whether it should be adopted exclusively, and which school should be followed. It is only when these questions are answered that it will be possible to earn unreserved enthusiasm from newer therapists who are strongly engaged in their work or in more experienced therapists who have worked for a long time with severely disturbed patients. However, answers to the above questions are not impossible.

Careful study of the literature concerning psychotherapy with schizophrenic patients reveals that no psychotherapeutic school has yet been able to obtain better results than any other, especially when results of long-term follow-ups are considered. Those authors who have reported case studies have obtained "good results" in between 50% and 75% of their cases, independent of their theoretical training and the method employed. Even when the difficulties in objectively evaluating the practical implications of these results are recognized (this by itself would require another book) and the results are accepted at their face value, one unavoidable conclusion is that the number of *truly successful* cases reported, even after more than 50 years of individual psychoanalytic therapy with schizophrenic patients, is no greater than three figures. (This number was estimated by Haugsgjerd, 1983.)

An understandable reason for the relatively small series that have been reported is that therapists who are wholeheartedly engaged in the treatment of schizophrenic patients are still very few and that therapy continuing for more than 10 years is the norm rather than the exception. In addition, most therapists have been selective in the choice of patients suitable for psychotherapy with regard to age, economic status, type of debut, duration of disorder, degree of earlier social adaptation, and motivation for therapy, so the fraction of suitable candidates has been severely limited. Furthermore, a not insignificant number of patients accepted for treatment have, for different reasons, discontinued it after a few months. Add to this changes in diagnostic practices, poor knowledge about the spontaneous course of the disorder in single patients, lack of adequate control over other confounding factors (e.g., other treatments administered, life changes occurring during the several years of treatment, etc.), and lack of consistency in defining "successful" or "good" outcome, and it becomes almost impossible to draw conclusions that can be generalized to the whole population of patients suffering from schizophrenic syndromes.

An example of the ambiguity of results is a report concerning shorter lengths of treatment provided by Rubins (Rubins, 1976; Rubins & Rucker, 1974), from Karen Horney's school of analysis, who described a larger group of patients who were treated for a maximum of 4.5 years (average, 22 months), and who were subsequently followed for a 5-year period. Rubins reported various improvements with respect to different measures); results were highest for psychotic symptoms (88%) and self-appraisal (72%) and lowest for independence and self-confidence (58%). However, it is not clear how these results should be interpreted since the program of treatment was not limited to individual therapy but included milieu therapy at a day center during the entire period, group therapy twice a week, and medication. Consequently, it is impossible to sort out what the specific contribution, if any, of individual therapy has been. However, Rubins's observation that positive results for most measurements were achieved within 2 years and were little affected by further treatment are thought-provoking as they would contradict the practice of endless treatment. An additional support to this opinion that significant improvement can be obtained in a relatively short time by experienced therapists is found in the results reported by Karon and Vandenbos (1970); however, their study has been criticized on methodological grounds (Gunderson, 1979; Tienari, 1986).

Matussek and Triebel (1974), on the other hand, found in a study of 44 patients that, among those 28 treated for 2 years, only eight showed improvement 2 years after the termination of treatment; however, among the 10 who had been treated for longer than 4 years, nine had improved. Once again, though, these results are difficult to interpret, because more variables were employed to gauge improvement than used by Rubins, more than half of the patients were reeiving regular medication (including only five of those who improved), and 14 of the patients had taken part in group therapy. Among the 30 who participated in individual therapy only 15 improved—but it is unclear to what extent and after how long a time. Furthermore, the length of the follow-up was too short to judge long-term effects.

Further relevant information can be extracted from the larger, more systematic investigations that are available. Since these studies have been recently surveyed (e.g., Tienari, 1986), only a few crucial issues are discussed here.

Even though the results of these larger studies must be treated with caution, there is much to indicate that they are, in general, hardly encouraging. First of all, they imply that engagement in intensive psychoanalytical therapy with schizophrenic patients, at least based on currently available theories, has lessened, especially in the United States (Carpenter, 1984; Gunderson, 1979), whereas the rate of use had been increasing (Karon, 1963). This recession probably does not depend only on overconfidence in the effects of psychotropic drugs or on economical considerations, as is occasionally suggested. It is more likely that attention has turned to more modern psychoeducational methods (e.g., C. M. Anderson *et al.*, 1986; Falloon *et al.*, 1984; McFarlane, 1983) that also involve the patient's family and that have proved to be effective in large groups of patients. Since these psychoeducational approaches are also relevant from a cognitive psychotherapeutic perspective they are discussed later in a special section (see "Contacts with Relatives of Patients," Chapter 7).

Even prior to reporting the results of his latest investigation, Gunderson (1979) admitted that a sufficiently flexible and comprehensive theoretical model that includes such factors as the patient's early development, his or her responses to medication, social and familial stress, and factors outside of dyadic relationships is still lacking. Such a model, according to Gunderson, should also include more complex social interactions as well as current knowledge of the diagnosis of schizophrenic disorders and their course.

The results of the study by Gunderson, Frank, Katz, Vannicelli, Frosch, and Knapp (1984) are thought-provoking. The study was an exceptionally well-designed ambitious investigation that lasted for over 10 years. It compared explorative, insight-oriented psychoanalytical therapy (IPP, n = 43) with reality-oriented supportive therapy (SP, n = 52), both conducted by experienced therapists. Unfortunately, there was a large number of dropouts, limiting the usefulness of the results. However, no major significant differences between IPP and SP could be demonstrated. If anything, markedly better social adjustment and fewer relapses after treatment was terminated were observed in the patients who had received SP therapy. Conversely, patients who had received IPP scored better on measures of ego strength.

These findings, together with the results of other competent studies employing practically oriented supportive psychotherapy (Hogarty & Goldberg, 1973/1974), raise the question of whether a continued investment in psychoanalytical therapy—with its demands for long-term training of therapist and personnel, prolonged engagement of both therapist and patient, and the comparative limitations imposed by the usual selection of patients—is really warranted.

## CONCLUSIONS

On the basis of what is known about psychoanalytical psychotherapy with schizophrenic patients, the following reliable conclusions can be drawn:

1. Psychoanalytical psychotherapy can, in isolated cases and in the hands of dedicated therapists, lead to exceptionally good results. These results cannot be ascribed to diagnostic errors or spontaneous remission alone, especially since those patients referred to here have been exposed, without success, to more traditional methods of treatment for extended periods. In many other instances, however, the methodological shortcomings mentioned above, especially the lack of appropriate outcome criteria, suggest cautiousness in evaluating the reported findings.

2. The establishment of a special patient–therapist relationship is regarded by most analysts to be an essential prerequisite for any effective psychotherapy with schizophrenic patients. It can be assumed that such a relationship extended over a period of several years might be one important determinant of improvement in many patients, if not the most important.

3. No acceptable reasons have yet been given that show that strictly individualized administration of psychotropic drugs is detrimental to the process of psychotherapy. Medication is presently used by a majority of the therapists who deal with schizophrenic patients.

4. Psychoanalytical psychotherapy cannot be regarded as a method of treatment that is applicable to all types of schizophrenic patients. Different selection criteria have been used by nearly all therapists, and it has been impossible to reliably identify prognostic criteria that allow the most suitable candidates to be chosen in advance of treatment. Judging from the data in the literature, as summarized by Gunderson (1979), it seems that patients who would not fulfill the criteria for schizophrenia in DSM-III and its more recent revision (DSM-III-R) have been frequently included among the patients accepted for treatment and that these patients have shown the best results.

5. No special theoretical psychoanalytical approach provides better or more permanent results than any other, and no particular method has been shown to be superior. The adequacy of current theories has, on the other hand, been questioned. In addition, warnings of pitfalls associated with overadherence to a specific theoretical model have come from analytical circles.

6. The duration of treatment is, in many cases, disproportionately long in relation to the results achieved. When therapy continues for several years, sometimes more than a decade, it becomes particularly difficult to identify the remedial components of the treatment.

7. Those few scientifically acceptable studies that are available indicate that reality-oriented supportive psychotherapy can produce better results than exploratory, insight-oriented psychotherapy.

8. Despite large variations, traditional psychoanalytical therapy, with its primary emphasis on intrapsychic processes, is reductionistic and not in keeping with modern scientific knowledge.

9. Training in psychoanalytical psychotherapy has become increasingly lengthy without producing significant changes in the results obtained. Attempts to identify the special characteristics of therapists suitable for psychotherapy with patients suffering from schizophrenic syndromes (e.g., the "type A" and "type B" therapists studied by Betz, 1967) have provided inconsistent results (Gunderson, 1978a, 1979); thus, the risk remains that after a large investment in time and money, a trained therapist could prove to be unsuitable for dealing with schizophrenic patients.

10. The basic theoretical training of assistant therapists in psychoanalytically oriented milieu-therapeutic programs also has problems (e.g., it requires at least some postgraduate training background).

Consideration of these points suggests that cognitive psychotherapy may represent a solution to many problems. The theoretical multifactorial standpoint discussed in earlier sections (see "A Dynamic Interactional Framework" in Chapter 2), together with information presented in later chapters about the practical application of this therapy, form the basis for this proposal.

# II

*Cognitive Psychotherapy*
*with Schizophrenic Patients:*
*Milieu Therapy*

# 6

# *Community-Based, Cognitively Oriented Treatment Centers*

In Part 1, it was pointed out that it might be advisable to begin individual psychotherapy with schizophrenic patients while they are admitted to an inpatient setting, which is therapeutic *per se*. There are several good reasons for doing this, as discussed below. Later on, an argument is also presented in defense of a cognitive therapeutic orientation to promote a therapeutic milieu that allows the utilization of all the powerful therapeutic processes that may develop in such a setting (see "Milieu-Therapeutic Processes," Chapter 7).

The focus of the discussion in this part of the book is the implementation and function of small, community-based, cognitively oriented treatment centers in Umeå in Northern Sweden. Since our pioneering work in this field a few years ago, centers of the type described here have been planned in several other places in Sweden. Although the development of such centers must be considered against the background of the National Health System in Sweden, there are two main reasons why their description is warranted in this book. First, centers of this type, as far as I know, are unique and represent a new, important application of cognitive therapy. Second, our approach can easily be generalized to other countries as well. Thus, it is my hope that this chapter will function as a practical source of inspiration and information for others. It is based on the development of three separate small centers, one for the treatment of patients with moderate to severe neurotic disorders and two for the treatment of patients with psychotic or postpsychotic syndromes. The latter type is described here since the former has been described elsewhere (H. Perris, 1986). For the sake of simplicity, attention is focused on only one of these centers, since they do not differ markedly in external form, treatment philosophy, or internal forms of treatment.

## RESTRUCTURATION AND ITS CONSEQUENCES

The development of small community-based treatment centers must be viewed within the framework of the restructuring of psychiatric care, with emphasis on the revolutionary changes in ideology taking place in most parts of the world. The general goals of these changes are well known. They include a gradual abolition of the large, traditional mental hospitals, decentralization of resources to bring them closer to those in need of care, and reduced support for traditional institutionalized care, thereby encouraging alternative solutions. In this context, the division of large catchment areas into smaller sectors is a necessary prerequisite for providing the community-oriented mental health worker with a better knowledge of the patients' actual social conditions. Smaller catchment areas also facilitate the continuity of treatment. Recent surveys of the restructuration of psychiatric care in Italy (C. Perris & Kemali, 1985) and in most of Western Europe (Breemer ter Stege & Gittelman, 1987) are available.

It is important to emphasize that one basic assumption is that patients to be discharged into the community should undergo adequate preparation; also, suitable alternatives to the traditional institutions should be developed for those most in need of specialized care. Unfortunately, it seems that neither of these fundamental prerquisites has been consistently provided. In particular, the planning of suitable alternatives for care of schizophrenic patients has been insufficient or nonexistent.

## ALTERNATIVE FORMS OF TREATMENT

The issue of alternative methods of treatment for patients suffering from "functional psychoses," including schizophrenic syndromes, has been extensively discussed in a meeting of the European Medical Research Councils in Italy in 1983 (Helgason, 1985). On this occasion, I was assigned the task of analyzing alternative treatments and initiating a discussion concerning for which patients the alternative forms of treatment were most topical. This issue was further discussed at an international meeting in Umeå in 1984 organized in collaboration with the World Health Organization's Section for Mental Health (C. Perris, 1984).

It emerged from these meetings, in agreement with opinions expressed in other countries, and in the United States in particular (Segal & Aviram, 1978; Stein & Test, 1978), that schizophrenic patients seldom require hospitalization, even in the acute stage, provided alternative forms of care are available.

For patients in an acute condition, there is some empirical evidence that *short* periods of hospitalization may produce better results, if followed with effective aftercare. However, it has been repeatedly found that length of stay is not a decisive variable in predicting survival in the community after discharge. Rather, the total time in the community has often proved to be longer for patients who received a shorter initial treatment (see C. Perris, 1985c, for review). Also, there is some evidence that hospital admission in itself might have a negative effect on the patient's later adjustment in the community (Test & Stein, 1975). Even though hospital admission of acute cases remains defensible for various reasons, there is nothing to recommend it for patients with more prolonged disorders once they are past the acute phase. The hospital environment is regarded by many as being hardly conducive even for "intensive rehabilitation." In particular, it has repeatedly been stressed that even the successful rehabilitation achieved in a hospital may not be maintained when the patient is discharged, and it is also not related to length of survival in the community (e.g., Paul, 1969).

Many hospitals in different countries have evolved toward a very high standard, and special intensive milieu-therapeutic units can easily be implemented in such settings. However, the experience that I have gained during the process of restructuration in the Swedish area where I work (see C. Perris, 1986c, 1987b, for details of this process) strongly supports the view that planning for more functional community-based alternatives should, whenever possible, be preferred.

## PATIENT GROUPS AND THE NEED FOR DIFFERENTIATION

The relatively young (usually 18–35 years of age) patients who are often regarded as eligible for intensive psychotherapeutic treatment represent, at present, only a minority of the schizophrenic patients for whom alternative forms of care must be planned. De-institutionalization mainly concerns older patients with disorders of a long duration who have been exposed to several years of continuous hospital care as well as other patients who, for various reasons, are judged less suitable for intensive psychotherapeutic efforts. If it is accepted that the number of acute cases tends to decrease in general and that the turnover in intensive psychotherapy units is relatively low, then the planning of alternative small care units must be preceded by a careful assessment of the different needs within each sector (or catchment area) and of which alternative forms of treatment are thereby required. Obviously, it would be a serious mistake only to focus efforts on the development of intensive psychotherapy units. Even though milieu-therapeutic considerations must pervade all care units independently of their location, as well as the types of patients for which they are intended, differences between centers will clearly arise.

At least four different patient groups must be considered in comprehensive planning:

- Somewhat older patients with very long periods of hospitalization who are judged unsuitable for discharge to their own homes (even with supervision) and for whom intensive psychotherapy is not of primary interest.
- Patients of various ages who, following treatment for an acute condition, are in need of a further period of care before being sent home. This group also includes patients with social networks who are not motivated for psychotherapy.
- Patients of various ages who, for different reasons, require special care and relatively long periods of treatment.
- Relatively young patients for whom intensive psychotherapy is indicated and who are themselves (at least to a certain extent) motivated for it.

Different forms of care may be planned in different countries for the first three groups, mainly depending on how the health care delivery system is organized at a national level. However, the principles for a therapeutic environment, as defined by the Health Standards and Quality Bureau of the National Institute of Mental Health (Brands, 1981), apply to all units designed for the care of the first three groups mentioned above.

From the cognitive therapeutic perspective, patients belonging to the last-mentioned group are probably the most relevant, even though older and severely impaired patients have also been included in cognitive therapeutic trials (Meichenbaum, 1977; Meichenbaum & Cameron, 1973). Treatment programs for younger patients have been implemented, or are being implemented, in various countries, including Switzerland and West Germany (Brenner, Hodel, Kube, & Roder, 1987), the United Kingdom (Feldman, personal communication, 1988), and the United States (Greenwood, 1983).

The treatment program developed by the German-speaking researchers is of particular relevance in the present context because it even represents a holistic approach. It includes, for example, the teaching of problem-solving, social skills, and verbal communication, along with the use of interventions aimed at promoting cognitive differentiation. Very promising results obtained by this group have been reported both by Brenner *et al.* (1987) and in a volume edited by Brenner, Rey, and Stramke (1983). A general survey of the treatment program can also be found in an article by Brenner, Stramke, Mewes, Liese, and Seeger (1980).

Two care units have been established in our sector (comprising some 90,000 inhabitants) for the final, younger group, both, able to accommodate a total of six patients of either sex. Further details concerning the other psychiatric facilities in our total psychiatric care system are available elsewhere (C. Perris, 1987b).

## CENTERS FOR INTENSIVE
## COGNITIVE–BEHAVIORAL PSYCHOTHERAPY

### Location and Dimensions

The location of small treatment centers for intensive psychotherapy is clearly dependent on the availability of suitable buildings. Experience from some countries (e.g., Greece) has shown that it is not necessary for such a center to be located in an isolated building; indeed, a center can be incorporated into an apartment building or within housing developments. One of the two cognitive centers in Umeå intended for schizophrenic patients occupies a slightly renovated semidetached house, while the other is made up of two adjoining, modern apartments in a row house. Since we were able to obtain these before completion of the buildings, no later alterations have been necessary.

The question of size must be taken into consideration if the unit is to function effectively. For a number of reasons, we have adopted a size that permits the accommodation of eight patients but that is utilized for six. Ideally, each unit should conform with a "normal" family environment as closely as possible, consistent with our treatment ideology. This goal might be better achieved with fewer patients, but this would result not only in unnecessarily high running costs (especially for the personnel required) but also in the loss of the establishment of social contacts between each patient and as many other people as possible. In addition, patients who have been treated at the center can visit it whenever they wish after discharge.

We have found that both single and double rooms can be provided with advantage for younger patients. We have attempted to provide adequate common space for indoor activities and to ensure that community social resources are within reach, at least by public transportation. In the planning stage, we regarded it essential to consider the need for rooms that permit meetings with family members and group activities to proceed undisturbed and rooms for personnel. The latter are discussed below since they are of particular importance.

We suggest that particular care be paid to the furnishing of the rooms to ensure a true family atmosphere. It is our belief that the care devoted to decoration and furnishing conveys in an immediate way a sense of respect for the patients who will attend the center. Such an attitude is consistent with recent research results obtained by environmental psychologists (e.g., Kasl, 1974) who have investigated the effect of housing quality on mental and physical health. Brands (1981), who emphasized the importance of the physical environment for psychiatric milieus, pointed out that our environment carries messages and therefore has an impact on our behavior.

## Relationships with Neighbors

Great attention must be given to relationships with neighbors if complete isolation of patients is to be avoided, even when the care unit is situated in a nonpsychiatric housing environment. Since patients may occasionally act out, it is essential that they are well accepted from the start. Just before the opening of each of our centers, several of the personnel visited the immediate neighbors to tell them something about the clientele expected to be accepted at the center and about its intended purpose. An open house was then arranged to allow those interested to visit the unit and learn about its activities. Also, reporters from local newspapers were invited, and further information about the planned activities of the center was released to the press.

These measures have been rewarded. For example, in the unit incorporated in a row house, which has a garden adjoining that of its neighbors', lively interactions occur, particularly during the summer. The patients feel completely accepted since no one questions their presence, and they enjoy genuine contacts with other normal people. Some 70 people accepted the invitation to the open house at the other unit. Among them was a woman who had grown up in that house and who was pleased that her childhood home could be used so purposefully.

## Personnel

The size of staff has depended, to a certain extent, on the personnel available as a consequence of the reduction or closure of wards at the mental hospital, which has taken place in parallel with the development of the new treatment centers.

Our treatment units are staffed predominantly by nurses who have been trained to act as therapists. One senior nurse is responsible for administration, beside functioning as a therapist. Five additional nurses share the daily schedule while two mental health nurses divide the night shift. In addition, an occupational therapist (full-time) and a physiotherapist (half-time) are attached to each center. A senior psychiatrist (myself) is attached part-time at both centers where he has medical responsibility and supervises ongoing therapies. The assistance of a social worker and of a psychologist is available on a consultation basis whenever required (see below).

## Staff Recruitment and Training

Many of the people recruited at the centers were already employed in other wards of the Umeå Department of Psychiatry and had broad experience working with younger schizophrenic patients. To a certain extent, each staff member was recruited personally, but no pressure was placed on anyone. It was important that staff members showed particular interest and aptitude for the special activities of the new units and were prepared to undergo appropriate training for new tasks. Staff members were also made aware that they could be assigned to other work if they found themselves unsuited to the special challenges of the center.

Since almost all the staff employed in all wards have received a basic training in cognitive psychotherapy and have gone through a special course in interactive skills for working with psychiatric patients, and since most already work according to a general cognitive therapy orientation, recruitment to the two centers has not met with problems. To those who want to start similar enterprises and do not have so many people to choose from, we strongly recommend that certain personality characteristics, in particular the ability to relate to schizophrenic patients, should be sought. A capacity for empathy, flexibility, tolerance of frustrations, and a preparedness to participate in extraordinary interventions outside of scheduled work time are invaluable personality characteristics that should always be given a high priority.

The most elementary basic training includes at least 50 hours of lectures and seminars in cognitive therapy followed by individual supervision and recurrent weekly inservice education. Most of our staff, however, were accepted for a further 2 years of training in cognitive therapy when they decided to work at the centers. A few were sent abroad for study purposes, and all were given the opportunity to visit the cognitive treatment center for patients with neurotic disorders that was already in operation. Furthermore, the staff of the second unit had the advantage of exploiting the experiences of those of the first, which had been operating for over a year.

Continued training also occurs in connection with supervisory seminars, which are held each week, and in connection with "planning days,'' which take place twice a year. Whenever there is an occasion, members of the staff attend national or international meetings relevant to their work. The courses and the travel are financed by part of the budget of the department set aside for this purpose.

Our experience training the personnel for our centers supports the view emphasized by Beck (1976) that cognitive therapy is relatively easy to teach to people who have good training in working with psychiatric patients and are motivated to learn a new approach. An essential prerequisite, however, is continued supervision on a regular basis (see below).

## Recruitment of Patients

This section considers the recruitment of patients for intensive psychotherapy. The criteria for selection of patients able to carry out a program of presumably long-lasting intensive psychotherapy need to be narrower than those required for other kinds of structured social training.

We accept patients of both sexes at our centers, almost exclusively between 18 and 35 years old and without any limitation due to social class. Since the centers are part of the public psychiatric services of our sector, there are no economic issues influencing the selection of the patients. We have found that a natural mixture of men and women helps to create a more natural environment, perhaps even more important here than in an ordinary ward. However, we do not impose a strict ratio, and the distribution between the sexes depends on demand. The age limits imposed do not concern the ability of older patients to benefit from some of our methods of treatment. Instead, we attempt to achieve as homogenous a group as possible so that each patient is able to recognize himself or herself in another. Also, younger patients have often not yet been admitted to the invalid pension scheme and therefore are more likely to attain economic independence. Many still live with their families and have never been given the opportunity to live self-reliantly, as is the rule for young people in Sweden.

Patients who come to these two centers are referred by a mental health worker from one of our two teams with whom they have had contact. Integration of inpatient and outpatient services has been described in detail elsewhere (C. Perris, Rodhe, Palm, Hällgren, Lilja, & Söderman, 1985) and need not be repeated here.

At the time of referral to one of our centers, a patient may be hospitalized for an acute condition or may be an outpatient with one of our mental health workers. Each patient is thoroughly informed of the treatment available at the centers and given ample time to decide upon enrollment in the program. Since we admit patients only twice a year, time is provided to well prepare patients before intake. Preparation, however, does not automatically guarantee a place. The decision to accept a patient rests finally with the staff at the center (see below), which means the patients can only decide to be prepared to spend several months in a special treatment center. The patient always visits once or twice before making a final decision. Such visits, however, only occur after the center personnel have arrived at a preliminary decision concerning admission. If the interval to the next admission period is long (e.g., several months), the patient is included in a special waiting list, which, in our experience, is quite short (comprising only a few names).

## Diagnostic and Other Inclusion/Exclusion Criteria

Since both centers were originally intended for patients suffering from schizophrenic disorders, these patients are given admission priority. The patient must be accessible, at least to a certain extent, through verbal contact, and it is important that he or she not be entirely burned out by prolonged hospitalization. The duration of the disorder in itself does not affect admission other than in cases of acute syndromes in usually well-integrated persons. Such patients, who according to DSM-III-R would be classified as having schizophreniform disorders or atypical psychoses, are excluded. Patients presenting mainly with negative symptoms (i.e., passivity, lack of initiative, emotional flattening, introversion, and social seclusion) and those with markedly productive symptoms expressed in the form of hallucinations and severe delusions are welcome. In short, since all our patients have a past history of illness lasting for years, they all meet the DSM-III-R criteria for schizophrenia.

Patients with established addictive alcohol or drug abuse, those with verified brain damage, and those with recurrent schizoaffective episodes are excluded. Also excluded are patients who meet the criteria for cycloid psychotic disorders (C. Perris, 1974, 1988a) independent of the duration of the current episode. Occasionally accepted are patients (not more than one at a time) with personality disorders of a schizotypal, borderline, or passive/avoidant type as defined in DSM-III-R. However, if there is a choice, we prefer patients suffering from schizophrenic disorders. All patients are admitted on a voluntary basis, and the cost of their stay at the center is covered by the National Social Insurance System.

## Admission Procedures

The patient is initially presented at a staff conference at the center by the mental health worker. The patient's past history, earlier treatment, and present status are discussed, and attempts are made to survey his or her global problems. The patient's motivation for being admitted at the center and his or her expectations are also considered. Exclusion factors such as those described above are noted. If the patient is judged to be unsuitable for the center, available alternatives are considered.

This initial presentation is greatly facilitated by the basic cognitive therapy training of our staff members. Because they are conversant with the psychotherapeutic treatment program at the center, they normally are able to assess the eligibility of the patient from a cognitive therapeutic perspective. If, at this first presentation, it is agreed that the patient is a suitable candidate for psychotherapy and admission is possible, the patient is invited to visit the center and meet those staff members who will function as his or her principal therapists.

Through interviews at the time of admission, one of which is usually videotaped, the patient has the opportunity to present his or her problems and expectations in person. The patient is told about the center and is encouraged to express verbally those elements of the treatment program he or she feels in most need of. The few basic rules pertaining to treatment at the center are also outlined. No patient may obtain overnight leave from the center during the first 4 weeks of attendance, and each patient must reside at the center for at least one term (5 months) and has to consent to the videotaping of individual therapy sessions. Also, each patient is expected to comply with a battery of ratings that are made at intervals at the center. All information is included in a contract that is signed by the patient after staff members are certain that he or she has understood its contents. Obviously, if a patient is grossly psychotic or his or her condition is particularly labile at admission, the admission procedure is simplified. For example, videotaping or the completion of rating forms may have to be postponed.

## The Concept of Motivation

The concept of motivation is often used, especially in a psychotherapeutic context, and some authors (e.g., Dewald, 1964) recommend using it for determining whether or not a patient should be accepted for treatment. However, it is not always possible to define "motivation" precisely. It includes both conscious and unconscious elements that are not easy to ascertain at the intake interview.

An initial problem regarding motivation often arises when an extended period of residence at a treatment center is suggested to a patient not in an acute phase or under pressure by other disturbing social factors. It is not easy for young people to make decisions when they are not greatly troubled by distressing symptoms.

A positive attitude toward a long period of treatment partly implies a recognition of possible negative consequences of the illness, partly a hope that the treatment offered can limit the impact of these consequences, and partly a willingness to work toward the solution of problems that are largely unknown. Problems remain even when a patient feels "motivated" for such an effort since it remains uncertain as to what is actually meant by this assertion; the patient may not easily understand what "working with himself" actually involves.

The patient may be influenced by the mental health worker who suggests intensive psychotherapy. First, the mental health worker must be convinced that at least some of the patient's problems depend on sociopsychological factors and that the proposed treatment can be beneficial. But how far should the mental health worker in charge of the patient go to influence the patient to accept the opportunity for treatment? Respect for the integrity of the patient plays an important role here as do issues of transference and countertransference.

What, then, is the possibility of evaluating motivation correctly? Even though a definitive answer is difficult because of the multiple issues involved, some general guidelines may be given. In the first place, the mental health worker in charge should be as objective as possible in presenting the proposed treatment. A suitable approach is to discover the patient's expectations and to compare them with thorough presentation of the possibilities offered by the proposed treatment. The mental health worker should also be able to recognize transference and countertransference reactions when they arise so as not to be influenced by them in either direction. Although most patients are able to decide by themselves, we suggest that the mental health worker should attempt to influence a shaky motivation when the patient is ambivalent.

More marginal, although not entirely without importance, is a genuine assessment of the overall situation of the patient. Since no one can identify in advance those patients who will respond favorably to psychotherapy and those who will not, it could be insensitive to recommend an extended interruption in ordinary life to a patient who, by and large, lives in a relatively stable social situation (with reference to both family relationships and occupation) and who only occasionally relapses into schizophrenic symptoms. In cases of this kind, even more than in others, the decision to enroll for treatment should rest entirely upon the patient. It cannot be ruled out, however, that considerations of this kind contribute to the undesired exclusion from treatment of patients who are socially more adapted and who could perhaps benefit from long-term psychotherapy. Admittedly, these patients can be treated on an outpatient basis; however, it is unknown whether therapeutic sessions scheduled more than once a week would become a cause of stress in patients who just manage to cope with the requirements of their work.

In the main, and regardless of problems of motivation, the mental health worker who refers a patient for treatment must at all times adopt a sober and realistic approach toward this referral. It is infinitely better for the patient to discover in due time that he or she has achieved much more than expected than to become disappointed by unfulfilled goals.

In practice, when motivation problems arise, the cognitive therapeutic approach of using a Socratic dialogue and other current therapeutic techniques can be exploited to help the patient to evaluate the pros and cons of the proposal for treatment and to reach a decision.

# 7

# *A Holistic, Intensive Cognitive–Behavioral Therapy Program at a Treatment Center*

This chapter provides a general outline of the holistic treatment program developed at the two cognitive therapy centers described in Chapter 6. Although such a program is, in our experience, both feasible and effective, what is described in this chapter is only a guide to the reader. In practice, the particular composition of the patient group present at a center at any given time might require occasional changes. Thus, flexibility should always be the leading principle.

Before describing the program, two general prerequisites must be discussed.

## TWO GENERAL PREREQUISITES

In order to understand our program of treatment, two general issues must first be understood. One concerns the schizophrenic syndrome itself while the other concerns cognitive psychotherapy. Wing (1974) suggested that the handicaps shown by a schizophrenic patient in relation to treatment and rehabilitation could be defined under three headings.

The first are primary handicaps that are directly related to the disorder, including the schizophrenic thought disorder. The second group includes those secondary handicaps that result whenever primary impairments are present, such as loss of self-confidence. Negative effects of institutionalism and late negative consequences of heavy medication are in this group as well. In addition, Wing pointed out that many patients, irrespective of diagnosis, suffer further handicaps in the form of lack of social skills and professional expertise because of the precarious conditions (not necessarily economic) in which many have grown up and the fact that many have never been given a chance to solve these problems. A very common example is found in young patients (especially males) who have been inhibited in attaining independence by their parents. Wallace (1984) recently published a comprehensive literature survey that clearly shows the inability of schizophrenic persons to deal with interpersonal relationships. Wallace asserted (in my opinion correctly) that this deficit represents an important contribution to overall vulnerability as defined earlier. On the other hand, one should not generalize the importance of defective social skills to all schizophrenic patients. A not negligible proportion of these patients has both social and professional skills before the disorder destroys what they have accomplished.

To apply a holistic approach to the patient's problems, the issue of social proficiency must always be examined carefully. Deficiencies must be identified, and adequate measures to remedy them must be included in the treatment program. It is in this context that cognitive-behavioral treatment differs clearly from treatment that focuses attention exclusively on intrapsychic processes. It is often insinuated that the practical orientation to which I refer wants to convert all patients to socially well-adapted persons according to stereotyped middle-class values. This view, in my opinion, is totally absurd. A milieu-therapeutic program would hardly be "holistic," if it did not systematically and purposefully include and try to repair deficiencies in social function; however, this does not automatically mean that the patient has to incorporate the values of the therapist, whatever they might be.

Much has been written on training social skills, and excellent reviews are available (e.g., Bellak & Hersen, 1979; Trower, 1984). However, exclusively behavioral training of social skills does not lead to radical and permanent changes that, without reservation, extend beyond the training situation itself (Marzillier, 1978; Shepherd, 1984). If such training is to be truly meaningful, a simultaneous assessment of the dysfunctional cognitions underlying the social skills deficits must be carried out, and efforts must be made to change these cognitions. This will be dealt with later in more detail (see "Group Therapy," below, and "Social Skills Training," Chapter 9).

The second prerequisite mentioned above has to do with the very nature of cognitive psychotherapy. When Beck, who was an experienced psychoanalyst, developed his cognitive therapy, he incorporated a number of techniques that were already in current usage in behavioral therapy and emphasized the need to document both the therapeutic process and its results. Such emphasis has its basis in the behavior therapy tradition. When Beck presented a comparison between cognitive therapy and behavior therapy in the beginning of the 1970s (Beck, 1970), intensive debate was occurring within behavior therapy circles as to whether cognitions should be taken into account. In his comparison, Beck compared his method and psychoanalysis by asserting the similarities (in scientific approach) to behavioral therapy rather than emphasizing the differences between the methods. The consequences have been unfortunate since many (at least in Europe) still have difficulty distinguishing between cognitive and behavioral therapies, especially since many behavior therapists now call themselves "cognitive–behavioral" therapists."

Beside certain differences in the therapist–patient relationship, the two forms of therapy differ markedly with respect to the purpose for which different techniques are used and in defining what changes occur as a result of therapy. The example above, concerning social skills training, should have already given an indication of the nature of this difference. Simply put, while the use of training techniques is regarded in behavioral therapy as a goal in itself, in cognitive therapy they are used to make the patient aware of the dysfunctional cognitions responsible for the handicaps and to begin to correct them. Role play is another example; in behavioral therapy, it is used to give the patient an opportunity to train a behavior to enact in a later similar situation. In cognitive therapy, the same role play serves to elicit the patient's dysfunctional assumptions that hinder performance and are later the object of treatment.

The reader interested in a comparison between cognitive psychotherapy and other major psychotherapy systems can find more information elsewhere (C. Perris, 1988c). However, it has been important here to point out that significant differences do exist. It is also important to stress that a distinctive feature of cognitive psychotherapy, as pointed out earlier by both Beck (1976) and Arnkoff (1981), is its flexibility, which enables the therapist to use those methods that belong to other forms of therapy when they appear to be particularly suited for some patient; however, their usage must not be haphazard but should coincide with the overall theory of cognitive therapy. It is in this context that the *Handbook of Cognitive Therapy Techniques*, by McMullin (1986), has to be understood.

## THE COGNITIVE MILIEU THERAPY PROGRAM

### Socialization Phase

Socialization of the patient within the therapy's rationale and procedures is an important component of cognitive psychotherapy. The functions of socialization are manifold. First, it provides an opportunity to assess the patient's expectations from and knowledge about the therapeutic procedure that is planned; therefore, it also gives the therapist an occasion to discuss goals and the main principles of cognitive psychotherapy with the patient. In other words, the patient is given a first opportunity to learn to identify relationships among thoughts, emotions, and behaviors and to recognize that dysfunctional cognitive processes may contribute to a negative self-image. To a certain extent, this socialization corresponds with the emphasis of psychoanalysis on "basic rules" with which the patient must become acquainted and conform if the treatment is to be meaningful. Further, it allows the therapist and patient to begin sharing a common terminology.

From a milieu-therapeutic viewpoint, socialization is even more complex since it includes the development of a trusting relationship between the patient and personnel (especially his or her nearest therapists) and also of trustworthy relationships with other patients. For this reason, we require that all patients admitted to the center stay at the center on weekends during the first 4-5 weeks. We assume that during this time the patient will come to regard the center as a "secure base" in Bowlby's meaning (Bowlby, 1973a, 1973b). By "secure base" Bowlby referred to the attachment person of the child. Because of reliance on such a person, human beings of all ages are "able to deploy their talents to best advantage when they are confident that, standing behind them, there are one or more trusted persons who will come to their aid should difficulties arise" (1973a, p. 407). Thus, from the secure base, the child dares explore his or her surroundings and eventually makes contact with strangers, always with the knowledge that the attachment person is nearby as a secure source of protection, if needed. We believe that such a relationship to the center must be established before the patient is prepared to regard it as his or her new (albeit transitional) home and is able to face the difficulties associated with the actual psychotherapeutic work (for further details concerning this topic see "The Family-Like Atmosphere," below).

During the socialization phase, the patient is also helped to regard his or her situation in terms of problems that can and will be solved, so an extensive inventory of problems is carried out.

Examples of problems that patients often describe include the occurrence of psychopathological symptoms, difficulties of assertion in various social situations, general uncertainty with regard to self-image and the future, possible conflicts with persons in the proximity, lack of lodgings or employment, and a wish for education. At this stage, we avoid drawing attention to problems that may have a deeper significance because the socialization phase also serves to allow a closer assessment of the level at which continued individual therapy is to proceed.

The problem inventory also enables us to survey those mechanisms that the patient has used earlier to deal with various problems. Similarly, the reactions exhibited in connection with these attempts are surveyed.

During this phase, the social worker who acts as a consultant at the center makes a thorough inventory of the overall socioeconomic situation of the patient. This includes the social assistance already received by the patient or his or her entitlement to such, a survey of the patient's financial situation in general, and a survey of earlier employment or the necessity for sheltered work opportunities. This inventory, together with the other information gathered, later provides the basis for an initial definition of the goals of treatment. In this context, it is important to observe that although the social worker contributes specific professional knowledge to the survey, he or she does not later take the measures necessary to correct possible drawbacks. Instead, the patient will work on these at a later stage as one part of the comprehensive treatment program.

Finally, during the socialization phase, the patient completes a battery of rating questionnaires. These are included in a continual evaluation program but are initially helpful in providing evidence of the patient's dysfunctional cognitions, which will later be the object of treatment.

## The Formulation of Preliminary Goals

During the socialization phase, the therapists, together with the patient, define preliminary goals. At this stage, we strive first for some relatively elementary goals that are within the patient's reach and toward which he or she can begin to work immediately. In connection with the formulation of goals, opportunities occasionally arise to bring to light the patient's unrealistic expectations. When this occurs, the therapists are given the opportunity to discover the patient's actual adaptation to reality and are able to apply some initial therapeutic intervention.

With regard to goals, an important question arises that must be focused upon. Although it has been mentioned that psychopathological symptoms may be present among those problems listed by a patient, it should be clear that the control of manifest psychopathology is not our prime purpose. Often, the control of psychopathological symptoms can be achieved with adequate medication without attendance at a special treatment center. Our general attitude toward medication is discussed below (see "Attitudes toward Medication," as well as the "Questions of Medication" section in Chapter 8); however, we do anticipate that our program of treatment will have an influence on the patient's manifest psychopathology in the long run.

A discusson of a more comprehensive goal, which may entail a restructuring of the patient's personality, is carried out with the patient only after a solid and trustworthy relationship with the therapists has been established and after the patient has acquired a feeling of security in contact with them. If and when the question of such a major goal arises, the time will be ripe for a discussion with the patient regarding an extension of his or her stay at the center. Such an extension may include one or several terms; this will depend on the patient. Obviously, the ambition of every therapist is to promote a restructuration of a patient's personality that may suppress morbidity in the long run if not forever. However, we believe that this goal cannot be attained with all patients at the same time as it is almost impossible to decide from the very beginning which patients are suited for such an endeavor.

On the basis of what has been said so far, the misunderstanding can be obtained that our goal is wholly pragmatic and more of a social-psychiatric than a psychotherapeutic nature. We are aware of the idiom that one shoots an arrow farther by sighting at a star than at the top of a tree. We accept the wisdom of this statement and aim at this desirable star, but we do not wish to miss the treetop. Our primary aim is to promote in the patient a condition that allows him or her to live as independent a social life as possible. We aim to correct as many of the patient's dysfunctional preconceptions as possible and to promote his or her self-awareness. We are conscious of our limitations and would never change this goal, which for others might appear modest (but which is not). We do not aim for the more uncertain goal of a thorough change of personality, which might hypothetically be achieved after years or decades of intensive treatment. In this respect, our humble opinion accords with those expressed by Fromm-Reichmann (1955) and Arieti (1974a, 1976) and with that Schmideberg (1970) stressed when she deplored the incapability of certain psychoanalytical colleagues to decide when a psychoanalytical treatment had to be stopped.

## Contacts with Relatives of Patients

Although family therapy as such lies outside our program of treatment, we plan to meet the patient's closest relatives during the early and later stages of treatment. The first meeting, which usually takes place during the socialization phase, has two purposes. The first is to obtain full anamnestic information on the patient and on the whole family, especially concerning facts or events that the patient might not know at all. The second is to be able to directly observe the type of interactions that occur between the patient and the relative(s) who respond to our invitation. At this meeting, the patient has an opportunity to talk about the goals that have already been set. This meeting can also reveal the attitudes of the relatives to the patient's plans and their possible cooperation. Attempts are made to avoid direct confrontations at this stage without, however, being too accommodating. In practice, our approach in dealing with the patients' relatives is a psychoeducational one, as recently emphasized by several authors (e.g., Anderson *et al.*, 1986; Falloon, Boyd, & McGill, 1984; McFarlane, 1983); it is easy to integrate in a more general cognitive therapeutic framework. Later on during treatment, meetings with a patient's relatives can occur both on request from the relatives and according to the wishes of the patient and therapists. One major purpose of these later meetings is to identify the kind of possible reactions that the patient's progress during therapy may cause in family members and to deal with them if those reactions are experienced as negative by the patient.

Other relevant issues concerning relationships with the patient's nearest relatives are discussed in connection with the presentation of individual therapy (see "Contact with the Patient's Relatives," Chapter 8).

## Attitudes toward Medication

It has already been stressed most psychotherapists' attitudes toward medication have changed. A strictly individualized and balanced use of psychotropic drugs is now regarded as being beneficial to the psychotherapeutic process rather than a hindrance. Such a beneficial effect is especially pronounced in patients suffering from schizophrenic syndromes who, in connection with their disorder, experience considerable difficulties in sorting and correctly processing the information to which they are exposed. Treatments carried out by psychoanalysts through the mid-1950s were greatly different than those carried out today because of the lack of psychotropic drugs. The primary goals of the earlier treatments were to withdraw the patient from his or her psychotic world; this was a major achievement that usually required a very long time.

The symptomatological improvements that can be obtained today with medication are both positive and negative as concerns psychotherapy. On the one hand, such improvements allow treatment to be initiated from a completely new starting point; most patients are much more accessible to the therapist's approach from the very beginning. Recent investigations (Orzack, Kornetsky, & Freeman, 1967; Spohn, Lacoursiere, Thompson, & Coyne, 1978) on the effects of arousal-reducing psychotropic drugs in schizophrenic patients support the view that appropriate use of these drugs improves attention and information processing. On the other hand, the symptomatological improvement obtainable with drugs is associated with two disadvantages: first, it often reduces the motivation of the patient for psychotherapy, and second, it occasionally distorts the perspective of the therapist who has encountered only medicated patients so that the severity of the patient's disorder may easily be underestimated.

Most patients referred to our treatment centers have been receiving medication for several years. However, they show symptoms that are not wholly controlled by the ongoing treatment. As a rule, no drastic changes in medication are made on admission to the center. We have found, however, that successive decreases to a minimum dosage can be carried out as the patient learns to employ his or her own resources to deal with disturbing experiences. Since participation in psychotherapy requires a certain degree of alertness from patients, along with a capacity to express emotions, it is our aim that attentional processes and emotional expressivity not be too negatively influenced by medication.

When and if a patient suffers a temporary relapse during the course of psychotherapy, we avoid turning to medication as a solution. Instead, the therapists and all the staff at the center increase their efforts to reinstate the patient's feelings of security. In other words, it is in those occasions that the staff's holding function, as conceived by Winnicott (1965), becomes most evident.

## Principal Functions of Personnel

All personnel act as individual therapists for different patients. We have adopted a system in which two persons are assigned to be principal therapists for each patient. The rationale for this is to ensure that one is always available. Another reason is that prolonged individual psychotherapy with a patient suffering from a schizophrenic syndrome is an emotionally demanding task for each therapist. By dividing the responsibility between two people, it becomes possible for each of them occasionally to adopt a smaller role if the emotional burden becomes too heavy. Also, we believe that a contributing factor to some patients' vulnerability is that they have been subject to conflicting messages from their original caregivers to whom they were tied symbiotically. Learning to establish contacts with two persons (with complementary attitudes) who provide a consistent approach can enhance patients' trust in people. Finally, during therapy, many messages transmitted by the patient, both verbal and nonverbal, might be missed by a solitary therapist. Since most therapy sessions are videotaped, there is an opportunity for both therapists to discuss the sessions and to supervise each other.

All personnel also adopt a holding role. This means in principle that personnel are always available to receive the patients' emotional reactions and to try to redirect them to something therapeutically productive. The personnel also serve as models for our patients, which means, for instance, that they take part in the patients' breakfast and dinner and eat one main meal with the patients each weekend. The model function, however, is not overemphasized as in behavioral therapy, but assumes the natural form of "good enough parenting" (Bettelheim, 1987). This also means that self-disclosure, that is, talking about oneself in various situations, is encouraged.

Even after only a few weeks, the relationship between the patients and personnel develops like that in a family that has a harmonic atmosphere, and the atmosphere at the center itself becomes relaxed. The patients very quickly learn to joke with the personnel while at the same time learning to recognize correctly when the personnel are joking with them. We agree with Isohanni (1986) that humor is an essential part of a mature and tolerant attitude toward life and, as such, is a natural component of the living–learning situation in a milieu-therapeutic setting. It should be unnecessary to stress that making jokes or being humorous, however, requires a very high sensitivity in all staff.

Although the personnel work according to schedule, no one opposes extra duty when required. We have found, however, that various agreements can be made with the patients so that encroachments in the private lives of the staff are kept to a minimum.

## Summary

From the description given above, the holistic characteristic of the treatment program at our centers should have clearly emerged. Therapeutic interventions are articulated at various levels and adapted to the needs of each patient during the different phases of the treatment. Furthermore, the particular flexibility of cognitive psychotherapy allows for shifting among these levels without the constraints imposed by adherence to a more rigid theoretical framework. How our program compares with the therapeutic approaches of other theoretical frameworks (mainly the psychoanalytic–psychotherapeutic) is illustrated in Table 7-1.

## THE TREATMENT PROGRAM

In the following sections, the different components of the treatment program of the centers is presented in detail. Some elements are discussed separately, while cognitive group therapy is only briefly pre-

TABLE 7-1. The Holistic Approach Versus Other Approaches

| Holistic Approach at the Centers | Psychoanalytically Oriented Psychotherapeutic Approaches |
|---|---|
| Emphasis on patient–therapist relationship | Object-relations theories |
| Emphasis on family-like atmosphere and on secure base | Object transference |
| Emphasis on training in interpersonal interactions (with correction of interfering cognitive–emotional dysfunctions) | Interpersonal theories; Sullivan's and Horney's approach |
| Social skills training focused on the correction of underlying dysfunctional cognitions | Ego psychology; ego-supportive theories |
| Restructuring of dysfunctional basic schemata; cognitive–emotional reconstruction of the patient's past experiences | Insight-oriented, explorative psychoanalytical theories |
| Validation of the patient as a subject | Humanistic/existential theories |
| Individualized medication | Biological theories |
| Interventions with families | Psychoeducational models |

This is a comparison of the holistic therapeutic approach implemented at the centers with corresponding approaches within a psychoanalytically oriented frame of reference. The flexibility of cognitive psychotherapy permits easy movement among the various levels of interventions without theoretical contradictions.

sented. A major reason for describing in detail the main components of the treatment program is that they are a general framework that can be applied in different treatment units, even those not primarily directed to intensive psychotherapy or intended solely for the type of patients considered here. On the other hand, a major reason for describing individual therapy separately is that cognitive psychotherapy with schizophrenic patients can naturally be used with both inpatients and outpatients, and descriptions must take into account both situations.

All the elements discussed here are included in our usual treatment program; however, the reader should remember the flexibility mentioned earlier. This feature of cognitive psychotherapy occurs also in the detailed weekly planning at the treatment centers. In practice, a balance is continuously maintained between flexibility and structure; the framework remains fixed but the contents can vary if necessary. Table 7-2 shows a general overview of how the weekly program is structured.

## The Family-Like Atmosphere

As already mentioned, one of our aims is to promote a family-like atmosphere at our centers. Sullivan (1931b) was one of the first people

TABLE 7-2. Weekly Activities at the Cognitive–Behavioral Psychotherapy Centers

| Time | Monday | Tuesday | Wednesday | Thursday | Friday |
|---|---|---|---|---|---|
| | | | Weekly Schedule | | |
| 7:45–8:20 A.M. | ← Breakfast → | | | | |
| 8:20–8:30 A.M. | ← Exercises → | | | | |
| 8:30–9:00 A.M. | ← Planning of the day → | | | | |
| 9:00–12:00 A.M. | Free for supervision | Therapy | Housework and therapy | Therapy | Housework |
| | | | ← Coffee break → | | |
| 12:00–1:00 P.M. | Free for supervision | Physiotherapy; bath | Social skills training | Physiotherapy | Summing up of the week; therapy |
| | | | ← Lunch → | | |
| 1:00–4:30 P.M. | Planning of cooking, shopping, etc. | Group therapy | Therapy | Whatever was planned in A.M. | Therapy |
| | | | ← Coffee break → | | |
| | Art therapy | Therapy | Therapy | Whatever was planned in A.M. | Planning of the weekend |
| 4:30–5:30 P.M. | ← Dinner → | | | | |
| Responsible for cooking, etc. | Name of patient on duty | Same | Same | Same | Same |
| Scheduled evening activities | Free | Badminton 7:00–9:00 P.M. | Theater or other activity (the whole group) | Free | Free |

Weekends are planned together by patients and staff and allow freedom of choice. Music interludes are not indicated since their planning may differ from week to week.

to stress the importance of making a new "home" for the patient suffering from schizophrenic syndromes. This conception was later expanded by Rosen (1962), who maintained that the place where the patient was treated should become a warm "foster home." There is no doubt that most young patients suffering from schizophrenic syndromes have grown up in environments that they have experienced as disadvantageous for a variety of reasons. Independently of whether the detrimental forces have been operating within the family or have been external to it, it often is in the original context in which the patient grew up that his cognitive–emotional growth went awry. Thus, since our major goal is to promote a functional redirection of cognitive-emotional growth in our patients, it becomes a logical consequence that we try to create an atmosphere that will help us reach that goal. However, we do not strive for "regression" (a concept that will be criticized at some length in "A Critique of the Concept of Regression" in Chapter 9).

Bowlby's concept of a secure base has already been mentioned; in addition, the atmosphere that we try to develop must allow the administration of what Fries (1946) once called "doses of life experience" (see also Anna Freud's concept of "corrective ego-experience," 1951) in such quantity and quality as are appropriate to the emotional status of each patient at different stages of treatment.

The work by Bronfenbrenner (1979a, 1979b) has also provided an important source of inspiration. In particular, his propositions concerning primary and secondary developmental contexts, conceived by him to characterize environments that promote the healthy cognitive-emotional growth of the child, are relevant. Bronfenbrenner defined a "primary developmental context" as "one in which the child can observe and engage in ongoing patterns of progressively more complex activity jointly with or under the direct guidance of persons who possess knowledge and skills not yet acquired by the child and with whom the child has developed a positive emotional relationship" (1979a, p. 845). The concept of "secondary developmental context" refers to giving the developing person opportunity, encouragement, and resources to engage in progressively more complex activities *without* the direct guidance of another person. Also other hypotheses advanced by Bronfenbrenner (1979b) seem to be applicable to settings discussed here. For example, those related to the patient's possible moving to new settings (e.g., school, work, etc.) when treatment has reached an advanced phase of improvement are relevant.

To apply the principles described above, all staff members have to act as "good enough parents." In practice, this implies that in addition to the scheduled individual therapy sessions, a continuous therapeutic preparedness is maintained by the staff. It is this preparedness, at all times determined by the cognitive therapeutic approach to the patients and to their problems, that gives the environment its therapeutic character. The patients always have someone to turn to when they wish to raise some problem, and the staff can offer both emotional and instrumental support depending on the patients' needs. Questions and deliberations raised by the patients are answered consistently and frankly, but questions requiring more extensive consideration of a therapeutic nature are referred, as a rule, to the next therapy session. Since it is generally acknowledged that patients suffering from schizophrenic syndromes experience particular difficulty in dealing with ambiguity, extreme care is taken at the centers to keep communication at a level that is comprehensible to all. This means that we strive to separate the individual therapy proper from other interventions that must more appropriately be considered in the context of our milieu-therapeutic approach.

## Social Training

Because patients are encouraged to regard the center as their home during their attendance, it is natural that they should participate in household duties. This means that they become responsible for cleaning, shopping, cooking, and laundry. Since almost all our patients are young and many have not lived alone, this type of training represents a first step to independence.

The patients themselves agree on a schedule for household chores at the beginning of each week; this includes a menu for each day, a shopping list, and a division of labor. The occupational therapist is present during this planning and helps with recommendations and guidance whenever required, but she does not carry out these tasks herself.

No patient is considered so ill as to be completely unable to do his or her share of the work. What differs is each patient's degree of assistance from the occupational therapist, which is proportional to the level of independence of each patient. Very frequently, patients spontaneously help each other, especially when one of them who is on duty goes through some emotional crisis. Each task is educational; for instance, the patient delegated to shop learns, with the help of the occupational therapist, to keep a budget and to become aware of prices.

It has been agreed by the patients that everyone should remain at the table until they have all finished eating; mealtimes are considered an important occasion for social interaction. As mentioned earlier, one of the staff is always present at breakfast and dinner. At lunch, however, each patient is permitted to eat what he or she likes and at the time he or she finds most suitable. This is in keeping with ordinary Swedish habits.

Other flexible components in social training include the booking of different localities for activities outside the center; visits to the cinema, to the theatre, to the library, and/or to restaurants or coffee shops, alone or with a fellow patient or member of the staff; the planning of excursions; and hosting the numerous therapists who pay study-visits at the center. Attendance during study visits is naturally not obligatory. The patients are aware that their wishes on this matter are always respected, although they realize that their presence at study visits shows that they need not be ashamed of their mental disorders and offers them the opportunity to meet strangers in a safe environment. At our longest running center, one or two study visits usually occur each month. Often, a patient makes a presentation of the center and summarizes the activities in which the patients are engaged. In subsequent discussions, the patients have reported that they found the experience rewarding.

Toward the end of their stay at the center, patients who plan to move out on their own receive assistance in finding an apartment and furnishing it according to their own taste. The patients are even encouraged to spend some nights in their new home and to make plans for the weekends. Other patients are encouraged to participate in this process. Often, fellow patients from the center are the first guests that a patient receives in her or his new apartment. This process is in keeping with Bronfenbrenner's assumption (1979b) that a person's development when moving from one setting to another is enhanced when some kind of continuity between the settings is established. In addition, the gradual passage from the center to the new flat mitigates problems related to separation.

## Pets

To enhance the family-like atmosphere at the centers, pets have been allowed in both—a dog at one center and a cat at the other. Of course, we first ascertained that none of the people at the centers suffer from allergic reactions to such animals.

There has been an increasing amount of empirical evidence suggesting that a companion animal has a great deal of social and psychological benefit, especially for the elderly (Brickel & Brickel, 1980–1981) but also for other target populations (Beck & Katcher, 1984; Corson, Corson, & Gwynn, 1977). In particular, Corson and coworkers pointed out that a pet humanizes the atmosphere on a ward, and Wilson (1987) emphasized that a pet's functions in facilitating psychotherapy include facilitation of rapport, provision of companionship and emotional support, and increasing the opportunity for sensory stimulation. Among other variables investigated in studies of patient–pet interactions, blood pressure and heart rate have consistently proved to be favorably influenced by such interactions, and petting an animal has been found to have a relaxation effect (Baun, Bergstrom, Langston, & Thoma, 1984; see also Wilson, 1987, for a partial review). Thus, taking into account that, according to our theoretical framework, most of our patients may be assumed to be hyperaroused, the presence of a pet at the centers is based on a sound rationale.

In addition to the pets mentioned above, we have allowed some patients to bring their own pets. This opportunity was utilized by a young man suffering from almost continuous frightening imperative delusional and hallucinatory experiences; he brought his canary, with which he was able to interact in a relaxed way. Also, a young woman brought her rabbit. This young woman experienced a feeling of chaos and impending catastrophe during the initial weeks of her stay at the center and had great difficulties in interacting verbally with the staff. However, she was able to speak of changes in the status of the rabbit to inform the staff of changes in her own feelings. Another young woman with a long-lasting severe impairment in her ability to relate to people seemed not to pay any attention to the center's cat. However, when the cat ran away, she showed increased anxiety, asked members of the staff to look for it, and went out herself to look for it until it came back safely.

## The Physiotherapist's Role

Both individual and group exercises are included in the treatment program. In addition to simple exercises every morning, the physiotherapist leads different activities outside the center, either in sport arenas or in local facilities that the patients can reserve for their activities.

The most important component of the exercise is the planning and execution of more individualized programs. These may include relaxation exercises, exercises designed to promote bodily knowledge, training to correct dysfunctional bodily deportment, and specially adapted programs for physical training. Since even the physiotherapist has received basic training in cognitive psychotherapy, individual training programs are complemented with the elicitation of dysfunctional cognitions that hamper the patient's performance, followed by corrective attempts by the physiotherapist.

## Painting

Picture language represents human's most immediate method of expression. Spontaneous paintings or thematic paintings can be a way to project perceptions of oneself and the surrounding world to an extent not always attainable through the spoken word. This knowledge has been used for a long time for both diagnostic and therapeutic purposes (see Refsnes-Kniazzeh, 1981, for a review), and Larsson (1986) has shown that it can be used with advantage within the framework of cognitive psychotherapy. Those drawings or paintings produced by the patients can be used directly as a starting point for the analysis and processing of the possible dysfunctional conceptions of themselves or their surroundings that the artwork reveals. For example, a house devoid of foundations can relate much of how a patient regards herself or himself.

The patients in our centers participate in a weekly session of creative painting under the supervision of the occupational therapist. They are allowed to paint spontaneously according to fancy or according to a previously decided theme (e.g., a house, a tree, a self-portrait, a man). The drawings are then displayed for all to see and are used to initiate a group discussion. The patients themselves comment on their pictures and indicate what they wished to express. They are made aware of the distinctive characteristics of the drawings and try to discover in their own creations, as well as in those of others, possible features that might reflect a dysfunctional self-image, for instance, that a tree lacks roots, a house lacks a door, contours are diffuse, or the drawing in general gives the impression of constraint and inhibition.

Since this activity is recurrent, it allows changes in the patients' self-image to be followed during the course of therapy. The occupational therapist helps the patient to recognize the implications of such changes and provides positive feedback.

## Musical Interludes

Irregularly, afternoon coffee breaks are used to listen collectively to music. The patients themselves choose the kind of music they listen to, but they may receive occasional guidance from the staff. The importance of music is strongly emphasized in other forms of therapy, for instance, in gestalt therapy, where the patient is trained to experience contact with unusual sensations and to perceive their different elements to form a gestalt, and in other therapies of various theoretical orientations (see Goodman, 1981, for a recent review). A thoughtful analysis, from a psychoanalytical point of view, of the enjoyment of listening to music has been published by Kohut and Levarie (1950).

The use of music is of relatively minor importance in cognitive psychotherapy, and no reports are available on its systematic use. However, Goodman pointed out that researchers have begun to confirm the effectiveness of an interrelated cognitive-musical framework in the treatment of severely handicapped children. That we include listening to music in our treatment program must therefore be regarded as a preliminary attempt to explore how it can be used; also closely connected is that the patients listen to transistor radios whenever opportunity permits. In our opinion, one function of listening to music is that, as a group experience, it contributes to group cohesiveness. Listening to music that is unfamiliar requires concentration, which might facilitate allocation of attention from dysfunctional thoughts to something that is enjoyable. Goodman (1981) suggested that cognitive organization is inherent in recognizing and enjoying the structure of music. Patients suffering from schizophrenic syndromes seem especially to experience the feeling that chaos is turned into structure.

Discussions following music sessions are often focused on the particular composition chosen and on its structure. The patients are led gradually into the therapeutic course by the personnel who take part in this activity. The patients are encouraged to talk freely about the feelings they experience and to discuss them with both other patients and staff members. The staff members thus have an opportunity to emphasize the intimate relationship between emotions and cognitive events (that is, moods, thoughts, and imageries) evoked by the music.

## Homework

Cognitive psychotherapy has borrowed the technique of assigning homework from behavioral therapy, but, as mentioned earlier, even psychoanalysts occasionally assign small tasks to patients. The content and aims of these tasks naturally vary from patient to patient, but the overall goal is to extend the therapy beyond the sessions and to observe whether the insight gained in therapy is generalized to behavior and situations outside. Also, the patient is given a chance to test the reliability of his or her conceptions and to recognize what happens in his surroundings outside of therapy. Involvement in homework also implies that the patient actively participates in the treatment.

Homework varies in content, especially according to its immediate purpose. For instance, it can require the patient to train himself or herself to monitor those situations that evoke unpleasant feelings and that are linked to the occurrence of automatic negative thoughts. The patient may also be assigned to read something that deals with his or her problems, to make another attempt to solve a previously impossible task, or to simply complete a task that has been continuously postponed.

In order for homework to be purposeful, certain conditions must be met. The most important are as follows:

- The content of the assignment should be closely related to some of the patient's problems discussed at the therapy session.
- The proposal of homework should come out of the collaborative effort of the therapist(s) and patient.
- The patient should be able to completely understand the purpose of the task so that he or she does not feel that it is an imposition devoid of any particular meaning.
- The task should be proportionally related to the resources of the patient.

Homework is even incorporated in the scope of the treatment program of the center. It may involve the completion of assessment forms, particular readings, or even a task outside the center that is particularly relevant to the patient's problems. The completion of the assignment is reviewed at the next therapy session, and its results are used as a basis for further therapeutic work.

## Weekend Planning and Weekly Summaries

After the socialization period, the patient is allowed to spend the weekend outside of the center, at home with parents, with a relative, or in his or her own home. Weekends are planned at a common meeting, so that the plans of each patient are discussed openly. Encouragement can then be given concerning any apprehension the patient experiences with regard to his or her initiative and possible alternatives can be suggested when it is difficult for the patient to plan something meaningful. Most often, homework assignments are stipulated for the weekends.

Weekly summaries have a different and more specific importance. They belong to the framework of cognitive therapy, which requires that each session be terminated with a summing up of the topics that have been dealt with. The purpose of this summary is to yet again draw the attention of the patient to the insight that has emerged during the session and to reinforce it.

A special meeting is arranged at the centers at the end of each week for the same purpose. Each patient gives a brief account of what he or she has experienced during the past week and is encouraged to decide to what extent and in which direction he or she has been affected by these events. The main purpose of the weekly summary, as with recapitulation in an isolated therapy session, is to make the patient aware of possible progress, to reinforce a positive experience, or to help the patient recover from feelings of failure when something has gone wrong. It should be added that the weekly summary is of great importance for the therapists as well since it represents an important source of feedback and allows continuous monitoring of the patients' progress.

## The Psychotherapeutic Work Itself

Those components that have been described so far constitute important parts of the overall program of treatment and contribute to the creation of a therapeutic milieu. The relevance of a cognitive therapeutic orientation in the therapeutic process is emphasized in a later section (see "Milieu-Therapeutic Processes," below). The psychotherapeutic work proper, however, includes not only those elements already discussed, but also group therapy sessions and individual psychotherapy. Since these latter form the nucleus of the treatment program, they are discussed separately. However, group therapy is described only in general while all of Part 3 of this book is devoted to individual therapy.

It is stressed, however, that all the procedures discussed in the previous sections are always performed according to a cognitive psychotherapeutic model and that the behavior of the personnel in all situations is consistent with this model.

Individual therapy sessions take place at least twice a week on scheduled hours. Two further sessions a week, which differ in major content, are devoted to group therapy. While group therapy sessions take place at the same time each week, the number and times of individual sessions may vary depending on the needs of the patient and the stage of treatment. It should, however, be obvious that changes in times or frequency of therapeutic activities are not made haphazardly but are planned jointly by the patients and the therapists.

## Group Therapy

Two weekly group therapy sessions constitute a consistent component of the treatment program. Each session lasts for about 2 hours, and all the patients are expected to attend. However, patients who feel particularly bad or are in a state of crisis are not forced to attend. Usually two and, more often, three of the staff participate in the sessions. This implies that the total number of people at a session is seven to nine at most; however, some patients who have been treated at the center continue to participate in the group sessions as outpatients. When this occurs, only two of the staff attend. In all, the patients participate in about 20 group sessions during each term that they spend at the center.

The content of the sessions is predetermined. One series of sessions is devoted to the training of social skills using a manual (unpublished) that has been developed for this purpose. However, the training of social skills, as we conceive it, is always related to a contemporary assessment of possible dysfunctional cognitions that may underlie any specific deficits. This approach is consistent with those of other authors (e.g., Dow & Craighead, 1984; Dryden, 1984; Shepherd, 1984) who have pointed out repeated failures in the transfer of skills acquired in a training situation to other situations when correction of possible dysfunctional cognitions is not taken into account. The special manual we have developed includes skills of increasing complexity and relevance and is designed to cover different aspects of social interactions. It includes aspects of nonverbal communication. Patients participating in the sessions are expected to evaluate the performance of each group member on a very elementary 5-point scale and to give a rationale of their evaluation. Within this series of group sessions, use is also made of psychotherapeutic games based on material that Weathers, Bedell, Marlowe, Gordon, Adams, Reed, Palmer, and Gordon (1981) have kindly put at our disposal.

The second series of group sessions is devoted to the expression of emotions and to an analysis of factors that may inhibit the expression of appropriate emotions. For this series, some appropriate readings are made available for the patients as a point of departure for the discussion. However, the emotion to be discussed is almost always suggested by the patients. Among the most common suggestions are the control and/or expression of anger, the expression and control of positive feelings toward persons of the opposite sex, and recognition of emotions that are not expressed verbally.

## The Use of Videotape

As mentioned in the earlier section on socialization, patients are made familiar with videotapes. This is of great importance to our work.

Videotaping is primarily done on two occasions—when the patients first enter the center (at the beginning of each new term) and at the end of each period of treatment. Videotapes are used to document changes in the patients. On the first occasion, efforts are made to ensure that the patient's problems and expectations with regard to the forthcoming treatment are clearly expressed. During the later recording, patients are encouraged to give an account of their experiences during treatment and to assess (on an imaginary 10-point scale) to what extent they have achieved their goals. The therapists' interviews on these occasions provide an overall impression of the status of each patient on the different recording occasions. These recordings are stored for future evaluation of the treatment program.

The videotaping of the individual therapy sessions provides an important basis for supervision. Obviously, not all therapy sessions are videotaped. However, we strive to record at least one session every second week.

In my experience as supervisor, I have become increasingly convinced of the value of such a praxis if supervision is really to refer to what goes on between the therapist and the patient. I am both skeptical and critical concerning the true value of supervision that relies only on verbal or written reports by the therapist. It is a truism for someone working from a cognitive perspective that no therapist can ever report correctly what has occurred between himself or herself and the patient during therapy, particularly when it comes to nonverbal communication. Even a thorough knowledge of the personal style of each therapist by the supervisor is not enough for the correct evaluation of the timing and appropriateness of therapeutic interventions that have occurred during the session.

Most often, recordings that are used for supervision purposes are subsequently erased. However, a few especially illustrative examples are retained. When appropriate, the patient may be encouraged to see these recordings, either shortly after the therapy session to reinforce what has been discussed or at a later time to demonstrate the progress that has been made. On these occasions, at least one of the patient's therapists is always present to deal with any reactions the viewing might instigate.

We have found patients to respond positively to these recordings and to viewing them during therapy, even though watching themselves, especially in the beginning, may prove to be a difficult experience. It seems that appearance on film often promotes a kind of dissonance, which the patients express by saying that they do not recognize themselves, and which is most tangible when the patients are still influenced by a pathological distortion of their self-images. There is much evidence, however, that suggests that repeated viewing tends to annihilate such dissonance and thus promotes a normalization of response.

An example illustrates this point. One of our patients suffered delusional ideas of reference that she attributed to the conviction that everyone was able to see that she was a sick person who behaved in a strange way. In support of this conviction, she reported that whenever she watched herself in a mirror, she saw a rigid, expressionless facial reflection, a clear indication that she was mentally ill. We had to wait for several weeks before she agreed to the recording of one of her therapy sessions, during which she behaved in a relaxed way after a few minutes of tension. When she afterward reviewed the recording, she was surprised to discover that she behaved in a relaxed way, and she was unable to point out how someone could recognize in her behavior that she was a mental patient. After that occasion, she insisted that each therapy session be recorded and spent some time in reviewing the recordings. In another few weeks, she changed her hairstyle, began to be more careful about her dress, and was able to criticize her previous delusional ideas.

## Supervision

Supervision takes up at least 4–5 hours a week, usually during a complete afternoon. It includes direct patient guidance and supervision related to the therapeutic process and in the form of seminars. Since the patients live at the center and treatment follows a certain predetermined course, emphasis in supervision is placed more on the process and on the occurrence of transference and countertransference reactions than on direct guidance concerning work with individual patients. All staff members present at the center at the time of the supervision sessions participate in it. Since supervision always includes the review of a videotaped therapy session, a lively discussion occurs at the same time a consistent therapeutic approach to the conduct of therapy is promoted.

## THE THERAPEUTIC ENVIRONMENT

### The Characteristics of a Therapeutic Milieu

What makes an environment therapeutic?

To answer this question, some conclusions reached by Rapoport (1960) following collaboration with Jones in a characterization of the first "therapeutic community" developed in Great Britain are considered. Although Jones's work was published in 1960, nothing that has been added since has significantly altered the basic understanding he expressed, which remains valid irrespective of the ideological orientation given to the therapeutic milieu. Rapoport summarized the factors that contribute collectively to produce a "therapeutic milieu" in seven main points:

- The environment must enable the patient to collect experiences that minimized his or her distortion of reality.
- It must promote a reality-based and meaningful communication with others.
- It must facilitate cooperation with others, leading to a sense of security and satisfaction.
- It must contribute to the reduction of anxiety and to the enhancement of feelings of well-being.
- It must promote the patient's self-respect.
- It must increase the awareness of the patient as to the possible causes and various manifestations of his or her disorder.
- It must support a mobilization of the patient's initiative to realize his or her potential creativity and productivity.

Other authors who have written on therapeutic milieus have, in principle, reemphasized Rapoport's conclusions (e.g., Fischer, 1972; Füredi & Kun, 1972). However, not all later attempts that have been made in the guise of a milieu-therapeutic ideology have attained the goals stated by Rapoport. Recently published reviews (e.g., Gunderson, 1980; Gunderson, Will, & Mosher, 1983; Gutheil, 1985; Islam & Turner, 1982; Mosher & Keith, 1979; Wilmer, 1981) have not been lacking in criticism. Wilmer (1981), for example, divided the various "therapeutic communities" into three main categories. He drew attention to the disadvantages associated with both those that were too permissive and bordering on the anarchistic and those that were clearly psychoanalytical and whose rather modest results stood in strong contrast to the extreme enthusiasm of the personnel. In between, he placed those units characterized by eclecticism and that gave priority to the "here and now" and were flexible. Islam and Turner (1982) drew even more drastic conclusions, reporting that no studies of acceptable scientific quality are yet available that demonstrate the therapeutic value of such a therapeutic milieu. Mosher and Menn (1978) reported a 2-year follow-up of patients treated in a particular therapeutic setting (Soteria House) compared with a control group. In their evaluation, no significant differences emerged between the groups. However, those treated at Soteria House appeared to need less medication and less outpatient support, had better working capacity, and were more independent.

Extensive and competent investigations of milieu therapy for schizophrenic patients were recently published in a series of articles by Vaglum, Friis, Karterud, and their coworkers at the Ullevål Hospital in Norway (e.g., Friis, Karterud, Kleppe, Lorentzen, Lystrup, & Vaglum, 1982; Vaglum, Friis, & Karterud, 1985). These studies emphasized that group meetings based on confrontation between the participants were destructive and that a greater emphasis on individual treatment is clearly preferable.

One major difficulty in evaluating results of milieu therapy is that the term has been used to designate a variety of treatment approaches in the varied settings with various kinds of patients. In most cases, therapeutic milieus were implemented in alternative to traditional wards in large mental hospitals and for long-stay patients; others, as for example Soteria House, were research projects concerned with the treatment of acute patients in an alternative setting. In some instances, the milieu was exploited as a complement to individual psychotherapy; in others, it was the only treatment approach; and in still others, it was a complement to drug treatment. Also, the goals of treatment and the underlying philosophy have all too often been ill defined.

Despite all of these problematic issues, consensus on some general characteristics conducive to better results seems to occur. Thus, small size, positive staff expectations, and a practical, down-to-earth orientation seem to be most appropriate for acute patients (Mosher & Keith, 1979, 1980), while milieus that are very structured, highly organized, and characterized by high expectations seem to suit chronic patients better (Füredi & Kun, 1972; Paul & Lentz, 1977). Gunderson (1980) underscored that distribution of responsibility, clarity in treatment programs, and high level of staff–patient interaction are sources of success for milieus designed for nonchronic schizophrenic patients.

One might wonder why a milieu-therapeutic approach, especially in small units, has not become more common in the treatment of patients with schizophrenic syndromes. Will (1968) enumerated some 20 years ago the main reasons hampering the development of small therapeutic centers. Among those, he included the fact that such centers do not have the support of governmental or private agencies, that few patients can pay for such care, that patients who are treated in these centers have often done poorly in treatment elsewhere and therefore do not respond rapidly to treatment, and that staff members require intensive and often prolonged training and may find other work more rewarding. There is reason to suspect that the reasons mentioned by Will are still valid in most countries.

Both the external aspects and the treatment ideology at our centers appear to meet the requirements that Rapoport placed on a therapeutic milieu. We mix supportive therapy in many aspects of the daily treatment program with restructuring therapy, which is included in the more direct treatment procedures. Both of these are based on a consistent cognitive therapeutic ideology, enabling our centers to cover a broad spectrum of the total problems of each patient. Since our centers are part of the public health services of our catchment area, and are thus covered by the National Health Insurance System, our patients have no economic reasons not to participate in the treatment offered to them.

## Milieu-Therapeutic Processes

From what has already been said, it is clear that not all types of environments are "therapeutic" for all kinds of patients and that various models must be developed if the needs of different patient groups are to be met in a meaningful way. However, to be able to choose the more useful model, it is necessary to attain some insight into those activities or attitudes that promote therapeutic processes in a care unit. Gunderson (1978b) published a most thoughtful study that identified and defined the most important therapeutic components in psychiatric milieus. The following adopts his description and attempts to show in what manner the different variables can be related to a general cognitive therapeutic attitude held by all staff members. An earlier description of the way in which these variables can be applied, even in ordinary acute wards, has been provided elsewhere (C. Perris, 1985b, 1988f).

In his article, Gunderson (1978b) commented on early attempts to describe ward climate in terms of functional variables that could be correlated with outcome, and he pointed out some of the inconsistencies he had found in several of the proposed formulations. In particular, Gunderson maintained that rating instruments supposed to reflect therapeutic actions frequently are descriptive in nature and not inherently related to therapeutic processes. He emphasized also that functional variables often are artificially separated into groups containing nonfunctional variables that are given equal weight. To help overcome any difficulties that might arise from the use of diffuse conceptualizations, Gunderson suggested a set of five functional variables, based on inferences drawn from clinical experience, that describe therapeutic activities that staff members employ with patients and that could be of use to clinicians as a model for developing milieu treatment programs.

The interested reader will find a thorough description of the variables in the original article. In the following, only a brief account is reported.

The first of the dimensions considered by Gunderson is containment. In this context, "containment" refers to the function of preventing destructive behavior, preventing dangerous accidents, and minimizing the chances of physical deterioration. Thus, this interpretation of the term is different from that used by object-relations theoreticians (e.g., Bion, 1977; Winnicott, 1965), who use the term "containing function" to refer to the function of the therapist (or nursing staff) to receive and accommodate all the strongly emotional expressions exhibited by the patients (see also Haugsgjerd, 1983). In the meaning used by Gunderson, the term refers to the use of restrictive measures (including medication) to prevent or contain destructive behavior or to the feeding of patients who refuse to eat. Containment is expected to enhance the patients' self-control indirectly. However, its misuse can easily obstruct the patients' initiative and generate a tendency to isolation.

Support is the second variable listed by Gunderson. It refers to all the activities of the nursing staff that are intended to enhance the patient's self-esteem and feelings of well-being. Examples include the availability of staff members whenever the patient needs help and encouragement given to him or her to participate in tasks that, in all probability, will be carried out successfully. A supportive approach to psychopathological manifestations could involve reassurance that they are symptomatic of an illness and other efforts to minimize their significance. Excessive support, on the other hand, can lead to negative effects, for instance, reinforcement of the patient's feelings of inadequacy and dependence.

Validation is a variable that to a certain extent is inversely related to support. It refers to a process intended to help the patient to assert his or her individuality while at the same time being aware of limitations. To put it in other words, validation refers to attempts aimed at conveying to the patient that his or her value as a human being is not based on the fact of being mentally ill. This implies that staff members do not refrain from relating their own weaknesses and that they encourage patients to participate in activities that lie at the limits of their abilities. In this way, patients are enabled to develop a tolerance for possible failures and to discover that they will not be devaluated as a consequence of such failures. Gunderson emphasized that validation helps patients to develop a capacity for closeness and a more consolidated identity. Füredi and Kun (1972) must have thought of validation when they emphasized that realistic interpersonal relationships with the staff gives a firm frame of reference that will promote the patient's functioning at the level of reality. However, validation is not indicated for very passive patients who could feel neglected.

Structure includes all the characteristics of a treatment unit that promote a predictable organization with respect to time, space, and person. Structure is reflected in the occurrence of clearly defined individual treatment schedules and routines, that is, variables that have been consistently found to be conducive to success (Fischer, 1972; Gunderson, 1980; Mosher & Keith, 1979). The most important function of structure is to promote changes in the maladaptive behaviors of the patients while simultaneously giving them a feeling of security. Emphasis on structure can, however, produce negative consequences; treatment routines may become too rigid and can severely hinder the patients' creativity and self-assertion. I have described elsewhere (C. Perris, 1963) one such therapeutic unit in which structure became unnecessarily elaborated in contrast to the outside world.

The last of the five variables described by Gunderson is involvement, which implies all those processes that promote the patients' participation in their social environment. Involvement's main purpose should be to reinforce the patients' self-esteem, to oppose passivity, and to correct dysfunctional patterns in interpersonal relationships. Too much involvement can, however, produce a feeling that the patient's integrity is being violated. Very likely, involvement is the variable that has been most exploited in the therapeutic communities criticized by Wilmer (1981), Islam and Turner (1982), and Gutheil (1985) for their tendency of becoming triumphs of ideology over methodology.

Involvement is related to another variable, called negotiation by Washburn and Conrad (1979). The latter, in principle, refers to the attitude taken by the nursing staff to regard the patient as a collaborator, especially concerning the planning of individual programs of treatment. However, it does not completely overlap with involvement because, according to my understanding of the concept, it implies a willingness to compromise by the staff that could be regarded as validation.

At the end of his article, Gunderson pointed out that, ideally, all these processes should occur at every milieu-therapeutic unit but that it is difficult to ensure that they are all equally well developed. I do not, however, share his pessimism, and I believe that a comprehensive cognitive therapeutic orientation, of the type applied in our centers, might very well serve to realize all these various processes.

One of the fundamental tenets of cognitive psychotherapy is that we are all controlled by incorporated preconceptions about ourselves and our surroundings that we continuously reaffirm and prolong by means of various cognitive distortions. The most common distortions are that we tend to draw far-reaching conclusions from isolated events (overgeneralization), that we tend to form opinions even when the evidence for them is scanty (arbitrary interference), and that we often tend to exaggerate the importance of some isolated event (magnification, minimization, or imagining catastrophies).

A cognitive therapeutic approach implies, first and foremost, that all personnel have been given the opportunity to become aware of their own attitudes and expectations concerning the patients and their behavior and that they have been trained to prevent themselves from being directed by unsubstantiated generalized opinions. Staff members must learn that their own opinions can become self-fulfilling and that their attitudes can indirectly affect patients' behavior patterns. Translated into psychodynamic conceptions, this implies that the staff should gain insight into their possible countertransferential motivations.

In practice, in restraining disruptive behavior in a patient in our centers, "regulated censure and praise," as stressed by Gunderson, is always applied. This means that the patient receives attention, is listened to with the aim of interpreting the message conveyed by the behavior, and is controlled in such a way that the expression of symptoms is not obstructed. The patient is helped to recognize the consequences (positive and negative) of his or her conduct but is never threatened with punishment. The choice of a positive functional solution by the patient is encouraged, but inability to do so is not punished.

Since the use of drugs is one of the components of the variable containment, it is important to briefly describe how a cognitive therapeutic approach can facilitate necessary medication. There should be no doubt that most patients entertain preconceived ideas concerning medication that are based on magical ideas about effects and on both factual and imagined opinions on adverse effects. When such attitudes occur, the nursing staff can help the patient to relate his or her opinions, to question and rectify totally incorrect ideas, and to arrive at a balanced opinion of the pros and cons of medication. Such an approach would probably be regarded as negotiation by Washburn and Conrad (1979).

Gunderson has quite correctly pointed out that many of the variables he has identified are interrelated. This interrelation becomes particularly clear when a tailored program of treatment and an agreement concerning goals are established with the patient. It is in this connection that mastery of different cognitive therapeutic methods and an overall judgment of the patient's problems and resources are best employed. Assignment of homework, for example, can fulfill a supporting and validating function in relation to the patient's actual condition, while the feedback to the patient after the homework's successful (or unsuccessful) completion can help to gradually enhance self-confidence. The nursing staff should always ensure that a meaningful balance is maintained so that the patient does not feel overprotected or subject to violations of his or her integrity.

Among the other milieu-therapeutic variables that have been identified by other authors, I would like to add one more, namely prevention, which, to a certain extent, is related to both support and validation. As is well known, the term "prevention" is used in many different contexts within psychiatry (Caplan, 1964). Here the term means a preparation of patients for their return to their circle of relatives and friends within the community after a stay at a psychiatric unit. It is well documented that many people entertain various dysfunctional preconceptions concerning how to behave and how they may be received back in an ordinary lifestyle. What is more important is that dysfunctional assumptions (e.g., "one does not speak about a mental disorder as one would about a physical illness," or "people who have been admitted to psychiatric units are always regarded as weak people, and thus weakness must be concealed") are often entertained by psychiatric patients and are accompanied by shame, which determines maladaptive behaviors. Luckily, even these preconceived ideas may be counteracted, both by using appropriate cognitive therapeutic techniques (e.g., problem-solving, reality testing) and by emphasizing openness at the unit (e.g., favoring visits to and from friends and relatives, visits to place of work, etc.).

Although the variables described so far are those that best characterize the therapeutic processes going on in their therapeutic milieus, this analysis would be incomplete without a reference to the family-like dimension described in previous sections and to the probable occurrence of unspecific factors of the type common to all therapies. The family-like atmosphere is already covered by the concept of support; however, it should be also regarded as nutritional in the sense that this concept is used in object-relations theory (Arieti, 1974a). "Nutritional" elements include the development of attachment to personnel and fellow patients, the concept of secure base, and the process of separation following cognitive and emotional growth.

Among the unspecific factors, I agree with Frank (1985) about the healing effects of faith and underscore that the very fact of being treated in a special unit may enhance hope in patients and have a curative effect. However, there are also dangers if the type of treatment and the setting where it is administered are experienced as unique, since this belief may reinforce possible grandiose ideas and make separation even more difficult.

# III

## *Cognitive Psychotherapy with Schizophrenic Patients: Individual Therapy*

# 8

# *The Principles of Individual Therapy*

In this section, the principles of individual cognitive psychotherapy with schizophrenic patients are described in detail. The section describes the use of this type of therapy for both hospitalized patients and outpatients.

Psychotherapy, whenever possible, should be initiated while the patient is admitted to a ward that is therapeutic in itself. This not only allows treatment to start when the patient is still in an acute phase, but also favors a quicker development of a good therapeutic relationship since it is easier to plan for more frequent, if shorter, sessions in the initial phase in a ward. As pointed out by Eldred (1972), the therapist can rapidly become a stable figure during acute psychosis, thus contributing to the patient's structuring of reality. In addition, the therapeutic potential of the ward's personnel can be profitably exploited.

Nevertheless, beginning therapy with patients referred to an outpatient unit is also straightforward, although it is necessary to devote a few sessions to obtaining as complete a picture of the overall problems of the patient as possible. These introductory interviews are extremely important since their outcome, that is, whether the patient continues therapy or simply disappears after the first meetings, largely depends on their quality. Because of this, the development of an optimum therapeutic relationship is discussed next.

The various therapeutic techniques of cognitive psychotherapy are discussed briefly here since therapists intending to work with schizophrenic patients are already well trained in the basic principles of cognitive psychotherapy as well as its most commonly used techniques. On the other hand, several aspects of therapy mentioned in Part 2 are considered in more depth so that the sections that follow can be read and used whether or not the reader has access to a treatment center of the type described earlier. In addition, aspects of the therapeutic process that markedly deviate from what is customary in short-term cognitive therapy are duly emphasized. This may lead to some repetition. However, such repetition can be compared with that in a piece of music, where the main theme recurs many times but where variations contribute to increased complexity.

At the end of the book, the therapeutic process is discussed in more detail from a cognitive perspective, with particular reference to schizophrenic patients.

## THE THERAPEUTIC RELATIONSHIP

"In the beginning is the relation" proclaimed Martin Buber (1970, p. 69), echoed by Yalom (1980). The quality of the therapeutic relationship, which is the most fundamental ingredient in all forms of therapy with all types of patients, becomes decisive in the psychotherapy with schizophrenic patients whether they continue to show psychotic symptoms or are in a nonpsychotic condition (Binswanger, 1942).

Some of the more important aspects of the patient–therapist relationship, upon which widespread agreement prevails within the psychoanalytical model, were discussed earlier. The importance of this relationship has been stressed many times by Beck (e.g., Beck *et al.*, 1979) and by other leading cognitive therapists, especially those who work on a long-term basis with patients with personality disorders (e.g., Freeman, 1986; Padesky, 1986; Simon, 1986; Young 1986). This section, however, enlarges on this subject further, mainly from the viewpoint of cognitive psychotherapy.

When one works with schizophrenic patients, more than a session is usually required to establish a meaningful therapeutic alliance of the type that is expected in cognitive psychotherapy (that is, one of "collaborative empiricism," see below), even though variations can occur depending on the actual condition of a given patient. One important source of variation might be whether the patient has applied voluntarily for treatment. Very often, the therapist encounters with the schizophrenic patient a similar problem as with very young patients (Bedrosian, 1981) who come for treatment not on their own but because of pressure from some important other in their immediate environment. Thus, a distinction has to be made between the development of a working alliance based on collaborative empiricism and the establishment of a trustworthy relationship as a necessary *prerequisite* to collaborative empiricism. It is invariably the case that, even though both types of relationships are continuously developed during the entire therapy in different ways, the foundations of a reliable relationship are laid at the first contact. The tone of the continued therapeutic cooperation is begun at the initial greeting.

Nicholi (1978) very perceptively described the importance of the first contact with his patient (irrespective of diagnosis):

Whether the patient is young or old, neatly groomed or disheveled, outgoing or withdrawn, articulate or inarticulate, highly integrated or totally disintegrated, of high or low socioeconomic status, the skilled clinician realizes that the patient, as a fellow human being, is considerably more like himself than he is different and that even if he understands only a fraction of a patient's mental functioning, that patient will contribute significantly to the therapist's understanding of himself and of every other patient. (p. 4)

Although the ability of the schizophrenic patient to send and receive normal communications, especially verbal ones, is often severely impaired, he or she is extremely sensitive to feelings and emotions and to the personal qualities of those nearby. This is one of the reasons for the repeated assertions of Fromm-Reichmann (1955). Searles (1958a), Arieti (1972), Cox (1986), and many others of the importance of being aware of possible countertransference reactions.

Since, as previously mentioned, schizophrenic patients seldom seek treatment voluntarily, it follows that the first task of the therapist is to break down a barrier of mistrust and doubt and to help the patient to establish a contact and to talk about his or her problems. For patients who are not spontaneously forthcoming, I agree with Arieti (1974a) that it is the responsibility of the therapist to take the initiative in conversation in such a way that the attempt at contact is unmistakable. However, it is important in this context to be extremely receptive to every form of nonverbal contact from the patient and to ensure that the patient is truly able to feel understood.

When a patient is very incoherent or talks only of hallucinatory or delusional experiences, I do not pretend to understand. One of my usual replies on such occasions is, "I understand that you are trying to tell me something which is of importance to you, but I am not able at the moment to understand what it is. I suggest that we speak about that later, when we have had an opportunity of learning more about each other. But now, would you tell me. . . ."

During my years of practice I have had the opportunity to learn that even the most talkative, incoherent patient is capable of supplying adequate replies when attention is patiently diverted to some neutral topic. Later, when the therapeutic relationship has been firmly established, replies to the patient's assertions of a delusional nature can be formulated according to cognitive therapeutic principles, and only then can attempts be made to analyze the deeper implications. The following vignette illustrates this point:

One of my patients with whom I have had a good relationship for many years telephoned one evening in a state of agitation to ask whether there was a risk that the bedroom ceiling could fall on her. When I asked what had caused this fear, she said, somewhat incoherently, that on an occasion when she had been compulsorily admitted to a hospital, a piece of plaster had fallen on her during a visit to the lavatory. After some discussion, she was able to analyze the difference between the two situations and to reach the conclusion that her fears were completely unreasonable.

I was not satisfied with her so-quickly attained insight, and I probed further to see if there was some other reason for the fear that made her call. She then admitted that she really wanted advice as to how to behave toward a neighbor who lived above her and who was disturbed by her early awakening every morning to go to work. This same neighbor had instigated the earlier compulsory hospitalization when she had been particularly troublesome.

Thus, she was actually afraid of getting into a dispute with her neighbor and risking rehospitalization. Even this second issue was easily resolvable, and she was induced to work out a suitable solution herself.

As mentioned earlier, a condition relatedness or secure base must be established between the therapist and the patient. This means that an atmosphere of mutual trust, warmth, and sharing prevails. The term "empathy" has become usual in characterizing good relationships, and much has been written about it (e.g., Beres & Arlow, 1974, Kohut, 1959, and Greenson, 1967, to name a few). The overall goal of cognitive psychotherapy is to help the patient to be conscious of his or her ruling convictions and self-opinions and to guide him or her to develop new and more functional meaning structures. For this purpose, the therapist should learn, through a consistent empathic attitude, to understand the way in which patients organize their wishes, thoughts, emotions, and preconceptions of themselves and the environment. In other words, empathy can be defined, in line with Schafer (1959), as the internal experience of sharing and correctly understanding the actual psychological condition in another person. It is important to remember that the most important signs of a person's inner experiences are reflected in nonverbal rather than verbal communication. Continuous awareness of nonverbal messages is, thus, just as important in cognitive psychotherapy as it is in other forms of therapy, since nonverbal signals often lead to timely therapeutic interventions.

Of course, it can be very difficult to start a dialogue with a severely disturbed patient. However, the therapist must be active and avoid getting caught in the patient's possible negativism, a mistake that, according to Schulz (1975), frequently occurs. It is also important to remember that the therapist's attempt to relate to the patient must always be attuned to the relating capability that is available to the patient. The "need–fear" dilemma of the freezing porcupines, described by Schopenhauer and reported by S. Freud (1921), perhaps best illustrates the experience of the schizophrenic patient in the initial contact with the therapist.[1]

Other aspects of the therapeutic relationship that become relevant when the therapeutic work has been in progress for a while are discussed below (See also "Analogies, Metaphors, and Other Stylistic Devices" and "Humor, Self-Disclosure, and Other Verbal Approaches," in Chapter 9.).

## COLLABORATIVE EMPIRICISM

The term "socialization" refers to that process by which a person who grows up in a certain cultural environment learns what is expected in certain situations and what may be expected of the persons with whom he or she interacts. If we transfer this sociological concept to the sphere of psychotherapy, socialization implies that the patient must recognize the roles to be played by himself or herself and by the therapist during therapy. A patient who has not understood what is expected or who has misconceptions about the therapist will, in all probability, experience some problems.

A research group at the Johns Hopkins Hospital in Baltimore under the direction of Jerome Frank has, over a period of many years, completed a series of experiments to investigate whether systematic preparation for therapy has any influence on patients' behavior during therapy as well as on the results of therapy. The results of these studies (e.g., J. Frank, 1985; J. Frank, Hoehn-Saric, Imber, Liberman, & Stone, 1978), showed that those patients who were systematically prepared were not only more busy and more active during therapy but also showed better results than patients who had received no preparation at all. A similar study, carried out by another group under the leadership of Sloane (Sloane, Cristol, Peppernick, & Staples, 1970), had less impressive results.

The importance of patient preparation prior to cognitive therapy has been repeatedly stressed by Beck and coworkers (e.g., Beck *et al.*, 1979; Bedrosian & Beck, 1980), who emphasized that the patient should be given the opportunity to understand the praxis of cognitive therapy with regard to planning, motivation, and special methods. Bedrosian and Beck (1980, p. 135) stressed that "demystifying the treatment process helps to define the patient as a more competent person who is fully capable of initiating and maintaining the steps necessary for self-improvement." This preparation or socialization is especially important in

---

[1]In the example described, porcupines huddled together on a cold day so as not to freeze to death; however, they were forced to separate by the pain of each other's quills.

cognitive psychotherapy since it requires that both the therapist and the patient be very active during the therapy sessions. It is important, preferably with some simple example, to help the patient to discover that there is a strong relationship between how one thinks and what one feels and that both affect behavior. An excerpt from a dialogue with a patient admitted to his first session serves as an example:

THERAPIST: How did you feel when you were waiting outside before coming in?
PATIENT: I was a little tense and apprehensive.
THERAPIST: Did you think of anything in particular?
PATIENT: I thought about our meeting . . . the start of therapy . . . that I did not know what was expected from me and that I would appear stupid.
THERAPIST: And how do you feel now that we have talked to each other for a while?
PATIENT: Well, I don't feel tense any longer.
THERAPIST: Is there any special reason that you are calmer now?
PATIENT: Yes, I now know a little more what to expect.

The last reply would allow the therapist to help the patient recognize that the earlier tension probably arose from lack of familiarity with the situation, uncertainty, and fear of appearing stupid. The therapist could point out that there are many situations or events that affect us simply because we do not know enough about them; with more knowledge, however, such situations do not affect us as much.

Socialization must take place successively and more gradually with schizophrenic than with other types of patients; also particular difficulties can arise with schizophrenics. One major obstacle is that some patients lack the ability to metathink (discussed in Chapter 9; see "Dealing with Automatic Dysfunctional Thoughts"), that is, the ability to reflect upon their own thoughts. Thus, in the dialogue reported above, a likely reply could be as follows:

THERAPIST: Did you think of anything in particular?
PATIENT: No, I just felt tense.

In such a case, an alternative intervention from the therapist could be the following:

THERAPIST: Well, I understand that you have some difficulty in thinking about your feelings, but I expect that you will learn that most of our feelings are related to some special thought. Now, would you tell me whether you have felt tense in similar occasions?

In other words, a patient unable at the beginning of therapy to focus on his or her thoughts must be successively trained in becoming aware of them. The rationale of the intervention reported above is to discover whether the patient is able to discover links among situations that arouse tension.

Socialization is often spread over many sessions, and only those aspects of cognitive therapy that are relevant are taken up in a particular session. On these occasions, the therapist should adopt a temporary role of teacher, but he or she should be judicious and not overwhelm the patient. In addition, it is crucial that relationships among feelings, thoughts, and behavior (including symptoms) be kept at a general level in the early stages and that no attempt is made to link them with a psychotic symptomatology. It has often been emphasized that self-disclosure is allowed for the therapist when in contact with schizophrenic patients; however, I have found it to be much simpler to refer to myself when exemplifying connections between feelings and automatic thoughts in the early stages of therapy. This approach is consistent with a focus on sharing, as emphasized from the psychoanalytical perspective by Arieti (1972).

Cognitive psychotherapy assumes that if the patient is able to identify distorted cognitions by name, it will be easier for him or her to recognize them and to report them to the therapist; also, therapeutic cooperation is promoted by the use of a common language. With schizophrenic patients, however, I have often chosen to avoid complicated explanations and the use of confusing terminology. Only much later in treatment, when the cooperation has become productive, do I introduce such concepts as "schema" or "cognitive distortions"; even then, I use vocabulary that is understood by the patient without difficulty.

In cognitive psychotherapy, Kelly's metaphor (1955) of "man the scientist" has been applied to a particular aspect of the therapeutic alliance. In his personal constructs theory, Kelly compared humans to a scientist who is continuously searching for meaning and context in all experience. In accordance with this similarity, people perpetually test their understanding of the world and restructure their picture of the environment progressively with the experience they gradually gain. This idea is used in cognitive psychotherapy to illustrate the cooperative work done by the patient and the therapist in putting forward hypotheses and testing their validity. Because the patient and therapist cooperate, the term "collaborative empiricism" is used to describe the continuous examination and testing of the patient's dysfunctional assumptions. Knowledge of this type of cooperation can be easily communicated to the patient in very simple terms.

Thus, to sum up, what is important in an early phase is that the patient is given the opportunity to learn the most elementary principles of therapy and to understand what is expected of him or her. Arieti (1972) stressed that the therapist must be a "peer" and that this is what collaborative empiricism is all about. However, I have found it appropriate to omit the term "scientist" or "researcher" when socializing excessively suspicious patients. Occasionally, I use the metaphor of the mountain climber and his guide proposed a few decades ago by Lungwitz (1980) to characterize the active work of the therapist and patient in correcting the latter's misconceptions.

## THE PROBLEM INVENTORY
## AND GOAL SETTING

It is important that the goal (or goals) of therapy and a time frame (even a very general one) be discussed with the patient at a very early stage; however, a formal contract cannot be established with schizophrenic patients as with other types of patients. Before formulating a goal, it is necessary for the therapist to make a problem inventory. In this context, the word "problem" acquires a meaning similar to that understood when one talks of "problem-oriented record." Thus, the various symptoms shown by a patient are counted as problems in just the same way the patient's lack of accommodation or job is counted.

The problem inventory can be established with the aid of a checklist or different rating instruments (e.g., a rating scale to evaluate symptomatology or a comprehensive scale to assess the level of social function). There is, in the context of psychotherapy, a certain resistance toward the use of rating instruments, often with the excuse that they disturb the therapeutic relationship. However, those who conquer their initial resistance quickly discover that different measures are not only of great importance for obtaining a more systematic appraisal of the course of therapy and its outcome, but are important to the patient who is always interested in receiving some measure of progress. We should never lose sight of the fact that, beyond the ambitious goal of helping patients to achieve an extensive restructuration of their personalities, lies the more modest goal of helping patients to increase their levels of social function so that they can lead a more satisfying life. Even when it comes to a restructuring of personality, cognitive psychotherapy permits an operationalization of that which is to be changed and enables measurements of the changes to be achieved.

Though some people fear that use of self-ratings or other operationalizations might disturb the therapeutic relationship, my experience is that the opposite occurs. In fact, engaging the patient in those tasks points out in a manifest way, and from the very beginning, that the therapist takes seriously the patient's opinions and evaluation of his or her situation and that the therapeutic work really is a joint effort.

Although the therapist should establish a thorough inventory of problems, he or she is not solely responsible for setting the goals of therapy. After the problem inventory is set up with the patient, the therapist recapitulates the most prominent problems to show that the therapist has understood all that worries the patient. Subsequently, the patient and the therapist must together define the goals that the patient wishes to achieve.

A delicate issue in this context is that some patients propose completely unrealistic goals, especially with regard to vocational training; often, the goal can be judged to be unrealistic regardless of the present mental condition of the patient. In such cases, I attempt to determine the patient's motives for choosing a particular goal, and I suggest that training or schooling be postponed until the patient becomes more independent and self-confident.

Ideally, several preliminary goals might be agreed on that the patient can realize in his or her present circumstances. Success in the efforts required for this work promotes the motivation for continued therapy. This approach is consistent with the emphasis on the healthy side of the patient previously discussed.

I would never be satisfied with an agreement based on the aims of the patient to "become a new person" or "acquire a new identity." Although sympathetic to Karen Horney's concept of "self-realization," I always insist on helping the patient to specify the meaning that he or she attaches to these goals.

It is not uncommon for the patient to ask whether the therapy will "cure" him or her. I try initially to determine what the term "cure" means to the patient. Then I explain that the patient will probably learn a lot about himself or herself and feel more self-satisfied, less dependent on others, and more able both to enjoy life and to confront its difficulties.

## AGREEMENT ON A PROGRAM AND TERMINATION OF THE FIRST SESSION

In agreeing on a program, it is important for the therapist to discuss with the patient how to proceed if either one or the other must be absent from a particular session. It is also important that the patient be informed of predictable interruptions caused by travel, vacations, or other factors known to the therapist.

It is quite common, especially at the beginning, that the schedule of meetings agreed to cannot be followed. Time after time, I have found that schizophrenic patients, particularly during initial stages when they still lack confidence in the therapist, feel a need to insure themselves against disappointment by testing him or her. This testing may be manifested in the form of a request for extra sessions or repeated telephone calls. In this respect, it is without doubt of great value to have an assistant therapist, as recommended by many psychoanalysts, so that the patient is associated with at least two persons on whom to rely. Such an arrangement should not be difficult if the leading therapist works within a team and another team member can function as assistant therapist.

Whether one or two therapists are involved, the patient must be made aware of when and under what circumstances it is acceptable to contact the therapist outside the therapy sessions. Many of my patients telephone me at home at varying intervals. However, it has not been difficult for them to accept that their telephone calls may, occasionally, be inconvenient and that I will not talk to them at those times. When this occurs, I ask them to call back at another, more suitable time. When the occasion is suitable, a short talk is often adequate and may be of great therapeutic value since it exemplifies a practical application of the concept of secure base.

Two other items are important at the first session. One is allowing the patient to experience how the therapy will proceed. This can be done by discussing one of the minor items discussed in the problem inventory. When no suitable topic can be found in this list, perhaps because of time constraints, a completely neutral subject can be adopted. For example, patients can be questioned concerning knowledge of cognitive therapy prior to the session and what they have learned during it; in this way, the future importance of what they have learned can be pointed out to them. Another option, repeated in each subsequent session, is to allow patients to briefly summarize what they have discussed and to ask them in what way the topic of discussion has been of value. Patients are generally also asked to verbalize their feelings about the session in general and about the therapist's understanding of their problems.

## QUESTIONS OF MEDICATION

The issue of medication acquires a different significance when the patient is seen as an outpatient than when he or she is admitted to a ward. It must be stressed, yet again, that a therapist who is also a doctor must assume responsibility for medication. In this respect, I completely agree with Eldred's opinion that "the guild-oriented model of competing therapies has no place in the total treatment of severely disturbed people" (1972, p. 155). Eldred also pointed out that the therapist should be well versed in the use of psychotropic drugs or changing medications" (p. 156). It is a little more complicated, however, when the therapist is not a doctor and therefore cannot be directly responsible for medication. In such cases, the two persons responsible for the patient must meet the patient together at the first contact to demonstrate that they will be working as a team and that they share similar attitudes. In this respect, it is important to remember that it will be more confusing for the patient to be treated by different people according to different principles than to accept that different people are working together within the frame of a comprehensive treatment program.

If medication has to be prescribed by another person than the primary therapist, it is necessary that the prescribing doctor share most of the therapist's values and knowledge of the therapeutic process. In fact, it is not uncommon that a patient may show an apparent impairment in mental status during the progress of drug therapy, which the therapist may be well able to deal with. However, a person responsible only for the patient's medication might view an occasional impairment from quite another perspective and unnecessarily increase the dosage of the drugs taken by the patient. Should this occur, the medication could negatively interfere with the progress of therapy.

Some patients assume that all medication will be discontinued automatically when psychotherapy commences. In such cases, I usually inform the patient of the possible favorable interaction between drugs and psychotherapy and suggest that all decisions regarding medication be postponed until we have had the opportunity to assess the extent to which he or she is helped by the psychotherapy. However, even with outpatients, one goal is to keep the patient on a minimum dosage of psychotropic drugs and to teach the patient to assume responsibility for the medication.

## CONTACT WITH THE PATIENT'S RELATIVES

Contact with relatives is different for outpatients than for inpatients, especially since many of our younger patients still reside with their parents. It is essential that at least one of the patient's closest relatives be invited to a meeting during the early stages of treatment. It has already been pointed out (see Part 1) that the emotional atmosphere in the patient's home is of great importance for the course of a schizophrenic disorder whether the patient is receiving regular medication or not. There is, thus, a clear distinction between a patient who is hospitalized and lives, at least temporarily, and a therapeutic environment and one who remains at home during treatment. The risk of negative influence is naturally higher in the latter case if the home environment is dysfunctional; it is thus important that an early meeting be arranged.

There exist differing opinions as to whether the therapist should meet the patient's relatives alone or with the patient; important reasons have been given for and against both practices. In principle, patients are entitled to hear, first hand, all information about them; also problems may arise for the therapist who has information obtained from sources other than the patients themselves. On the other hand, it is also important, in certain circumstances, to collect as extensive information as possible on the patient, and this possibility would be limited if close relatives were compelled to express their opinions in patients' presence.

The answer to this question is entirely dependent on the sensibility of the therapist and on the type of relationship that has unfolded with the patient. Also important is what the patient is told about the aim of the meeting with the relatives. My own solution is to include both a separate meeting alone with relatives and one with both the patient and relatives present. I inform the patient that I wish to first meet the relative(s) alone in order to obtain an understanding of their opinions concerning the problem and to form a direct assessment of the relatives' reaction to the patient's illness.

I believe that the advantages of this procedure outweigh its disadvantages. One advantage is that one can gather, at leisure, anamnestic information on the family as a whole, on the circumstances surrounding the patient's conception and birth, and on his or her development. In addition, one is able to gain a first impression of the relatives' attitude toward the patient and the disorder and of other problems that may exist in the family. A clear disadvantage is that a suspicious patient may assume that some agreement has been reached between the relatives and the therapist from which he or she is excluded. I attempt to repair such possible damage during the joint session; first I recapitulate what the relative(s) told me and ask the patient whether he or she has anything to add or correct. Depending on the actual condition of the patient, I can then pose additional questions to all parties to obtain an insight into how direct the communication among them really is.

During early contacts with the patient's relatives, the therapist can assess their expectations and correct any unrealistic ones that are expressed. The therapist can also assess, as far as possible, what the relatives' reactions will be should the patient occasionally relapse and how their response to the overall goal for treatment set by the patient. Since I work almost exclusively with individual patients, I refer the relatives who need and wish support to some suitable psychoeducational group.

Whether one achieves this goal of making some psychoeducational intervention or not, repeated meetings with the patient's most important relative must be planned during treatment. The purpose of these meetings is primarily to assess how the relative reacts to changes in the patient so that measures can be taken if the reactions appear dysfunctional. Also, these meetings serve to prepare the family if the patient plans to move from the parental home at the end of treatment or to follow a course of action previously disapproved of by the family (e.g., changing jobs or commencing studies). I always prefer the patient to be present at these meetings, even when a risk of confrontation exists. (Incidentally, the use of a direct confrontation technique is not new in psychotherapy with schizophrenic patients.)

In those instances when the arrangement of several meetings with the patient and his or her most significant relative is warranted (for example, in the case of a married patient living with his or her spouse), the principles of cognitive therapy with couples and families (N. Epstein, 1983; Waring, 1981) should be applied to avoid therapeutic inconsistency.

## THE GENERAL STRUCTURE OF THERAPY SESSIONS

Differences occur in therapy sessions depending on whether the treatment involves an outpatient or a hospitalized patient. Ideally, inpatients live in a therapeutic milieu that represents a secure base. In this environment, access to an assistant therapist is easy, and the development of a therapeutic relationship is greatly facilitated. It follows that therapy sessions proper can be less frequent than for an outpatient who may reside in a completely dysfunctional environment.

In deciding about the frequency of the therapy sessions, one receives very little help from the literature. It seems, in fact, that all possible variations occur, and the results are more in keeping with the personal style of the therapist than based on a solid rationale. My own approach to this issue is to let the patient decide how often he or she would like to meet me, at least in the beginning phase of the treatment. Having at least two weekly sessions seems ideal, especially during the period when relationship is building. Since many schizophrenic patients are unemployed when they begin treatment, even daily sessions (if necessary) do not produce severe disruptions in their daily routines.

When patients work, however, I judge it to be more destructive to require them to leave work than to meet them less often.

The frequency of the sessions can change if the condition of the patient changes. In particular, frequency can be reduced when treatment approaches termination and the therapy proceeds more or less routinely.

A detailed agreement on the frequency, length, and times of sessions should be established at the start and should cover, to the degree possible, the entire treatment period. If a long-term plan is not possible, some agreement should be reached for the initial period.

It is important that the patient be informed that the planned psychotherapy may last for years and that he or she may experience euphoric periods along with periods of hard work during this time.

Much has been written about the importance of adhering to a strict schedule, a definite location, etc., but I suspect that this excessive emphasis on rigid planning occasionally conceals a protective attitude; unforeseen changes in our plans are a part of everyday life, and the frustration that such changes entail need not be antitherapeutic. Naturally, I am not suggesting that a schedule should be changed haphazardly and without warning, but I know that my patients have been able to accept changes when I have provided them with satisfactory reasons. It is hardly likely that any therapist is able to plan for several years in advance without unforeseen events disturbing his or her routine.

If a date for termination is discussed, an agreement on eventual booster sessions should be reached. It is highly appropriate that the first of these be held within a few months of termination.

In principle, the structure of the therapy sessions does not differ from that commonly adopted with other kinds of patients. Therapy's main principles have been repeatedly described in the literature (e.g., Beck *et al.*, 1979, C. Perris, 1986b, 1988e) and need not be repeated in detail here. Briefly, each session should begin with the patient discussing delayed reactions since the previous meeting along with his or her homework. Subsequently, an agenda for the session is mutually agreed on, and when the meeting approaches its close, time is spent on a brief summation and the assignment of new homework (if this has not already occurred at some appropriate occasion during the session). In practice, it is often necessary to allow for some alterations in this structure. Clearly, the condition of the patient (and the sensitivity of the therapist) will dictate the degree of flexibility to be applied. Both shorter and longer (up to two hours) sessions may be required. The former become necessary when the patient is unable to concentrate on the therapy. There is no need for the therapist to undergo long training to become able to detect when the patient is unable to sustain attention any longer. On the other hand, longer sessions should always be considered when the discussion is on an important subject and should not be interrupted.

Flexibility is a necessary prerequisite for the therapist who wants to work with patients with schizophrenic disorders. This is one of the reasons why it is not advisable to accept more than a few patients of this type for treatment at one time.

# 9

# Conducting the Therapy

The different cognitive therapeutic techniques used with schizo-phrenic patients are similar to those employed with patients suffering from other disorders. It is even more important for work with schizo-phrenic persons, however, that the techniques to be adopted are ex-plained simply and clearly and that the patient understands their purpose. In the following sections, the most commonly used ap-proaches are described in detail with special reference to their applica-tion to schizophrenic patients. Even though many of them are inter-correlated, they are discussed separately. In addition, although a logical order is followed in the presentation, this does not mean that the same order must be used in practice; in reality, the therapeutic approach should be attuned to the condition of the patient rather than the patient being stuck in an inflexible therapeutic schedule.

## CHARACTERISTICS OF THE COGNITIVE PSYCHOTHERAPEUTIC DIALOGUE

### Use of the Socratic Method

In the cognitive psychotherapy literature, a great emphasis is put on the use of questions to promote patients' collaboration, enhance the observing selves, and help them to widen their perspective. This ap-proach is commonly referred to as the "Socratic method" (Beck & Emery, 1985; Golden & Dryden, 1986; Guidano & Liotti, 1983; Ja-remko, 1986). Other than short fragments of therapeutic interviews to illustrate this principle, however, no more general guidelines have been reported in the literature so far. Therefore, the following deals in some detail with the Socratic method of teaching. The use of the word "teaching" is not accidental, since use of all kinds of therapy is a learning process (C. Perris, 1988d).

The origins of the Socratic method of teaching are in the Meno dialogue of Plato. In this dialogue, Socrates elicits the solution of a complex geometrical problem from the unskilled young slave Meno through skilled questioning. Socrates used his approach to suggest that knowledge existed in the young slave even without instruction. In other dialogues, for instance, those with Thaetetus and Parmenides, Socrates defined his method as "maieutic" to emphasize that his approach to bringing an idea to birth could be compared with the work of a midwife assisting a delivery. Dillon (1980a) pointed out that Socrates held it essential for inquiry that the participants share a regard for each other in order to join in a mutual search for a satisfying truth.

The Socratic "elenchus" (strategy) aims at moving the respondent from (a) "I know" to (b) "I don't know" to (c) "I desire to know" and (d) "I wish to inquire." It is important to notice, however, that questioning in itself does not stimulate curiosity and inquiry. According to Dillon, the questioned person must be bothered by not knowing, knowing must be personally important, and knowing must also serve to solve some problem presently being experienced as troublesome. There is no doubt that the Socratic requirement for inquiry and the "I have to know" that Dillon (1980a, p. 18) adds to elenchus both fully apply to the therapeutic situation.

The Socratic method is frequently used in formal teaching (e.g., Collins, 1977; Dillon, 1980a, 1980b, 1982; Stevens & Collins, 1977) on the assumption that, through its use, the student learns specific information about a variety of cases, the causal dependencies that underlie these cases, and a variety of reasoning skills (Collins, 1977). The reasoning skills that are particularly relevant for cognitive psychotherapy include the ability to form and test hypotheses, making uncertain predictions, and determining their reliability. Stevens and Collins (1977), in discussing the advantages of the Socratic method of teaching, emphasized that the kind of knowledge thus acquired by students cannot be earned passively. With this method, students must actively try to deal with problems, and they must make mistakes that reveal their misunderstandings. Obviously, this approach is highly pertinent in a psychotherapeutic context.

To achieve these educational goals, however, questioning according to the Socratic method cannot occur haphazardly. For tutoring purposes, Collins and coworkers (Collins, 1977; Stevens & Collins, 1977) developed a computational theory of the Socratic method comprised of 24 production rules based on the strategies used in tutorial dialogues they analyzed. The main goals included a refinement of students' causal model and refinement of their predictive ability. Subgoals included the diagnosis of "bugs" in the students' knowledge and their correction. Whereas for a detailed description of all 24 rules the reader is referred to Collins's original article (1977), a few examples are provided in Table 9-1.

The set of procedural rules proposed by Collins are intended for Socratic tutoring in formal teaching, but the guiding principles be-

TABLE 9-1.   Collins's Production Rules

---

Case selection
   Ask for a known case
   Ask for any factors
   Ask for prior factors

Prediction
   Ask for a prediction about a particular case
   Ask what are the relevant factors to consider

Information rules
   Question a prediction made without enough information
   Point out an inconsistent prediction

Probe reasoning strategy and hypothesis testing
   Probe for a necessary factor
   Probe for differences between two cases
   Request a test of the hypothesis about a factor
   Ask for consideration of relevant factors

---

Adapted from Collins's computational model of Socratic tutoring (1977).

hind their development are easily generalizable to the therapeutic situation. On the other hand, it is seldom necessary to make use of all 24 rules, and Collins himself was aware that they might be in need of further refinement. Of major relevance in connection with psychotherapy are those rules that refer to the assessment of the patient's ability to make predictions, those that refer to information collection and those that probe for reasoning strategy and hypotheses testing.

Correctly applied, the Socratic method is one of the most powerful tools in cognitive psychotherapy; a note of warning is, however, in place. The use of the Socratic method requires time. There is also a risk that it can become stereotyped, thus impairing communication. In practice, one should develop the skill to be able to shift between a Socratic approach and other styles of interviewing in order to keep the dialogue as alive as possible. The use of the Socratic method, however, is an effective approach to elucidate the patient's most common cognitive distortions and to guide him or her toward their correction; furthermore, it is the most useful method with which to teach problem-solving.

## Hypotheses versus Interpretations

One clearly distinguishing feature of cognitive psychotherapy is the use of hypotheses instead of interpretations to promote the patient's progress in acquiring self-knowledge (C. Perris, 1988d). Opinions about the use of interpretations with schizophrenic patients are contradictory among analytically trained therapists to the point that some of them (e.g., Lichtenberg, 1963; Zimmerman, 1982) have characterized interpretation as "poisoning" (see also Federn, 1943, and Spotnitz, 1986, for a negative opinion and Gunderson, 1979, for a critique of the controversy).

The technique of cognitive psychotherapy is different from the psychoanalytical technique in this respect, mainly because of the particular characteristic of the therapeutic alliance, which is fundamentally based on a working partnership or collaborative empiricism.

The use of hypotheses in the course of treatment is explained to the patient at the time of socialization, when the main principles of the therapeutic conduct are clarified. Later, the use of the Socratic method (or other approaches to dialogue) allows the derivation of hypotheses that can be subject to verification. The verification of the validity of such hypotheses can be reached through further deductive questioning or, whenever feasible, by some kind of homework assignment to be done by the patient in between sessions.

In a sense, one could maintain that an interpretation is also a hypothesis formulated by the therapist and submitted to the patient for confirmation. Obviously, such an opinion would be quite correct. The analyst Peterfreund (1983) has poignantly commented, however, on the all too frequent use of theory-bound interpretations in the analytic process. He suggested as an alternative that a set of strategies be used in the therapeutic process so that the therapist can formulate in his mind hypotheses about what is going on in the patient. Peterfreund emphasized that the analyst should give an interpretation only when he or she has verified the validity of any such hypothesis.

However, cognitive therapists maintain that a major difference exists, in both nature and purpose, between giving interpretations and deriving hypotheses. In fact, the primary purposes of a hypothesis are to act as a tool and to suggest a test: It looks forward and raises questions that demand answering. An interpretation instead looks backward: It represents a tentative explanation applied to something that the therapist assumes to have already observed or discovered. Indeed, an interpretation often does not involve testable consequences.

There are also other issues in the distinction between using hypotheses and giving interpretations. First, there is the much-debated risk of acquiescence from the patient when confronted with an interpretation received from an expert (Grünbaum, 1984). Also, and of crucial importance to the schizophrenic patient, there is a high risk that an untimely or wrong interpretation may become reminiscent of a dysfunctional pattern of communication experienced with a significant figure in the past. Thus, when receiving an interpretation, patients could feel that others are yet again more able than themselves to understand what their real feelings or thoughts are. Of course, this strikes a blow against their already low self-esteems. In contrast, hypotheses derived in a joint effort with the therapist, which can eventually be rebutted, are experienced as less threatening and less anxiety provoking and are thus less likely to provoke resistance. In addition, since the verification is carried out by the patient, the patient's self-confidence is enhanced as it also becomes easier for him or her to assimilate the results.

## Analogies, Metaphors, and Other Stylistic Devices

It is a long-accepted notion that the psychotherapist influences the patients (J. Frank, 1959). Nevertheless, the issue of how such influence can best be conceptualized is still unsettled. Though psychotherapists are well aware of the possibility of directly imposing their own ideas on the patient, and behave in such a way as to diminish this possibility, it cannot be neglected that persuasion still is an important compo nent of the psychotherapeutic healing process (J. Frank, 1973). Didactic persuasion is one major approach in Ellis's rational emotive therapy, and various techniques have been conceptualized to pursue it (Harrell, Beiman, & LaPointe, 1981; McMullin, 1986). Thus, side by side with Socrates, it is necessary to acknowledge a link with Aristotle's rhetoric. For instance, Glaser (1980) has attempted to conceptualize the rhetorical potency of a therapist (that is, the capacity to influence), and she suggested that four devices contribute to determining such potency: (a) the extent of "ethos" appeal (i.e., the charismatic nature of the therapist); (b) the extent of logical appeal; (c) the extent of tension release mechanisms; and (d) the extent of stylistic devices. Stylistic devices are discussed below; see the work of Frank (1973) and Glazer (1980) for a more thorough study of the other devices.

Stylistic devices include balances, antitheses, metaphors, and sensory images. They are used to intensify the content of therapeutic discourse. Of particular relevance of the present context is the use of metaphors—and their close relatives, similes and analogies. As pointed out by Ortony (1975), these have been used in teaching since the earliest writings of civilized humans. Similes, analogies, and metaphors are also frequently used in cognitive psychotherapy. One of the most well-known analogies is that of conceptualizing the therapeutic alliance as the partnership between two researchers or scientists. Other examples of the use of such stylistic devices are the reference to the mountain climber and his guide mentioned earlier, or picturing the unfolding of the therapeutic process as a long road to be traveled together by the patient and the therapist, who must both always be alert to the road blocks and to other hidden obstacles they will meet on their path.

A review of the psychological literature concerned with metaphor was published by Billow (1977), who emphasized that metaphor supplies a language with flexibility and expressibility, that is, it helps language expand. Since metaphors use words in multiple meanings, it follows that to be able to comprehend metaphors, one must be familiar with the word in its widest context or, to use Aristotle's words, have "an intuitive perception of the similarity in dissimilar" (Aristotle, 1958). In addition, metaphors may induce attitude shifts by functioning as a set that emphasizes some facts and suppresses others. Levy (1963) suggested that therapist's metaphors bring into therapy an alternative frame of reference that may permit a patient to redefine a situation in a way that makes it possible to change his or her behavior. A further analysis of the function of metaphors in facilitating constructive behavior change in psychotherapy has been made by Lenrow (1966). Lenrow said that metaphors give language an intimate or personal quality, permit the therapist to communicate about sensitive characteristics of the patients without appearing intrusive, and highlight subtle social roles that a client takes.

The language and thoughts of schizophrenic patients are often metaphorical (Arieti, 1955; Searles, 1962) and may reveal past forgotten experiences that would otherwise be difficult to verbalize. On the other hand, there is also a risk (at least in certain phases of the course of illness) that the patient, being unable to think in figurative terms or in abstractions, may interpret a therapist's metaphor in the literal sense. Thus, therapists should always be alert not only to catch the meaning of the patient's metaphors, but also to ascertain that the patient has really understood the meaning of the therapist's metaphors.

## Humor, Self-Disclosure, and Other Verbal Approaches

The therapeutic use of humor has been beautifully illustrated by Shakespeare in his play *King Lear*, in which the "fool" attempts (albeit unsuccessfully) to help his king who is rapidly moving toward mental deterioration. However, humor's use in modern therapeutic context is still a matter of discussion ever since Freud (1905b; 1927) emphasized the abreaction of mainly aggressive impulses concealed in a joke. Kubie (1971) emphasized the destructive potential of humor in psychotherapy and issued a warning against its use. Other authors, on the other hand, have taken a different stance in this connection, maintaining that the appropriate use of humor can have a powerful therapeutic impact (e.g., Grotjahn, 1971; Kaplan & Boyd, 1965; Rose, 1969; Rosenheim, 1974). Rosenheim (1974) emphasized that humor in therapy is characterized by a measure of warmth, which demonstrates to the patient that the therapist can tolerate naturalness. The aim of a therapist's humorous remarks is to challenge the sturdiness of the patient's reality testing at two different levels: "first, in regard to his self-concept (or 'observing ego'); secondly, in regard to his perception of others" (Rosenheim, 1974, p. 586). A related opinion was maintained by Rose, who stressed that the use of humor has a double aspect: "a genial, kindly side is allied with the observant ego, and a critical, mildly ironic side is directed toward resistances" (Rose, 1969, p. 932).

Undoubtedly, humor has to be used carefully and must never represent a subtle way for the therapist to manifest hostility. Both Kaplan and Boyd (1965) and Rosenheim (1974) have stressed that the unique value and potency of humor in the therapeutic situation derive from its intrinsic attributes of directness and humaneness; also, it creates a feeling of intimacy and provides a means of social approval.

Being foreign-born, my spoken language still contains elements that easily reveal my origin and that are easily observed by natives. It is not infrequent that some patient, when our relationship has grown to one of sincere mutual understanding, makes some joke imitating my pronunciation. I firmly believe that it would be destructive not to laugh at such an imitation, which I do not interpret as an expression of hostility but rather as an attempt by the patient to test the trust and openness that prevail in the relationship. In such instances, I willingly join in the joke, accentuating my bad pronunciation to demonstrate that I share the patient's intention.

On one occasion, a very intelligent patient of mine phoned one evening for a short chat, and I realized from her tone of voice that she felt well. In the course of the conversation, she mentioned that a few days before she had had the feeling of possessing telepathic power. I answered, "Then you could have saved the cost of the telephone call and got in touch with me telepathically." She laughed wholeheartedly and assured me that she had been able to counteract on her own those "foolish feelings."

Cognitive psychotherapists do not condemn the use of self-disclosure in the contact with their patients. With schizophrenic patients, self-disclosures are used by psychoanalysts to establish a relationship based on humaneness and relatedness. Schwartz (1975) reported a conversation with other analysts in which Otto Will participated. Will told his colleagues that he was always willing to speak with his patients about himself and his family and to recount bits of his daily life. Beside the fact that self-disclosures represent a powerful, indirect type of modeling, it would be impossible to keep the relationship close with a schizophrenic patient if the therapist were to maintain an aloof, impersonal attitude.

Other interventions that can be profitably made in the course of the therapeutic dialogue include the use of therapeutic tales. These can be well known or specially invented in order to convey a therapeutic message that is particularly attuned to the patient's problems. H. Perris (personal communication, 1986) has obtained challenging results in patients with severe personality disorders by using this approach.

# THERAPEUTIC STRATEGIES AND TECHNIQUES

## Breaking Passivity and Structuring the Day

An initial therapeutic intervention most often involves a breaking of patients' passivity and lack of initiative by helping them to plan their day—that is, helping them to build structure in their lives. The intervention may require a patient to get up earlier in the morning, to refrain from withdrawing excessively during the day, or to work hard at some form of preplanned activity.

To achieve all of this, it is necessary for the therapist to be aware of how patients spend their days and whether they have shown any particular interests earlier. Information about these matters is usually collected by direct questions. However, many patients show a tendency to give diffuse answers, especially as concerns their daily schedules. They may, for example, tell the therapist that they go shopping or to meet people, but it may remain unclear how often patients do these things. Whenever uncertainties arise, the patient should be asked to complete a schedule of daily activities to bring to the next session.

When it is clear that a patient has, for example, difficulty getting up in the morning, or in going out, the next step is to try to identify what kinds of interfering thoughts are responsible for this behavior. Suitable questions for this purpose include the following:

- When you are about to get up in the morning, what thoughts stop you from doing so at once?
- What do you think may happen if you go out?

If patients are unable to answer these simple questions, ask them to imagine that they are lying in their bed and that it is time to get up. This visualization can help, through simple cognitive rehearsal, to capture and relate the dysfunctional thoughts (or images) that hinder their actions. The same technique can, of course, be used to extract information on the obstacles they see before them when they are about to go out or to meet people.

If feasible, a patient may agree to have sessions at morning hours to motivate him or her to get up earlier and go out. When this new behavior has stabilized, the sessions can be scheduled at another time.

In order to determine, in a systematic fashion, how patients spend their days, it is appropriate, as mentioned above, to ask them to make notes of all their activities from the time they wake until the time they sleep. On the same form, patients should also note the activities they prefer and that they carry out with a feeling of satisfaction. Subsequently, therapist and patients together can attempt to reach an agreement about what can be added or changed in the daily schedule. If patients adopt a low level of activity, only very simple tasks should initially be added. When patients comply with any agreed-on addition to the schedule, it is important to refrain from praising them too much for their efforts; their own satisfaction should be their major reward.

## Distancing

Many patients beginning psychotherapy do not question their convictions and conclusions and equate their inferences, that is, the interpretations they make of different situations, with reality. This occurs frequently with schizophrenic patients whether or not they suffer from delusional and hallucinatory experiences. Among this group of cognitive disorders I include the fact that patients often identify themselves with their basic disorders and symptoms as if they were an integral part of themselves. Very often, patients feel that they cannot get rid of the symptoms without losing their identities. This fear is especially common with certain hallucinatory experiences that have lasted for a long time.

In most of the respects just mentioned, the patients' thought processes can be defined, in Piaget's terminology (Piaget, 1932), as nondimensional, absolutistic, and moralizing—for example, when a patient says "I am lazy" to excuse himself or herself for having been idle during the day. Beck *et al.* (1979) and myself in an earlier book on cognitive therapy (C. Perris, 1986b) have drawn attention to the fact that absolutistic expressions of the type "I am lazy," "I am a coward," and the like reveal a logical fault and an unwarranted globality since they can never refer to all situations that one meets in daily life. Belonging to the same category is the error patients make when they say, "I am a schizophrenic." That patients are capable of such a statement constitutes a paradox, since they are not behaving schizophrenically when they make it.

"Distancing" implies the therapeutic process aimed at helping patients to question dysfunctional nondimensionality or absolutistic and moralizing thinking, as in, for example, pointing out the incongruence in the affirmation of being exclusively schizophrenic. At the same time, the therapist must help patients to become conscious of their potentialities and to dissociate themselves from their disorder. In the same way, patients can be easily led to realize that they are not lazy 24 hours a day; instead, they have a behavior, or a problem, on certain occasions that they can get rid of or learn to solve.

That distancing often leads to a successful result does not mean, naturally, that patients automatically gain insight into their disorder. What is important is that the patients' way of thinking starts to move toward becoming multidimensional and more relativistic and flexible, at the same time as their attention is diverted from the assumption that the disorder and symptoms are an inseparable part of themselves. Ideally, patients move toward a position in which they regard them as problems that can be solved.

Questioning the patients' dysfunctional convictions and the subsequent reattribution should not be conducted at a purely abstract level. Patients must be guided in such a way that they find confirmation that a change of thinking is both warranted and correct. For example, if one wishes to help patients dissociate themselves from the idea that they are lazy, it will hardly help to only try to persuade them on a theoretical level. Instead, they should be given the opportunity to identify the occasions when they behave lazily and to demonstrate that they can achieve something if motivated. Sometimes, patients can, when made aware of their cognitive fault, provide examples of situations in which they have not been lazy; in other cases, it may be necessary to provide homework as a means of obtaining this confirmation. In the same way, it is not difficult to help patients to realize that they are not thoroughly crazy. The strategies of logical analysis, evaluation, and reduction to absurdity (e.g., "Do you mean that you are crazy even when asleep?") may be helpful in this context.

Irrespective of the strategy adopted, the therapist must always be prepared to provide feedback to patients so that the escalating insight is secured.

## Dealing with Automatic Dysfunctional Thoughts

In his studies of depressed patients, Beck (1963–1964) discovered that an important component in their cognitive disturbances was negative thoughts, which may arise suddenly in different situations and generate a feeling of sorrow, hopelessness, and resignation. These thoughts are automatic in the sense that they are not preceded by any deliberation, and they are involuntary and persistent in the sense that they recur in a stereotyped manner in a number of different situations. To a large extent, these thoughts occur out of focal awareness, and, thus, are unconscious. The occurrence of automatic dysfunctional thoughts is not, however, limited to depressed patients. On the contrary, automatic negative thoughts may occur in every one of us when we experience a particularly trying situation. The only difference is that, with patients, these thoughts occur more frequently and more intensely even in situations that most persons would regard as quite ordinary. In addition, it is more difficult for persons with mental disorders to apply corrective and more functional deliberations. Automatic negative thoughts also produce a more deleterious effect in patients with mental disturbances than in psychically healthy persons; in the former, the thoughts are, as a rule, similar to more deeply rooted negative self-images. In other words, these negative thoughts are congruent with the patients' more basic preconceptions of themselves.

The higher frequency and greater intensity of negative thoughts in patients with mental disorders are probably related to the fact that they commit more cognitive errors than mentally healthy persons in comprehending and processing information. What these cognitive errors are and how they may be corrected is described in detail later (see "Recognition of Cognitive Distortions," below). The present discussion focuses on that part of the therapeutic process that deals with helping the patient to recognize his or her own automatic dysfunctional thoughts and to record the situations where these occur.

Many schizophrenic patients are already conscious of some of the dysfunctional thoughts they have in various situations. Patients who are reluctant to go out among others, for instance, may relate that whenever they want to do so, they abstain because they "feel" that everyone regards them as abnormal. Or patients who do not talk in the company of others may say that they "feel" stupid. Other patients say they have no thoughts at all, even in trying situations; they only "feel" that the situation is trying.

The first instance implies the patients' inability to distinguish between thoughts and feelings and is often easy to correct since it only reflects the influence of everyday language. Sometimes, however, a period of training is required before patients become aware that what they express in terms of an opinion or a feeling is nothing more than a negative thought.

More difficult to tackle is the second instance, because patients' difficulty in verbalizing any thoughts might be mistakenly regarded as an expression of poor motivation or lack of cooperation. Jacobs (1980), in an article on the cognitive approach to persistent delusions, pointed out that some schizophrenic patients lack what he defined as "meta-thinking," that is, the ability of "thinking about one's own thinking" or "thinking about how one thinks." Although Jacobs discussed meta-thinking in the more complex context of delusional experiences, his observation is particularly relevant for the situation considered here. If a deficit in metathinking is suspected, the therapist must try to assess whether patients are unable to answer questions aimed at mapping what they think about other people. Should a lack of metathinking be verified, it becomes necessary to train patients to become aware of their deficit and to help them to correct it.

Different techniques have been developed in cognitive therapy to identify the occurrence of negative thoughts and to make patients aware of the detrimental influence such thoughts have on their feelings and behavior. During a therapy session, for example, sudden changes in a patient's nonverbal behavior may suggest the occurrence of some automatic thought and thus provoke the therapist's direct questioning. Or a patient may be asked to close his or her eyes and imagine in detail a situation usually experienced as trying and then to focus on the thoughts that arise. This last-mentioned technique is one of the many in which one exploits, as in behavior therapy, the use of "imageries." The difference between the two therapies is that in cognitive therapy the method is used to induce the patient to focus on the negative thoughts in order that these may become available for treatment.

With patients who, despite all efforts, still have difficulties in focusing on their negative thoughts, the use of the Automatic Thoughts Questionnaire (ATQ) developed by Hollon and Kendall (1980) might be warranted, even if the test was originally constructed for the assessment of negative thoughts in depressed patients. The content of most negative thoughts is (to a certain extent) similar in patients suffering from different mental disorders, and the questionnaire acts as cue to help the patient to recognize dysfunctional cognitions and to better understand what the therapist is asking.

When patients have learned to recognize their negative thoughts, the therapist can reach an agreement with them that, prior to the next session, they should try to identify and record those situations they have found to be difficult and what thoughts they have had in connection with these situations. A simpler alternative is to request patients to keep a record of the number of times they have negative thoughts. Of course, the therapist cannot expect an exact list of all occurrences of negative thinking. The task serves, however, to make patients aware that such thoughts exist and that they are adversely affected by them.

## Fighting Procrastination and Task-Interfering Thoughts

The tendency to postpone necessary tasks is often prevalent in patients with schizophrenic disorders. This may stem from a lack of initiative, the expectation of failure, or the fact that the task itself generates anxiety because patients feel uncertain of how to carry it out. The difficulties become greater as time elapses, and the patients brood over what they feel compelled to do. In these circumstances, it is not difficult for the therapist to discover that the patients' dysfunctional thoughts and expectations contribute greatly to the procrastination.

Various methods are available that may be used to deal with this type of problem. It is most usual to begin with simple questions of the kind, "What have you got to lose if you make an attempt?" or "What would be the worst consequence of failure?" Even such elementary questions can, in many cases, induce patients to reveal the reason for their anxiety, so that the therapist is given the opportunity to correct the dysfunctional assumption and, eventually, to "decatastrophize."

In a similar manner, the therapist and patients may together attempt to elucidate the kind of thoughts and deliberations that hinder action. Again, it may be a question of negative expectations, fear of the reactions of others, or other negative consequences, which are maintained and strengthened both by automatic dysfunctional thoughts and by mistaken assumptions about others' reactions. When these become evident, the therapist is able to direct patients to question their factual validity.

When dealing with attempts to counteract procrastination, the therapist should always make sure that the patients' behavior is not dependent on an actual lack of skills. If such is the case, and if a specific task is under scrutiny, then the use of role play or modeling might be indicated.

With patients suffering from a serious lack of initiative, and who postpone even very simple tasks, the therapist may use cognitive rehearsal, allowing the patients to imagine the task and to relate the difficulties that they anticipate at every stage of it. Patients are then given the chance, through appropriate questioning, to suggest how they would overcome these problems in a satisfactory manner.

With more active patients who know something of cognitive techniques, a method that requires them to make a list of the pros and cons of carrying out a certain task can be used. If this approach is adopted, it is usually good practice to train during a session with an actual or fictitious example so that the therapist is certain that patients can use it. The value of this method rests on the fact that the patients themselves are required to judge, and to express, the eventual positive consequences of the actions.

One major reason for the suitability of some of these techniques in the early stages of therapy is that they are relatively simple and concern relatively superficial problems. Patients thus receive an opportunity to feel that they actively participate in the therapy, and small changes occur that they experience as positive. It is, however, important for the therapist to recognize the types of tasks patients postpone as well as those for which the degree of difficulty and their capabilities coincide. In other words, therapy at this stage is mainly supportive, as it contributes to the further socialization of the patient by using the technique of cognitive psychotherapy.

Finally, it should be yet again emphasized that the use of different techniques should never be a goal in itself and should not be regarded as an alternative to continuous observation of, and response to, the different signals and needs communicated by the patient.

## Recognition of Cognitive Distortions

Most of the cognitive distortions that Beck (1976) described in the perception and processing of information in patients suffering from emotional disorders may be found in schizophrenic patients, as pointed out by Greenwood (1983). That this is the case is not surprising since the occurrence of these cognitive faults has already been established in patients suffering from many other mental disturbances. Beck (1963–1964) himself suggested this hypothesis in his original description of cognitive distortions in depressed patients. Furthermore, cognitive distortions of the type described by Beck could be assumed to be distributed over a wide spectrum in the general population.

If these errors are so common, what is it that makes them so relevant to the present context? A reasonable first assumption is that different types of cognitive distortions occur simultaneously in psychically vulnerable persons and with higher frequency than in psychically stable ones. This hypothesis is supported partly by the fact that different cognitive errors of the type considered here have consistently been observed in patients suffering from different kinds of mental disorders. To understand their relevance, it becomes necessary to consider the mechanisms we employ to confirm our identities. Our self-concept or "identity" or "self" consists of all the basic meaning structures, basic assumptions, and schemata that we, little by little, have assimilated, as Sullivan (1953) emphasized, in our interactions with other people of significance in our environments. Markus (1977) defined the "self-schema" as the specific combination of knowledge and preconceptions we have of ourselves, which originate in our earlier experiences. Lecky (1945) stressed that self-concept includes organized values that are mutually consistent. That the self-schema is influenced by experience implies that it is not static but dynamic. S. Epstein (1973) wrote that the self-concept tends to assimilate more and more information while at the same time he emphasized that it is essential to the well-functioning of the individual that the internal consistency of the self-concept be retained. Liotti, Onofri, Spadafora, and Tombolini (1984) discussed at some depth the issue of "personal identity" and continuity versus discontinuity, and they suggested that self-schemata should be treated as the building blocks in a continuous constructive process. I strongly agree.

Although most authors agree that the self-concept to a certain extent is changeable and shows a tendency to grow and develop by means of the mechanisms of assimilation and accommodation, it is also assumed that a kind of hierarchy exists in our meaning structures and that the more fundamental of these are relatively stable and difficult to influence. In this connection, Kelly (1955) wrote of impermeable core constructs, while Greenwald (1980), in his thought-provoking article on the fabrication and revision of personal history, referred to "cognitive conservatism."

Several of the mechanisms that support the idea of conservatism are "confirmation" and "transcription of memory," two processes that are akin to the cognitive biases in scientific theory (Lakatos, 1970). Confirmation is that cognitive bias that is associated with our tendency to select that information that validates or confirms our preconceived ideas at the cost of other information. Extensive research work by Crary (1966), Swann and Hill (1982), and Swann and Read (1981) lends support to this assumption. Such a cognitive bias manifests itself not only in the perception and processing of new information but also in the retrospective judgments of our memories, which thus become continuously revalued on the basis of our fundamental meaning structures. It was probably the latter mechanism that Arieti (1968) referred to when he asserted that patients' reports of their early relationships with their mothers are mostly a product of their imaginations.

Greenwald (1980) aptly pointed out that cognitive conservatism functions to preserve organization and to assure intrapsychic survival. He stressed, however, that this conservatism is, in the long run, disadvantageous since it "will produce cognitive stagnation in a person who is capable of greater developmental achievement" (p. 614).

A graphic illustration of the self-confirmatory mechanism, with special reference to the most common cognitive distortions considered in the cognitive psychotherapy literature, is provided in Figure 9-1. A similar diagram can be used with advantage when one wishes to illustrate these particular aspects of a patient's problems to him or her.

Since a short description of the cognitive distortions most frequently considered in cognitive psychotherapy has been already given in Chapter 3 of this book, I will not repeat it here. It should pose no problem to the trained therapist to recognize these and other common

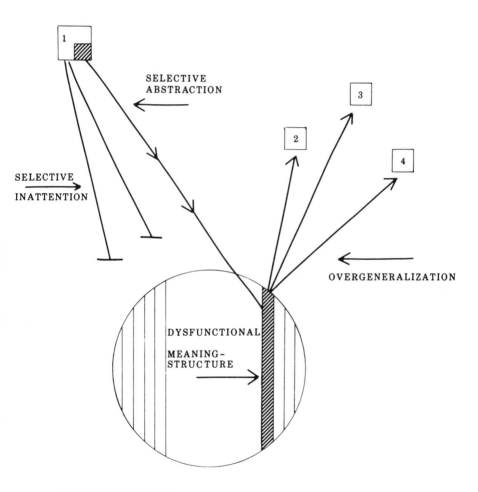

1,2,3,4 = SITUATIONS

FIGURE 9-1. Various cognitive distortions promote dysfunctional schemata, which contribute, in turn, to the continous validation of the distortions.

cognitive distortions during conversations with the schizophrenic patient, but some of the techniques mentioned earlier can also be employed. A common three- or four-column technique (i.e., pinpointing a trying situation and recording the feelings and thoughts related to it) is as feasible with schizophrenics as with all other kinds of patients. What is important is that patients become aware of their errors and learn to identify them by name. This is relevant for various reasons: in the first instance, it allows patients to identify and question their cognitions outside of the sessions; secondly, the dialogue between the therapist and the patient becomes easier if both agree about the meaning of certain concepts and thus speak the same language.

While some cognitive distortions can perhaps be corrected through use of the Socratic method, others may require that simple experiments be carried out to help the patient to understand the distortions' invalidity in various concrete situations. The nature of the situations and experiments chosen depends entirely on the condition of the patient, the level reached by the therapy, the situations in which the cognitive distortions most commonly arise, and the patient's preparedness to participate. The therapist must rely on his or her own sensitivity. A few basic precepts can, however, be given. In the first place, one must be capable of recognizing the boundaries between an arbitrary inference and a paranoid experience. Even though the latter can be treated in a similar manner, it is not advisable to begin a cognitive restructuration from a psychotic symptom. Second, and related to the first point, one should always attempt to begin with a distortion that is of less importance emotionally to the patient and gradually approach those that are more central, at a later time. This approach allows the patient to learn to master the technique in relatively less important situations, and, thus, it will be easier for him or her to apply the same technique later on distortions of a paranoid dimension. Finally, no experiments outside the therapy sessions should be planned before the patient has become familiar with his or her errors in thinking and has begun to question them under the guidance of the therapist.

In addition to the cognitive distortions mentioned earlier, I have discussed elsewhere (C. Perris, 1986d, 1987a, 1988b, 1988e) a few others that, while not necessarily specific for schizophrenic patients, are encountered more often with this type of patient than with others. Since these have a particular theoretical and practical importance in therapy with schizophrenics, they are discussed below. The order in which they are presented is without special significance.

*Predicative Thinking.* As discussed by Arieti (1948), this belongs to the logical errors in the patient's thinking that were described earlier by Von Domarus (1944). According to Arieti's modification, the principle stated by Von Domarus entails that, while the normal person accepts identity on the basis of identical subjects (i.e., follows the formal laws of logic), the schizophrenic patient accepts identity on the basis of identical predicates (i.e., follows an archaic form of logic or "paleologic"). If we state, for example, that "all presidents of the United States must be American-born," and that "Roosevelt was an American President," it follows that Roosevelt was American-born. A schizophrenic patient may, on the other hand, draw the following type of conclusion: "Björn Borg is a tennis player," "I am a tennis player," "I am Björn Borg." In this context, it is important to point out that Arieti (1968, 1974a, 1974c, 1976) emphasized that the "predicate" may refer not only to the inherent properties in the identified object in general, but also to objects that are related to it in time and space. For example, a patient of ours believed that God is present within a church to praise the pure of spirit and to punish the sinners. He further believed, being himself a member of that church, that he was God and thus entitled to praise or punish others. Since most patients coming for psychotherapy are already on medication, this cognitive distortion is not so frequent or so markedly pathological as the above examples might lead one to believe.

*Premature Assignment of Meaning.* It is well known that most schizophrenic patients experience considerable difficulties in being faced with ambiguity. As a consequence of this difficulty, they tend to prematurely assign meanings to external stimuli (for example, an occasional remark or the first part of a sentence) before they have had a chance to understand them completely, so that distortions in the comprehension of information result. It is not unreasonable to assume that this particular cognitive disturbance is one of the factors that contribute to the development of delusional ideas, especially when it is combined with arbitrary inference.

*Egocentric Overinclusion.* The term "overinclusion" was introduced by Cameron (1938) to define the inability of the schizophrenic patient to exclude from a thought sequence material that is irrelevant to the major theme of the thought. Maher (1966) pointed out that overinclusion may be regarded as an instance of schizophrenics' inability to keep their responses to the external world separate from the fantasy processes that are going on at the same time. More generally, overinclusion may be defined as the tendency of the patient to include (or respond to) a much greater number of objects (or stimuli) that really belong to a given set (e.g., Rabin *et al.*, 1979).

Lidz (1974) drew attention to the fact that the schizophrenic over-inclusiveness is predominantly egocentric in a Piagetian sense; he also emphasized the regressive character of egocentrism. In this context, Lidz wrote, schizophrenic patients typically believe that what others do and say is always centered on themselves, as, for example, in connection with ideas of reference or persecution. Or patients may believe that they can affect not only others in their immediate environment but the whole world with their thoughts. The use of the concept of egocentrism is very suitable in this respect since all egocentrism is linked by reliance on the all-pervading power of thought. From this perspective, the psychoanalytical conception of the child's feeling of omnipotence should be easy to understand in cognitive terms. However, I dislike the term "regressive" and prefer to interpret egocentrism in schizophrenic patients as the result of defective "decentering," which persists during the entire lifetime of the patient if it is not treated in therapy. According to this assumption, other cognitive distortions in schizophrenic patients can, as discussed later, be regarded from the perspective of egocentrism (see "Critical Remarks on the Interpretation of Certain Cognitive Distortions" and "Decentering and Egocentrism," below).

*Failure to Distinguish Between Meanings and Causes in Arriving at Certainty.* This type of cognitive disorder has been described by Jacobs (1982) and to a large extent is closely related to the cognitive fault described earlier under the label "personalization" (see Part 1). This is also related to the development of ideas of reference or persecution. In practice, this fault consists of replacing a cause by a personal meaning when attempting to reply to the question "why?" when confronted with an external situation. For example, patients who are turned down when they ask someone to dance may interpret the rejection to be a consequence of their own clumsiness or ugliness instead of considering that the other person was already engaged or had decided to rest for a while.

*Loss of Symbolic Thinking (Desymbolization).* The term "desymbolization" was introduced by Searles (1962) to refer to that process, which has been reported many times in the psychiatric literature to be associated with schizophrenic patients, in which previously assimilated symbolic or metaphorical meanings lose their symbolic value and the patient reacts toward them as though they are concrete (see, for example, Chapman, 1960, and Maher, 1966, for a thorough discussion of the concrete–abstract hypothesis). For example, a patient who overhears someone say "Joe wanted me to believe he finished the dishes but I saw through him" may conclude that this person is really capable of seeing through people. On the other hand, early metaphorical concepts seldom lose their symbolic value. Many studies have been carried out to assess the correct comprehension of proverbs by schizophrenic patients. Although, on occasions, the patients appear to encounter difficulties with this task, the results have generally varied so that no consistent picture has emerged (Rabin *et al.*, 1979). Even though this kind of cognitive disorder is probably less common than it was 20 or 30 years ago, it is important to remember its possible occurrence, especially in cognitive psychotherapy since this technique frequently involves the use of metaphors or other figures of speech.

*Concrete Concepts and Their Transformation to Perceptions.* This type of cognitive disorder was described by Arieti (1959) who called it "concretization and perceptualization of the concept" and judged it to be an expression of regression. This refers to the reluctance of the schizophrenic patient to maintain a level of abstract thought and the tendency to transform concepts to perceptual phenomena. According to Arieti, this disorder resembles dreams as visual transformations of paleological thoughts, that is, thoughts that do not conform with the formal laws of logic. It appears to be Arieti's opinion that the thoughts of schizophrenic patients can "regress" to the perceptual level and manifest themselves in hallucinations. In effect, what Arieti described seems to be (at least as concerns a transformation in auditory hallucinations) nothing more than the psychopathological phenomenon that has been well known in the German psychiatric literature since the beginning of the century under the name "Gedankenlautwerden" (Haring & Leickert, 1968). This concept implies that patients experience feelings that they hear their own thoughts expressed as if by loud voices within their heads. Arieti's interpretation of the phenomenon is clearly inspired by the classical psychoanalytical approach to primary processes, which is examined in the next section. Again, I prefer to avoid the term regression in this context, and I would like to propose an alternative hypothesis to that given by Arieti for this cognitive disorder; this alternative hypothesis is presented in the next section.

## Primary and Secondary Processes and Regression

According to a widely accepted psychoanalytical tradition, which may be traced back to Freud, the distorted cognitive processes observed in schizophrenic patients are regarded as expressing "regression" to a ("primitive" or "irrational") primary thought process. However, neither the term "regression" nor the term "primary process" (let alone the characteristics primitive and irrational) is necessary to describe the cognitive disorders of schizophrenic patients. Both regression and primary process, in the senses in which they are commonly understood in psychoanalytical theory, are, on the basis of a developmental and information-processing perspective, obsolete concepts that may be abandoned. In suggesting this I feel, in spite of the controversial nature of this idea, on quite solid ground since the opinions of some contemporary psychoanalysts (e.g., Peterfreund, Noy, and Holt) largely support my viewpoint. Even though differences exist among these authors with regard to their opinions and goals, their writings have been of great help to me in forming my own ideas.

### Criticism of the Concept of Primary Process

Primary and secondary thought processes (Freud, 1895, 1900) are considered within psychoanalytical circles to be two of Freud's greatest discoveries (e.g., Arlow, 1958). Jones (1953) actually suggested, with his characteristic enthusiasm, that the discovery of primary process represents "Freud's chief claim to fame: even his discovery of the unconscious is subordinated to it" (p. 213).

Other authors, such as Hilgard (1962), claim that the distinction between illogical and impulsive thinking and the logical and rational is much older knowledge that can be traced much farther back in time than Freud; however, it remains undebatable that Freud's characterization of primary process laid the grounds for a better understanding of thought development in normal people and of psychopathological manifestations in mentally disordered persons. Primary process is a system of cognition that has principles and mechanisms of its own; however, this does not automatically imply that it is correctly defined as chaos, a random mixture of disparate elements, or a special way of binding energy.

Freud defined the primary process in terms of three main mechanisms: condensation, displacement, and symbolism. He regarded the secondary process as subordinate to the laws of formal logic. Understandably, the primary process was originally described within the framework of the economic theory, but Freud never reappraised this concept, not even when he adopted his later structural theory (Freud, 1923). Neither has any radical (or universally accepted) revision of the concept been made during more recent times, despite extensive discussion in psychoanalytical circles during the 1950s (see Arlow, 1958, for a report of a panel and Noy, 1969, 1979, for a partial review of the literature). Noy drew attention to the fact that the development of the primary process has been consistently neglected in a most remarkable way. It has apparently been taken for granted that it was constitutionally determined and that it remained unchanged from its original form. Somewhat ironically, Noy (1969) commented that the primary process is unique in that it is assumed to "develop from nothing and progress toward nothing" (p. 158). Although Noy's opinion is too drastic, especially as concerns the later development (see in this respect the thorough investigations carried out by Lehtinen, 1981, 1983), other authors have also focused their criticism on developmental aspects.

Holt (1967), for example, pointed out that the primary process hardly exists at birth but must grow at the same rate as those structures responsible for the secondary process. A similar viewpoint was put forward by Noy (1969, 1979), who stated that the course of development of these two processes is determined by the same inherent maturational factors.

Both Klein (1976) and Noy (1969, 1979) used the concept of information processing and feedback in their attempts to define the secondary thought process. Noy extended Klein's viewpoint further and proposed that feedback in particular may be considered an important criterion for defining both the primary and the secondary process. Accordingly, the secondary process is regarded by both Klein and Noy as being continuously controlled by, and dependent upon, feedback information. Klein (1976) suggested that the secondary process depends on "the consequences of self-generated activity" (p. 244). In this respect, the primary process is regarded as being independent of such feedback. Peterfreund (1971) adopted a similar viewpoint in a discussion of the differences in thought activity during sleep and waking periods when he drew attention to the fact that the input of information from the external environment is greatly reduced during sleep.

The principal thesis of Noy was that the primary process does not disappear completely or remain unchanged when the secondary process becomes operative; instead, both processes develop side by side and coexist during a person's complete lifetime, even though the level of organization and function changes. Similar ideas have been expressed by other authors, including Burstein (1959) and Rapaport (1967). Quite correctly, all are aware that at least some contribution from magical thinking occasionally occurs in most people irrespective of age or cultural origins.

One problem associated with regarding the primary process as regressive is that such an opinion does not do justice to its occurrence in artistic expression. To avoid the problems caused by considering the primary process to be regressive, primitive, and underdeveloped in an exclusively negative fashion, the concept of "regression in the service of the ego" has been introduced by Kris (1952). Arieti (1964, 1969, 1974b) preferred to talk about a "tertiary process" in the context of creativity and artistic expression. Arieti (1964) maintained that the creative process "allows man to liberate himself from the fetters of secondary process responses" (p. 52). He pointed out, on the other hand, that whereas in the primitive or psychopathologic use of the primary process there is no consciousness of abstraction, in art the use of primary process does not eliminate the abstract. Accordingly, Arieti looked at creativity as depending on a special mixture of primary and secondary processes that he saw as a tertiary process.

If, in accordance with Holt (1967), the primary process is considered to be a specific system for processing information to serve a synthetic need, it becomes easier to understand its main characteristics—condensation, disregard for space, and time, etc.—at a time when the complex cognitive meaning structures are not yet fully developed. Peterfreund (1971) discussed the formal properties of the primary process at some length in his work on dreams and maintained that they can be easily explained within a theoretical framework that includes information processing. Noy (1969) suggested that one should quite simply ignore the attribute primitive in all discussions of primary processes. He stated, instead, that the primary and secondary processes are different since their purposes and functions are different. Noy implied that the primary process develops in such a way that it is able to cope with everything connected with the self and the experiences assimilated within the self, while the secondary process develops in such a way that it can deal with those things connected with the external world. Noy (1979, p. 180) further asserted that objects, events, and phenomena are organized as experience by the primary process while they are organized as knowledge by the secondary process. A very important corollary of Noy's assumption is that use of the term "regression" becomes completely inadequate. In fact, it would be more proper to speak of a shift from one type of process to the other rather than of a regression.

Before concluding this survey, it may be of value to point out that one of the characteristics of the primary process, namely condensation, has been treated from another viewpoint by Ryle (1978). Ryle referred to Bartlett's distinction (1932) between verbal thinking and pictorial thinking and stated that one of the characteristics of pictorial representation or visual images is that they are normally composed according to atmosphere and interest and not according to temporal or spatial dimensions.

### A Critique of the Concept of Regression

It is well known that Freud borrowed his analogy of psychic regression from Jackson's neurological theories, probably because it fit in well with assumptions concerning a fixation at different stages of development as a pathogenic component in the growth of neuroses. Regression is thus regarded as a return to the mental functioning at the stage at which fixation took place. Since fixation at one of the classic stages of development has not been established in schizophrenic patients, it has been assumed that fundamental disturbances occur at a very early stage of growth. In consequence, parallels have been drawn between psychopathological manifestations in schizophrenic patients and characteristic psychic functions in infants, implying that schizo-phrenic symptoms exist as regression to an even earlier stage of development.

Criticism of the traditional psychoanalytical approach to psychic processes in infants has been expounded by Peterfreund (1978), who stated that many of the terms and concepts commonly used in psychoanalytical literature are completely unacceptable since they express nothing but an "adultomorphization" of early childhood. The term used by Peterfreund implies a tendency to characterize early, normal stages of development in terms of psychopathological phenomena that arise later in life (e.g., when one talks about autism with regard to a stage of development of a normal child). Such terminology, characterized by the use of the same concepts to describe both normal conditions in children and pathological behavior in adults, is, in my opinion, deceptive since it promotes circular reasoning; the concept of regression applied to schizophrenic symptomatology is one example. My assumption is consistent with the opinion expressed by Rubins (1969). In fact, Rubins was very critical of the concept of regression. He pointed out that this concept assumes that "symptomatic schizophrenic behavior which *resembles* that of an infant, is in *reality* infantile, and more specifically a behavior which the patient has previously had" (p. 135, italics in the original). Rubins criticized the fallacy of considering the adult as returned to an infantile state and pointed out that a simple similarity is taken for an actuality.

If we consider the concept of regression applied to schizophrenic thinking, we realize that it contains at least two implications: that the schizophrenic patient thinks and acts primitively and that he or she has regressed to a precivilized mode of thought. This assumption is particularly evident in Arieti's formulation of a definition of predicate thinking, in which he changed the term "paralogical" used by Von Domarus (1944) to "paleological" and substituted the term "logician" with "the normal person," thus implying that the formal laws of logic are representative of how normal people think (see also Maher, 1966, for a discussion of the consequences of these subtitutions). The second implication, already discussed above, is that the patient's thinking has regressed to a mode used early in childhood; this assumes that the source of the intrapsychic processes that lead later to the development of a schizophrenic syndrome have to be sought for in the childhood of a person's development. Whereas the first implication has been proved to be completely unwarranted by several anthropologists, the second is difficult to sustain unless one can demonstrate that the patient "has regressed to a form of behavior which he had exhibited before but had since abandoned" (Maher, 1966, p. 411). I have already argued, in accordance with Noy (1969), that this last thesis is untenable. In addition, it has clearly emerged in several studies (see Maher for a partial review) that similarities between the performance of children and that of the adult schizophrenic are more apparent than real.

Arieti (1955, 1974b) apparently tried to circumvent the controversial issue of regression by proposing the concept of "progressive teleologic regression" in his attempt to explain the reemergence of the primary process in the schizophrenic patient. According to Arieti's conceptualization, regression is no longer regarded as a return to earlier stages of fixation, but rather as the renewed availability of functions belonging to lower levels of integration. In other words, while Arieti retains the term regression, the attribute teleologic implies that the regression is purposeful, intended to remove excessive anxiety and to reestablish some kind of psychic equilibrium. The term progressive implies that regression often fails in its purpose and repeats itself. Even though Arieti's conceptualization points to a positive function of regression (similar to the concept of 'positive disintegration' used by Dabrowski, 1964), his view about the reemergence of primary process, paleologic thinking, and concretization of the abstract, is not flawless. Two problems in this view are his unwarranted equation between paralogic and paleologic and his unsupported assumption concerning the use of logic by "normal" people and the lack of logic of "primitive" people.

Use of the term regression is completely unacceptable for everyday language. Its use may easily result in a patient who is considered to have regressed being treated as a child instead of as an adult. Because of this risk, I strongly support the view that any characterization of the schizophrenic patient's behavior as regressive should be dispensed with altogether.

### Critical Remarks on the Interpretation of Certain Cognitive Distortions

The preceding remarks about the concept of primary process allow a reconsideration of the interpretation given to cognitive distortions detected in schizophrenic patients as described previously.

One major source of confusion concerning, for example, predicative thinking is the assumption that it is paleologic (i.e., primitive) instead of just a deviation from the laws of formal logic. Another problem is the implicit assumption that primary process is the mode of thinking of the irrational unconscious. Other authors have been concerned with defining the language of the unconscious, prominent among them being Matte-Blanco (1954) and Lacan (1960). Lacan approaches the unconscious from the perspective of linguistics and equates condensation with metaphor and displacement with metonymy. On the other hand, the major thesis sustained by Matte-Blanco (1959, 1965, 1976) is that schizophrenic primary process thinking, even though it does not follow the laws of Aristotelian logic, is by no means irrational; it is consistent with the principles of generalization and symmetry stemming from symbolic logic. In studying schizophrenic thinking, which he considered a particular application of the formal characteristics of the unconscious, Matte-Blanco (1959) detected a conformity to two main principles. The first of these principles (i.e., the principle of generalization) states that "the thinking of the system unconscious (and accordingly, of the schizophrenic patient) treats an individual thing as if it were a member of element of a class which contains other members; it treats this class as a subclass of a more general class, and this more general class as a subclass of a still more general class, and so on" (Matte-Blanco, 1959 p. 2; 1976, p. 213). The second principle, that of symmetry, states, "the unconscious treats the converse of any relation as identical with the relation. In other words, it treats asymmetrical relations as if they were symmetrical" (Matte-Blanco, 1976).

While it is beyond the scope of this book to report in more detail all the corollaries that Matte-Blanco (1976) derived from his main principle and his concept of bi-logical structures, it is important to point out that, judged from the perspective indicated by Matte-Blanco, predicative thinking is nothing but one of the structural disturbances that can be derived from the principle of symmetry. The cognitive distortion labeled "desymbolization" (for example, the literal interpretation of metaphors or other figures of speech) represents a combination of the first and the second principles.

The concept of predicative thinking was discussed by Mallinger (1974) in his attempt to establish a cognitive explanation of transference reactions. He proposed that the cause of a transference reaction in a given person toward another is that the first person, on the basis of a specific characteristic, mistakenly identifies the other person with someone of significance in the past who possessed a similar characteristic. Mallinger even referred to Piaget's concept of "transduction" (Piaget, 1962) and to "pars pro toto," which is one example of diffuse thinking (in contrast to the more mature, articulated thinking) taken into account by Werner (1948). Both concepts refer to the child's tendency to establish identity on the basis of a detail (or attribute) instead of on the basis of the whole (e.g., all men with beards are doctors since the first doctor the child met had a beard). Mallinger maintained that a child who grows up under trying circumstances (or a situation characterized by insecure attachment) learns to focus only on a few characteristics of the parents (facial expression, tone of voice, etc.) and to identify them from such characteristics. This restricted repertoire becomes a schema that the child uses later in life in interactions with other important people. Thus, the child learns to categorize rather than identify.

Both Arieti and (less explicitly) Matte-Blanco suggested that syllogistic reasoning errors such as predicative thinking belong to schizophrenic psychopathology. Even this type of cognitive distortion, however, has been repeatedly found in normals (see Gottesman & Chapman, 1960, for a partial review), and this finding has been invoked to question the validity of Von Domarus's (1944) and Arieti's hypotheses about the difference in syllogistic errors between schizophrenics and normals. It should be stressed, however, that syllogisms used in research have been rather neutral in content and that a delusional identification on the basis of the predicate has never been reported in normals as it occurs in schizophrenic patients. The results obtained by Gottesman and Chapman (1960) and by other research workers, on the other hand, are consistent with the thesis that there are no cognitive distortions pathognomonic of a particular disorder; instead, cognitive distortions are distributed along a continuum in the general population and contribute in various degrees to the development of individual vulnerability. In the case of predicative thinking, it could yet again be maintained that what distinguishes schizophrenic patients from normals is only a matter of degree.

Concerning the perceptualization of concepts described by Arieti (e.g., Arieti, 1959), an alternative hypothesis could be taken into account. Thus, this cognitive distortion may be regarded as a form of private (or internal) dialogue or private speech in the sense given to this concept by Piaget (1923) and by Vygotsky (1934, 1980). Both of these authors used the concept to refer to the commonly known fact that, during their development, children talk to themselves and give themselves encouragement or criticism during their actions. Hand in hand with cognitive development, these conversations become internalized and transformed to abstract thoughts. The difference between Piaget's ideas and Vygotsky's lies in the fact that the former asserts that this private dialogue disappears completely when the child learns to think abstractly, while the latter (see also Luria, 1976) proposes that the stage at which the child audibly repeats instructions is followed by an internalization of this behavior, which is thus transformed to an inner dialogue. If we take into account that the cognitive–emotional development in persons who later develop a schizophrenic disorder may have been negatively influenced by various environmental stresses, it is not unreasonable to assume that these particular individuals may have learned to use their inner dialogues as an adaptive mechanism to cope with these stresses or with stressful situations in general. It is well known that normals resort to inner self-instructions or other types of inner dialogue in stressful situations; accordingly, it is not unreasonable to assume that a similar inner dialogue may become even more vivid in hyperaroused schizophrenics and be mistakenly interpreted as inner voices.

Vygotsky, who drew attention to the intimate relationship among higher psychic functions (symbolization, language, problem-solving, etc.), emphasized that this reflects an early interpersonal relationship. This postulate and Fuson's proposal (1979) that the inner dialogue fulfils a function, for instance, in the expression of different emotions, are both compatible with the hypothesis presented here. Unfortunately, however, I am not able at the present time to advance a corresponding hypothesis for the experience of other types of hallucinatory experiences. On the other hand, Arieti has made reference almost exclusively to auditory hallucinations and has not dwelled on other hallucinatory phenomena.

### Summary

Is it possible to apply these discussions of clinical manifestations to patients with schizophrenic disorders? Without doubt, such possibilities exist, and the contents of the sections above support this viewpoint. I maintain, consistently with other authors, that we do not need the concept of primary process, and we need even less the assumption that it expresses the illogical language of an irrational unconscious. Noy's notions of experience and knowledge mentioned earlier appear to be very similar to the concepts of semantic and episodic memory (Tulving, 1972) that are now used in cognitive psychology. I agree with Noy, on the other hand, that the secondary process may be considered to be dependent on feedback from the external world. For such a feedback to be meaningful, a decentering in a Piagetian sense must occur so that reality is comprehended not exclusively from one's own perspective. From what has already been said, it should be apparent that the schizophrenic patient's assessment of the environment is egocentric and that various cognitive distortions really occur. In the circumstances just mentioned, it is not surprising that the corrective feedback mechanism needed for the secondary process becomes markedly reduced, while at the same time, "egocentric feedback" may well promote an activation of and shift toward other forms of thought. My hypothesis in no way contradicts Noy's proposal that the primary process in schizophrenic patients becomes prominent as a result of a disturbance in the development of the secondary process by various unspecified factors.

## DELUSIONS AND HALLUCINATIONS

Delusions and hallucinations are quite common occurrences, although they are not necessarily found among the clinical symptoms of all schizophrenic patients. Traditionally, both of these phenomena, the contents of which are totally unreasonable and which are manifested with great conviction, are regarded as being largely inaccessible to rational counterarguments. If such a definition, which prevails in most textbooks, is accepted without question, it becomes necessary to discuss to what extent these phenomena may be considered amenable to cognitive therapeutic interventions.

### Delusions and Their Characteristics

A few earlier studies of the use of cognitive therapy with patients suffering from delusions indicate that even those that are long-lasting are capable of being influenced (Adams, Malatesta, Brantley, & Turkat, 1981; Beck, 1952; Hole, Rush, & Beck, 1979). The results reported are in complete agreement with those of Arieti (1962b) and Jacobs (1980), who referred to the treatment of delusory patients according to a cognitive approach applied within a psychoanalytical frame of reference. Before these investigations are discussed, however, it is necessary to define "delusions" more precisely, particularly since some of the more precise characterizations can be easily generalized to include hallucinations.

First of all, it is important to emphasize that delusions can be recognized on the basis of various characteristic dimensions. According to Hole *et al.* (1979) and Kendler, Glazer, and Morgenstern (1983), the more important of these include the following:

- "Conviction," which is the extent to which the patient is certain of the validity of the delusions.
- "Extent," which is the degree to which the delusion includes different aspects of the patient's life.
- "Pervasiveness," which is the extent to which the patient is preoccupied with the delusions; included is the degree to which the patient is guided by goals dictated by the delusions or interprets different experiences on their basis.
- "Disorganization–sytematization," which is the extent to which different delusions are internally consistent and thus structured as a system.
- "Absurdity," which is the degree of absurdity of the delusion and to what extent it deviates from the sense of reality of all others within the patient's cultural sphere.

Besides these dimensional aspects, additional fundamental cognitive processes of importance to delusions should be taken into account. Among these, Jacobs (1980) included thinking, knowing, metathinking, and the forming of erroneously controlling assumptions, that is, the development of basic dysfunctional core schemata.

Jacobs referred to the neo-Kantian philosopher Arendt's work (Arendt, 1978) in order to stress the difference between thinking and knowing. He stated that thinking normally precedes knowing, since thinking assigns meaning to what we perceive. During the initial experience of delusion, this order is reversed; knowing precedes thinking. The term metathinking refers, as mentioned earlier, to that process by which we think about our thoughts. This process in turn is divided into various subprocesses, the most important of which are assumed to the following: the ability to select and direct the contents of one's thoughts and to avoid selective inattention; the ability to survey a broad cognitive spectrum of alternative explanations; the ability to shift easily from the concrete to the abstract; and the ability to distinguish between cause and effect when one draws conclusions. According to Jacobs, it is primarily metathinking that is severely impaired in schizophrenic patients.

The last cognitive process Jacobs considered is the growth of fundamental controlling preconceptions (i.e., basic dysfunctional schemata). He assumed that these dysfunctional (delusiogenic) preconceptions are developed early in life and predispose to the later development of delusions. Jacobs tended to equate his viewpoint concerning dysfunctional controlling assumptions with Klein's ideas (1970) on peremptory ideation, that is, thoughts that are experienced as imperative and demanding and that preclude all doubt and do not admit refusal (see, however, Peterfreund and Franceschini, 1973, for a critical discussion of the concept of peremptory ideation). If the term "peremptory ideas" is interpreted only as described, without inclusion of additional assumptions concerning psychic energy (which Rapaport, 1960, has used to explain the origins of these ideas), it becomes quite similar to the term "automatic thoughts" as used in cognitive psychotherapy.

Although Jacobs was not fully explicit, I have interpreted his emphasis on erroneous controlling assumptions and the fact that he equated them with Klein's peremptory ideas to imply that he referred to the knowing process in schizophrenic patients. Klein's definition of peremptory ideas, given above, with its stress that these ideas preclude questions or doubts, appears to support my viewpoint. If correct, it becomes easy to understand why one can maintain that knowing precedes thinking in schizophrenic patients suffering from delusions. Jacobs pointed out, however, that the fact that erroneous controlling assumptions are operative is not sufficient to establish the occurrence and persistence of delusions; additional factors play an important role. Among these factors, Jacobs included a defective growth of the autonomous metathinking process in persons who grow up within families where they are obliged to incorporate dysfunctional assumptions. Examples of the dysfunctional assumptions are, according to Jacobs (1980), "a relationship is either successful or a failure," "growth leads to catastrophe," and "to leave you means I will cease to exist" (pp. 559–560).

Jacobs's hypothesis is elegant and conforms to what has been described in terms of the cognitions taken into account in cognitive psychotherapy. He seemed, however, to erroneously equate the peremptory ideas with the delusiogenic schemata, while they are, in my opinion, nothing more than the automatic thoughts described earlier. A more precise definition of the hypothesis, accordingly, should comprise some additional steps as follows:

- Dysfunctional (delusiogenic) schemata of the type described by Jacobs generate, when instantiated, dysfunctional automatic thoughts with the characteristics attributed by Klein to peremptory ideas.
- Because of a lack of metathinking, the patient is unable to correct severe schema-congruent cognitive distortions (selective inattention, arbitrary inferences, etc.).
- The automatic thoughts are thus reinforced through a dysfunctional feedback mechanism and become even more frequent, also assuming a delusional dimension.

## Therapeutic Interventions and Delusions

In 1952, Beck reported one of the first cases of chronic delusions in a schizophrenic patient who was successfully treated by a cognitive technique within the framework of an analytically oriented psychotherapy. In short, the report concerned a 28-year-old patient with a 7-year long history of persecutory delusion treated in a phase of acute decompensation. Beside dynamic interpretations, the treatment, comprised of a total of 30 interviews over a period of 8 months, focused on leading the patient to realize that his delusional experiences were strongly intensified by his turning to the "idea" that a group of men were "looking out for him" (p. 310). As will become apparent later, the approach followed by Beck is strongly reminiscent of that proposed by Arieti, described in more detail below.

A further case report was published by Adams *et al.* (1981). During nine therapeutic sessions, these authors applied a variety of techniques intended to make the patient aware of suitable internal and external stimuli away from his delusional thoughts of reference, persecution, and being controlled. Both at the termination of treatment and at a follow-up session 6 months later, the patient was completely free from thought disorders.

Milton, Patwa, and Hafner (1978) compared a direct confrontation approach with an approach aimed at belief modification (by means of an inductive–deductive dialogue technique) in 14 patients with persistent systematized delusions divided into two comparable subgroups. Both methods produced a slight fall in the delusional beliefs with a further fall 6 weeks later in the belief modification group. The authors did not report follow-up data, so it is impossible to know how long-lasting the results have been. Worth noting, however, is that patients with persistent systematized delusions showed detectable changes in their delusional experiences as a consequence of a cognitive approach.

Further support to the assumption that delusional experiences are amenable to influence by a cognitive approach can be found in an article by Hole *et al.* (1979). The aim of their study was to investigate to what extent various characteristics of delusions—that is, conviction, accommodation (the degree to which the content of delusion can be modified by external events), pervasiveness, and encapsulation (a decrease in pervasiveness without a decrease in conviction)—could be influenced by a cognitive approach using such techniques as focusing, questioning the validity of delusional contents, and reality testing. At the end of the trial, which included eight patients and stretched over seven 1-hour sessions, four of the patients had markedly improved; they showed reduced pervasiveness, and two even showed an additional reduction in conviction. It should be remarked, however, that this study was performed to determine whether or not chronic delusions could be influenced by external events (in this case, the cognitive therapy techniques) and was not a straightforward treatment.

Jacobs (1980) did not report any cases of his own, but he proposed a cognitive therapeutic strategy to be used with patients suffering from delusions. This strategy, used during the initial phase, is intended to help patients to be aware of and to train the various components of metathinking; in the second phase, it is used to help patients to recognize and gradually correct their specific controlling preconceptions.

Arieti (1962b) described four cognitive therapeutic strategies that may be used with patients with delusions:

- To help patients to be aware that they adopt a referential attitude.
- To make them aware of the tendency to make concrete the indefinite mood of being threatened.
- To allow them to recognize situations where they use paleologic to maintain their delusions.
- To make them conscious of their punctiform insight.

"Referential attitude" is the label assigned by Arieti to that process that takes place before delusions have acquired full strength. This process means that the patient almost seeks external cues that can justify his or her frame of mind. In other words, it might be said that the patient commits many of the errors of perception and processing of information described earlier. According to Arieti, the patient should be helped to discover his or her frame of mind and the expectations entertained prior to the onset of delusions in order to be able to remedy them. The patient should also be helped to become aware of the other types of cognitive errors he or she makes and to learn how these can be corrected.

Arieti (1962b) used the term "punctiform insight" to refer to the fact that certain patients intuitively appear to perceive different stimuli in their environment correctly even when they are under stress; however, this insight remains a grain that does not expand to a full insight. In other words, "instead of enlarging the insight to an abstract level, the patient generalizes it at a concrete level, actually distorting the rest of reality" (p. 58).

The strategy one adopts to deal with delusions in patients depends on the pervasiveness and extent of the delusions. When they dominate the clinical scene to such an extent that meaningful communication with the patient becomes extremely difficult, the initial therapeutic effort must be directed toward influencing their breadth and pervasiveness; efforts to affect the degree of conviction must be deferred to a later stage. One of our patients, for example, despite adequate medication suffered continuously from massive anxiety-generating delusions that hindered him from even sitting with others; our initial efforts were aimed at training him to differentiate those situations in which he found himself to be most affected from those in which he was free from such influences. Later he was made aware that events he was fully convinced had happened never, in fact, occurred. The patient himself then suggested that briefly written notes would help him to maintain this limited insight, and he began to exploit this possibility. However, probably because he used paralogical thinking, he was incapable of benefiting from this insight. The only significant result that we were able to achieve was that the delusions gradually became less extensive and less pervasive to a degree that allowed the patient to participate meaningfully in the resocialization program. His conviction of the truth of his delusions could not be affected to any great extent even though he himself admitted some doubts on several occasions. One thing that may have hindered any further improvement was that the patient lived in a severely conflictive environment that we were unable to modify.

With patients suffering from less extensive and relatively limited delusions, we have found that it can be meaningful not to focus attention on them at all during the first stages of therapy. Our therapeutic work with one such patient was aimed at helping him to develop and reinforce a more functional self-image. During this phase of therapy, the patient learned the most common cognitive therapeutic techniques with which to recognize the occurrence of dysfunctional automatic thoughts and how to identify several cognitive distortions that he made. When this was achieved (during a period of almost 3 months), the patient himself reported that he had become aware that he could exploit the newly acquired cognitive techniques to question the validity of his delusions; with the help of these techniques he could neutralize them. This patient had discontinued medication prior to the commencement of psychotherapy and never did resume it afterward. He has been able to return to the occupation he was engaged in prior to the onset of his disorder (almost 3 years before coming for psychotherapy) and he has reported during his 2-year follow-up that he is able to live an ordinary life and that he has learned to cope with occasional mild ideas of reference that arise in stressful situations.

With other patients whose delusions do not constitute a dominating component in their clinical picture and do not prevent them from functioning socially, it is probably not of prime importance that the delusions be the object of direct therapeutic intervention. While it is important to be alert to their possible communicative implications, it is not necessary to focus attention on them unless the patient suggests it. If one realizes that the patient is attempting to express a punctiform insight and that the message is distorted by concretization or the use of paralogical thinking, it may be helpful to inform the patient that one understands that he or she wishes to communicate something but that one does not completely grasp what it is. On several occasions, I have found that the patient has been able to reformulate his or her thoughts in more comprehensible language.

Jacobs (1980) suggested that a psychoanalytical interpretive approach to delusions most often does not give any positive results. In addition, Jacobs maintained that attempts at interpretations may be received by the patient as if the therapist said, "Everything can be explained. My explanations must be more accurate than yours"

(p. 561), thus reinforcing rather than resolving the delusional problems. I completely agree with Jacobs.

No matter which strategy is adopted, eventual corrections of delusions is an arduous task that cannot be rushed and that can only be performed within the context of a well-developed, trusting relationship; the therapist must assume the function of a "beacon of orientation," as described by Mahler (1968) rather than push the patient beyond his or her actual preparedness. Untimely and confrontative approaches easily lead to "sealing off" or "passing"—that is, patients may act as if they have lost their delusions while retaining their convictions in private.

## Hallucinations and Psychotherapeutic Interventions

The possibility of influencing hallucinatory experiences with cognitive therapeutic interventions has only occasionally been discussed in the literature. On the other hand, several of the dimensions employed to characterize delusions can, without difficulty, be generalized to hallucinations and can also be used as the basis for treatment. These factors include conviction, pervasiveness, extent, and degree of absurdity.

Arieti (1962b, 1974a, 1976) stated that hallucinatory experiences most often occur when the patient expects that they will occur (with the exception of patients in very advanced stages of schizophrenia). Since he used auditive hallucinations as examples in his writings, Arieti used the term "listening attitude" to define this expectation; this is an analogy to "referential attitude," which Arieti used for patients with delusions. Arieti maintained that when a good therapeutic relationship has been established, it is not at all difficult to help patients become aware that they adopt a listening attitude before they experience a hallucinatory phenomenon. When a therapist succeeds in helping patients to recognize the relationship between these two conditions, a major step has been taken toward a meaningful treatment of this kind of disorder. In Arieti's opinion, the same approach can be used for other types of hallucinations as well.

During recent years, I have not come into contact with patients suffering from nonauditive hallucinations except when in a very acute stage, where medication is a more suitable method of treatment. In previously medicated patients with whom I have worked therapeutically, only auditive hallucinations have occurred. In such cases, I have had the opportunity to confirm the validity of Arieti's ideas. Thus, I have found it to be possible to gradually increase the awareness of patients that the intensity of their hallucinatory experiences increases when they feel themselves to be stressed and to expect that "the voices" would become audible. Long-lasting auditive hallucinations were spontaneously described by one of my patients as her own thoughts that "spoke aloud inside her head"; in an earlier stage, the "voices" were regarded by the patient as coming from somewhere else she was unable to define. This patient then discovered that she was able to (according to her metaphor) "switch on and off" her auditory experiences depending on whether she was able to control her train of thoughts.

In classical textbooks on psychopathology (e.g., Jaspers, 1913; Schneider, 1959), the experience of hearing one's own thoughts has been treated at some length. Jaspers referred to reports in the early literature to maintain that a distinction should be made between "inner voices" (or "voices of the mind") and "voices proper," and he assigned to the former the label of "pseudohallucinations." According to Jaspers, inner voices are nothing but a special kind of imagery. Schneider (1959), on the other hand, regarded hearing one's own thoughts as a first-rank symptom. More recently, less attention has been paid to this distinction, and "loud thoughts" have probably been equated with hallucinations, especially when patients report their experiences as "hearing voices" and no further probing is made to describe the nature of these voices.

Obviously, there is a possibility that the two phenomena are not as distinct from each other as is maintained in the literature. The auditive hallucinations of my patient described above seem to suggest, in fact, that a transition can occur moving the location of the voices to the inner subjective space or elsewhere. However, if a distinction does in fact exist, it would become necessary to evaluate more precisely which kind of hallucinatory experiences can be influenced by a psychotherapeutic approach.

Patients who have experienced auditive hallucinations for extended periods often report that they are afraid to lose a part of their own identity if the voices disappear. Reports of this type support the assumption that patients are to a certain extent aware that the voices are not alien but are part of their own cognitive processes. In such cases, I do not insist on focusing on hallucinatory experiences until the patient is ready for such work. In my experience, hallucinatory experiences can disappear without any direct work on them as the patient improves.

## MISATTRIBUTIONS AND THEIR CORRECTION

The term "misattribution" refers to that process by which patients show a tendency to seriously underestimate the degree to which they control their behavior (Bedrosian & Beck, 1980; Greenwood, 1983). It is derived from Rotter's original ideas on internal and external control of reinforcement (Rotter, 1966) or what is called "locus of control" (LOC). LOC is the individual propensity to regard one's source of reinforcement as an integral part of one's behavior (internal) or as dependent on external factors such as chance, fate, or the power of others. A person who adopts the attitude that "I can do anything if I set my mind to it" shows internal LOC, while one who believes that "nothing helps no matter how hard I try, since everything I do depends on chance" shows external LOC.

There is empirical support that people's conception of LOC is markedly dependent on the relationship that existed between them and their parents (e.g., Austrin & Aubuchon, 1979; Davis & Phares, 1969; MacDonald, 1971; Rohner et al., 1980). Persons who have experienced their parents as stern and punitive, but also as nurturant, affectionate, and predictable tend to display internal LOC. Such a conception of inner control is also developed in a relationship to the extent to which a person has felt himself to be accepted by his parents and has grown up in an atmosphere of security. In contrast, people who have experienced their parents as punitive, dominating, and without affection tend to display external LOC. In contrast, not-yet-published results of my own, obtained in a group of 42 healthy medical students, did not show any significant correlation between experienced parental rearing attitudes and LOC. It should be noticed, however, that my subjects could be regarded as high achievers since they had succeeded in a very hard competition for a place at medical school. Thus, it cannot be excluded that compensatory mechanisms might have been operating at an age when our subjects were less dependent on their parents.

In a number of studies of schizophrenic patients (e.g., Harrow & Ferrante, 1969; Lefcourt, 1976; Levenson, 1973a, 1973b), it has been found that, on average, they are more external than the healthy controls. Greenwood (1983), however, suggested that both internal and external characteristics can be found in such patients; they may assume that they have no control over their thoughts or behavior, which are determined by external factors, while they are also convinced that they can control others by acts of will. One of our patients provides an illuminating example. On the one hand, he believed himself (through paralogical reasoning) to be completely under the control of God and the devil; on the other hand, he was fully confident that he could influence his surroundings both positively and negatively.

It is worth remarking that the results of studies of LOC carried out with schizophrenic patients, taking into account the relationship between LOC and the fostering attitudes of the parents, are consistent with the general theoretical ideas described in the first part of this book; that is, the parental influence is not a unidirectional phenomenon, but is the result of an interplay between dysfunctional rearing attitudes in the parents and a vulnerable child. Judged from this perspective, the lack of correlations in my sample of healthy medical students makes some sense. Finally, it should be observed that the experience of being internal, as found in some schizophrenic patients, is strongly egocentric in a Piagetian sense.

As mentioned earlier, "personalizing" is one of the more frequent cognitive distortions, especially in depressed patients. In practice, this cognitive fault implies that patients attribute negative events to themselves ("It was my fault") even when these events clearly are beyond their control. This cognitive error is incorporated, for example, in Abramson and coworkers' revised theory of learned helplessness (Abramson, Seligman, & Teasdale, 1978), where it was considered with the addition that patients attribute to others the merit for events turning out well; this inclination reflects a mixture of internal and external LOC.

As pointed out earlier, personalizing is closely related to the inability to distinguish between cause and meaning, described earlier. Although no direct studies have yet been reported concerning the occurrence of this cognitive error in patients in relation to the fostering practices of their parents, it is not unreasonable to assume that such faulty thinking can readily develop and persist in persons who grow up exposed to ambiguous messages of the double-bind type, as described by Bateson and coworkers (Bateson *et al.*, 1956).

Misattributions of this kind are amenable to therapeutic interventions using the many techniques discussed by Beck and his colleagues (e.g., Beck *et al.*, 1979; Bedrosian & Beck, 1980). One suitable approach is a skillful application of the Socratic method. Suitable experiments can also be planned as homework, in which the patient is given the opportunity to test different alternatives. Before introducing experiments of this kind, the patient can be trained to question distortions by means of questions such as, "How do you think others would see the problem?" or "Do you think everyone sees this as you do?"

Since misattribution in schizophrenic patients is often integrated in a negative self-image, therapeutic interventions designed to produce a reattribution contribute to a more marked restructuration of the patient's personality. It should not be forgotten, however, that the possibility of succeeding with therapeutic strategies of this kind greatly depends on a well-established therapeutic relationship; that this dependency becomes stronger (according to studies that link attribution style and security in relationships; Austrin & Aubuchon, 1979) when the misattribution is connected with a deep-rooted dysfunctional belief concerning self-image. In other words, these therapeutic interventions allow the therapist to approach the core of the patient's disorder.

It is important to point out (as in Greenwood, 1983) that attempting a reattribution of convictions based completely on delusions tends to be less successful. In our experience, attempts aimed at modifying misattributions based on delusions should be postponed to a later stage of treatment when the patient has learned to alter other beliefs of a more peripheral nature.

## DECENTERING AND EGOCENTRISM

"Decentering" is the developmental law hypothesized by Piaget (1932, 1936) to account for the maintenance of a balance between assimilation and accommodation. In the sensorimotor stage, for example, decentering refers to the development of the concept of the external object separate from oneself. In the stage of concrete operations, decentering means that the child, in the course of interactions with peers (e.g., when playing a game), is forced to assimilate their communications, that is, their rules, with his or her own rules until equilibrium is achieved (that is, a set of mutually agreed-upon rules is established). In this instance, the child decenters from his or her own rules toward the establishment of new ones through a process of negotiation that takes into account the rules of the other children. In this context, egocentrism is defined as a deficit of differentiation in some aspect of subject-object interaction (Piaget, 1923) or as the inability to shift attention to consider more than one aspect of an event (Feffer, 1959).

The term egocentrism, as used in a Piagetian frame of reference, should be interpreted without negative or moralizing overtones. It is a completely normal phenomenon characteristic to certain stages of cognitive development (Elkind, 1970). Thus, it does not possess the same meaning as in everyday language, where it is most frequently used to describe someone who is selfish or self-preoccupied. Looft (1972) suggested that the very meaning of egocentrism is an embeddedness of one's point of view. Thus, the child in a stage of egocentrism is convinced that others comprehend things and experience feelings in the same way as he or she does. Egocentrism implies that the child (and, in a similar fashion, the egocentric adult) assimilates experiences from the external world into a pattern that is determined by the child's own view of the world; the child sees everything in relation to him- or herself without any pronounced accommodation (that is, the child sees only similarities without grasping differences). Consequently, children easily ascribe life and feelings to all objects, including stones and other inanimate items. They are convinced of their ability to influence distant objects by their desires, and they believe that their thoughts and emotions are directly available to other people without having to talk about them. In addition, they think that they do not need to explain anything, since everyone thinks as they do. Certain similarities between egocentric thinking and primary process thinking are easily discerned.

Elkind (1970) proposed that there exists a correlation between children's egocentrism and how positively they experience their parents. Although such an assumption may be valid in many cases, egocentrism nevertheless contributes to a situation in which children tend to think well of their parents even when the actual conditions are negative. In other words, since egocentric children are unable to comprehend things from a perspective other than their own, they may ascribe to their parents those feelings and attitudes that they feel toward them. According to Elkind, this phenomenon could be regarded as an example of denial, which implies an inability to discard an assumption despite evidence of its invalidity. The situation can best be described by saying that assimilation predominates over accommodation and that children are unable to grasp differences; thus, they cannot adapt their schemata to incorporate experiences that contradict their egocentric conceptions.

Even though Elkind's hypothesis is suggestive and may be valid in many cases, it neglects other important aspects of the parent-child relationship for which the concept of egocentrism may be relevant. Earlier Arieti's interpretation of the reports of schizophrenic patients concerning their mothers was discussed. It was emphasized that Arieti's opinion was consistent with a hypothesis on the development of a dysfunctional meaning structure in the patient that was based on a *pars pro toto* perception of the mother's attitudes and behavior that was later repeatedly reinforced by cognitive distortions acting as a confirmatory bias. There is, however, another possible interpretation, related to Elkind's hypothesis discussed above—namely, a situation completely opposite to that described by Elkind may occur. Accordingly, preschizophrenic, egocentric children may view their mothers negatively because they equate her feelings and attitudes with those they may have toward her. This negative view later persists if children fail to decenter; it can be even more reinforced by confirmatory bias. Even the frequently held assumption that schizophrenic patients' dependency on their mothers is based on the dysfunctional assumption that any attempt at separating from her would provoke her death can be interpreted as a consequence of a lack of decentering; thus, it shows the persistence of the egocentric belief of the power of the patients' own thoughts.

Only at the beginning of the stage of formal operational thinking do children become capable of freeing themselves from that which is phenomenologically possible; in their own minds, they now examine different steps that would be impossible in reality. The concept of decentering refers to this widening of perspective and, thus, to a gradual decline in egocentrism. At 7-8 years of age, children become able to shift easily between their own perspective and that of another; they now realize that others may look at things differently. This does not mean, however, that egocentrism disappears completely. On the contrary, as described in more detail below, egocentrism grows again during later critical stages of development and especially during the teens. In this context, however, it may be worth adding that findings reported by Verkozen (1975) suggest that children at age 3-6 years may be able to realize the existence of distinct points of view of other persons.

Although Piaget's theories have long been underrated in the psychoanalytical literature and have been regarded by some authors as irrelevant to psychotherapy (e.g., Friedman, 1978), there have been, on the other hand, serious attempts to assimilate Piagetian conceptions in the psychoanalytical domain (e.g., Greenspan & Lourie, 1981; Wolff, 1960). For instance, there have been several attempts to define the psychopathological manifestations of schizophrenic patients in terms of Piaget's conceptions (e.g., Blatt & Wild, 1976; Feffer, 1967; Freeman & McGhie, 1957; Kilburg & Siegel, 1973; Lidz, 1972). Feffer (1967), for example, discussed different aspects of the schizophrenic symptomatology; in particular, he focused on ideas of reference and other delusional and hallucinatory symptoms from a perspective that takes into account the process of decentering. In a similar way, Freeman and McGhie (1957) attempted to explain schizophrenic thinking in relation to the stages of cognitive development described by Piaget. They emphasized that both the degree and the type of cognitive disorder in the patient can be assumed to be linked with the degree of disturbance in human relationships. A similar opinion has been maintained by Lidz (1972, 1973), who pointed out that different types of disturbed families actively promote egocentrism. Lidz (1974) also underscored that egocentrism normally increases every time the child enters a new situation that requires new kinds of cognitive processes (probably some further accommodation) and later declines when the child has learned to cope with the new environment. Even though Lidz does not make this connection, it may be assumed that egocentrism increases during the various life crises described by Erikson (1953) and subsequently decreases when these crises have been solved in a meaningful way.

The egocentrism shown during the early teenage years, which Elkind (1970) has ascribed to the development of abstract thought, is of particular importance for understanding schizophrenic manifestations. Teenagers who experience identity problems during this sensitive period miss a meaningful decentering and retain a conviction of the unlimited power of their own thoughts (Piaget & Inhelder, 1969). Two theoretical perspectives have been advanced in an attempt to explain an increase of egocentrism in adolescence (Riley *et al.*, 1984). The first one is consistent with the Piagetian classical notion that egocentrism increases in the transition between the stages of intellectual development. The second one is based on the assumption that egocentrism increases as a consequence of parental rejection and, conversely, diminishes in relation to parental support and affection. Findings reported by Riley *et al.* are consistent with this second perspective even though they do not contradict the first one.

Recently, Rund and Blakar (1986) published the results of a study indicating that egocentrism is an often prevailing characteristic in the communication patterns of nonparanoid schizophrenic patients.

Remarkably, the similarities between egocentric thinking and primary process thinking have not been emphasized enough in the literature. When these similarities are taken into account, one easily realizes that modern assumptions related to the development of primary process thinking (Noy, 1969, 1979) closely correspond to assumptions concerning the reemergence of egocentrism in critical situations.

Among other authors who have looked upon schizophrenic symptomatology from a Piagetian perspective, Kilburg and Siegel (1973) concluded that schizophrenic patients exhibit less developed and less complex cognitive structures on the basis of an empirical study. Blatt and Wild (1976) suggested, on the other hand, that the psychotic state is associated with important correlations among the degree and type of disorder in various cognitive–perceptual functions, the level of the person's definition of self and others, and the level and nature of interpersonal relationships. Sollod and Wachtel (1980) proposed that a withdrawn, introverted individual can be regarded as a person who has not been able to develop and adequate schema concerning social reality and instead retains childish egocentric characteristics.

To assess the level of egocentrism, the Adolescent Egocentrism–Sociocentrism Scale (AES) was developed by Enright, Shukla, and Lapsley (1980). Egocentrism is operationalized in this scale in terms of three components: the personal fable, the imaginary audience, and general self-focuses. Baron (1986), who used this instrument, reported the occurrence in 157 healthy teenagers of a moderate but statistically significant correlation between AES scores and scores on a measure of more habitual dysfunctional attitudes. There are no available comparative data concerning patients suffering from schizophrenic syndromes; however, it is reasonable to assume that a similar correlation will also be found. Meanwhile, data already available support the assumption that egocentrism is a construct of great relevance for the understanding of cognitive distortions in schizophrenic patients and represent a rationale for the use of cognitive therapeutic techniques aimed at promoting decentering.

A cognitive distortion that occurs frequently in schizophrenic patients and that, as far as I know, has not been treated in terms of egocentrism—despite the fact that it may well be interpreted as reflecting egocentric thinking—is the patients' lack of awareness of the asymmetry that exists in human relationships. Jacobs (1982) drew attention to this type of cognitive disorder and maintained that the schizophrenic patient engages in interpersonal relationships with the erroneous assumption that they are symmetrical. He stated that such a mistake may arise from the following incorrect misconception: "If I love you it means that you and I become identical from the viewpoint of what we understand, what we feel and think and in the way we behave" (p. 99). It should be noted that this error may also be conceptualized in relation to the second principle of symbolic logic discussed by Matte-Blanco (1965). It is also worth mentioning that one of the earliest descriptions of the possible occurrence of this type of cognitive distortion in schizophrenic patients was made by Jung (1928) who used the term "participation mystique" to label it.

It is clear that some degree of egocentrism occurs quite commonly in schizophrenic patients; this egocentrism can without doubt be considered an important foundation for many of the cognitive disorders observed in such patients. Furthermore, the results of studies that suggest a significant correlation between egocentrism in the subject and certain fostering attitudes in the parents, as well as a correlation between egocentrism and dysfunctional attitudes in general, are in complete accord with the theoretical framework presented in the first part of this book. In addition, acknowledgement that egocentrism may be (normally) present during critical periods in older ages than early infancy—and, consequently, that failure in decentering may be a result of traumatic experiences in those periods—lends further support to the criticism of the concept of regression voiced earlier.

Since it can be safely assumed that many of the patients' cognitive distortions are characterized by egocentrism, therapeutic interventions aimed at promoting decentering become an important component in the therapeutic process. The value of these interventions has been repeatedly stressed in the cognitive psychotherapy literature in connection with depression (Beck, 1976), compulsive neuroses (Guidano & Liotti, 1983), and anxiety (Beck & Emery, 1985).

In practice, the aim of the therapeutic strategies is to teach patients to question the assumption that they are always at the center of all events (e.g., when they think, "Everyone is looking at me because I am strange") and to help them quickly shift between their own and another's perspectives to facilitate the development of interpersonal relationships. Although many of the commonly used cognitive techniques already mentioned may be effective in this respect, I expect, on the basis of my own experience, that the use of the Socratic method (complemented with appropriate homework) represents the most powerful approach. It should always be kept in mind, however, that decentering demands a shift in cognitive processes from assimilation to accommodation; consequently, it is a lengthy and difficult process. It is thus especially important that the therapist always be aware of and recognize that patients must be given adequate time and assistance to be able to adapt their thought patterns to the new insights that decentering entails. It is also worth remembering that schematic accommodation provoked by incongruent stimuli (or events or situations) engenders—as illustrated in Figure 4-1 earlier in this book—an increase in arousal and a rather intense emotional response.

## FUNDAMENTAL DYSFUNCTIONAL CONCEPTIONS

Everything written so far is based on the assumption that there are a number of basic dysfunctional meaning structures that control the patients' conceptions of themselves and their environment. These fundamental preconceptions may also be called basic dysfunctional schemata or, if one wishes, dysfunctional working models, in the terminology of Bowlby (1973a). In his definition of the (cognitive) working model, Bowlby stated that "in each individual, working models of his environments and his position within it are developed and are used to enable him to comprehend events, predict future situations and make plans" (p. 236). Bowlby hypothesized that it is not uncommon for individuals to operate simultaneously with two or more working models of themselves; he also pointed out that the hypothesis of multiple models, one of which is highly influential but relatively or completely unconscious "is no more than a version, in different terms, of Freud's hypothesis of dynamic unconscious" (p. 239). Bowlby's emphasis on prediction of the future is suggestive of the concept of "memory of the future" proposed by Ingvar (1985) to label (cognitive) programs that form the basis for anticipation and expectation was well as for short- and long-term planning and that seem to have their neurophysiological basis in the frontal–prefrontal cortex. Peterfreund (1983), who adopted Bowlby's terminology, maintained that "working model" is particularly appropriate since it clearly implies something more than a simple mental representation or map with which we evaluate our environment. Although I have no special preference and use basic schema, (silent) basic assumption, and core structure synonymously, I do not conceive of these cognitive structures as being static. Rather, I share with many others an understanding that takes into account both continuity and the possible occurrence of transformational processes.

In his discussion of working models, Peterfreund emphasized that these are altered by the information that they receive and that they become continuously updated, adapted, and readapted to maintain internal consistency. Although I accept this characterization in principle, I again emphasize that early assimilated conceptions or rules of life (whether dysfunctional or not), especially those connected with self-appraisal, are, because of their inherent nature, quite persistent. This was also stated by James (1890) during the last century. One of the most important properties of basic schemata, pointed out by Bartlett (1932) and reemphasized by Neisser (1962) and many others, is that they systematically distort new constructions. Consequently, it is to be expected that, if the basic meaning structures develop dysfunctionally, the mechanisms described earlier tend to reinforce rather than diminish dysfunctionality.

Goldfried and Robins (1983), who thoroughly discussed the concept of self-schema, called attention to its ability to (selectively) ignore all information that does not concur with one's self-image. These concepts are highly important in understanding the therapeutic process and, above all, the resistance that may be encountered with patients, which may well be explained on the basis of a cognitive theoretical approach (Liotti, 1987).

Up to the present, little has been specifically written concerning fundamental dysfunctional conceptions in patients suffering from schizophrenic syndromes. Jacobs (1980), who used the term "erroneous controlling preconceptions," listed several that he regarded as delusiogenic, that is, underlying the development of delusions. Examples of such include, "If you are not responsible for something negative then I must be to blame," "If I were to lose you I could not exist any longer," "If I need you it means that you cannot live without me." Jacobs stated that these and similar ideas are commonly encountered in children who grow up in dysfunctional family environments and that several of them clearly reflect a disturbance in individuation–separation in the sense used by Mahler and coworkers (Mahler, Pine, & Bergman, 1975).

In addition to the misconceptions described by Jacobs, others are intimately connected with the patient's self-image. Common examples include, "I am not worth anything," "I cannot be loved, thus it is meaningless that I try to relate to people," "I must be careful since others wish to harm me," "If I keep to myself I cannot be hurt," "I will not rely on appearances because I will be deceived." These and many others of a similar nature are easily recognized since they are often reflected by the patient's behavior.

It can often be observed that these and similar rules of life are largely accessible to the patient's consciousness. This is not surprising, since it has long been known in the psychoanalytical literature that the contents of the unconscious in schizophrenic patients are easily detected because they become part of the conscious during the psychosis. Accordingly, a conceptualization of the patient's basic dysfunctional assumptions to be used as a foundation for the conduct of therapy is seldom difficult.

In a discussion of basic dysfunctional assumptions in patients with personality disorders (borderline, narcissistic, etc.), J. E. Young (1986) stated that these are often unconditional. I am inclined to believe that a similar opinion is warranted concerning many basic dysfunctional assumptions in schizophrenic patients (for example, "I am unlovable," "Nobody sees me"). Although the attribute unconditional may be debatable—since, as Lundh (personal communication, 1987) pointed out, it may conceal conditions for self-acceptance and self-evaluation—I think that this concept is, nevertheless, theoretically acceptable on the basis of the discussion of primary process presented earlier. Primary process thinking, among its other characteristics, includes the absence of negation and of conditional and other qualifying conjunctions (Peterfreund, 1971). Primary process cognitions also include a tendency to replace complete perceptions with partial perceptions (as in *pars pro toto*, used by Werner, 1948, and transduction by Piaget, 1962), to confuse similarity and identity, and to do that which Arieti (1968) (with a term borrowed from linguistics; see Rosch, 1975, and Rosch, Mervis, Gray, Johnson, & Boyes-Braem, 1976, for a thorough discussion of this particular topic) calls "primary class formation"; this refers to the patient's generalization of certain qualities of the mother to other women. All these characteristics of the primary process can be explained on the basis of a cognitive theoretical model, and psychoanalytical interpretations are not necessary.

There is no doubt that a radical restructuring of the patient's personality implies a radical change of fundamental dysfunctional assumptions. For the present, very little is known concerning to what extent and in which patients such a restructuring can be achieved. It is also not known whether such a restructuring would imply an accommodation of the dysfunctional schema or any other of the transformation processes hypothesized by Neisser (1962). On the other hand, the possibilities for such a restructuring are hardly smaller for cognitive psychotherapy than for other forms of psychotherapy. At this time, I would like to express restrained optimism with regard to this question, since long-term follow-up studies of schizophrenic patients who have participated in intensive cognitive psychotherapy of the type described here are not yet available.

## ADDITIONAL THERAPEUTIC STRATEGIES AND TECHNIQUES

The disability of schizophrenic patients often includes different components. This complexity, which should always be kept in mind, and which is underscored in the holistic approach we pursue in our community-based treatment centers, is especially prevalent in patients who have a history of long periods of hospitalization, but it is not uncommon among younger patients who have not been hospitalized at all. For this reason, several therapeutic techniques are discussed in this section that are particularly valuable in treating some specific disorders in schizophrenic patients that may be encountered in ordinary psychotherapeutic situations. These techniques include self-instructional training, training in social skills, and training in problem-solving, that is, active procedures that are sharply focused on altering the dysfunctional behavior. Since social skills and problem-solving are, for practical reasons, taught more often with groups than with individuals, and since their use with schizophrenic patients does not markedly differ from their use with other kinds of clients, only a few important principles are summarized to serve as a guide for their use with individuals; I refer the reader to more specialized literature on the subject (e.g., D'Zurilla & Nezu, 1982; Trower, 1984). All these techniques are aimed at enhancing deficient ego functions from an ego-analytical perspective.

### Self-Instructional Training

All information that is received and processed, both from external sources and from internal sources, as in ruminations or imagery, is coded as pictures or as verbal sequences. It appears to be generally accepted that what is stored is not only pictorial representations of the outer world but also the verbal information (including meaning) that different messages convey. Since the meaning experienced is affected by our fundamental meaning structures, the stored representation is consequently colored by our very personal and idiosyncratic way of interpreting various situations and stimuli. Verbal representations, since they are restricted to words, are assumed to be more coherent and regular than pictorial ones, which are not only more changeable and less bound to such rules as grammar, syntax etc., but, as mentioned earlier, are less dependent on laws of time and space. The process of verbal thought, the silent inner conversation or monologue that occurs when we assess different situations or events, occasionally assumes the character of instructions, recommendations, or exhortations to ourselves. The importance of such exhortations for our efforts has been known since antiquity, but only during the last decades have they been exploited both in popular forms of therapy as positive thinking and in more scientifically based therapeutic approaches.

It has been predominantly the developmental psychologists (e.g., Piaget, Vygotsky, Luria, to mention a few) who, through their studies of the cognitive development of children, have fully appreciated and clearly stressed the importance of these often silent self-instructions for the control of our behavior. On the basis of this knowledge, it is not surprising that attempts to influence this phenomenon in a purposeful way have been introduced into serious forms of psychotherapy. This has been the case in behavioral therapy in particular, where the inner conversation is regarded as "covert events" or "concealed events," which are open to similar interventions as manifest behavior. Since the inner dialogue without doubt belongs to our cognitive processes, the strategies designed to affect or change it are rightly considered to be cognitive–behavioral techniques.

What is perhaps somewhat more surprising in this context is that this particular strategy has been one of the first to be applied systematically to chronic schizophrenic patients undergoing cognitive–behavioral therapy. Meichenbaum and coworkers are to be credited for having first used this application (Meichenbaum, 1977; Meichenbaum & Cameron, 1973).

Meichenbaum (1977) began with the assumption that we all show a tendency, to a greater or lesser extent, to engage in irrelevant thoughts and imageries, which divert our attention and thus affect our ability to concentrate. He stated that similar phenomena frequently occur in patients with schizophrenic disorders, although with the important difference that the latter were less capable of disregarding irrelevant ideation that hindered the execution of various tasks, including social interactions.

Meichenbaum and Cameron (1973) attempted to treat patients who were chronically and seriously disturbed in order to assess the feasibility of improving their conduct in interpersonal relationships by modifying their self-instructions. The patients were trained initially to recognize those situations in which they exhibited "schizophrenic" behavior and then to integrate a set of corrective self-instructions. The results of this experiment, which comprised only eight training sessions, showed that it was possible to achieve a significant improvement in the patients' behavior using this technique. The improvement was still apparent at a follow-up examination 3 months later, when it had been consolidated rather than diminished. The training of more functional self-instructions was carried out by using a modeling technique followed by practical exercises.

The same approach was used with equal success by Meyers, Mercatoris, and Sirota (1976) with a patient who spoke incoherently. After 15 training sessions, the patient was able to control his speech, and his improvement was retained 6 months later. I have observed a similar result with a patient whom I described in my earlier book (C. Perris, 1986b); after 7 years, she has not relapsed (apart from very short periods of deterioration during a more general relapse) into the markedly pathological speech she used at the beginning of treatment. In this case, I used the technique suggested by Meichenbaum, letting the patient repeat aloud the self-instructions until I felt sure that she had learned them.

Apart from the instance mentioned above, I have not used this method in the systematic way proposed by Meichenbaum to any great extent. Occasionally, I have enquired about the occurrence of dysfunctional inner monologues or dysfunctional self-instructions in the patients I have treated, and I have suggested the possibility of substituting them with more adaptive instructions, but I haven't used modeling. In these instances, the main aim has been to make patients aware of chains of thought with negative contents that interfered with his or her behavior in various situations. The patients were also taught to question the validity of the reasons alleged to be responsible for the occurrence of the thoughts and subsequently to attempt to formulate within themselves more adaptive self-instructions. I expect, however, that for more complex behavior, patients can be trained to give themselves silent instructions step by step to obtain better control of their conduct.

## Social Skills Training

There should be no doubt that significant defects in social skills are observed in both young schizophrenic patients with a short history of illness and in older patients who have experienced long periods of hospitalization. The training of social skills in schizophrenic patients has enjoyed prolonged popularity, especially in the field of rehabilitation, and an extensive literature has been accumulated, particularly with reference to the process of deinstitutionalization that has occurred (or is in progress) in many places (Bellak & Hersen, 1979; Brady, 1984; Liberman, Mueser, & Wallace, 1986). However, many of the excellent results reported in the literature are often not retained when patients are discharged from the hospital where the training has taken place; that is, the results are not generalized to cover situations that differ from those in which the patients have been trained.

A probable cause for the transience of these therapeutic gains arises from the fact that most of this training relied on role playing and modeling, without much attention being paid to the dysfunctional cognitions underlying the deficiencies. Such problems have been considered more recently, however, and modern training programs consistently attempt to correct prevailing cognitive distortions (for a review of modern research, see Trower, 1984). Training of social skills in social interactions is included in the multilevel cognitive treatment program adopted by Brenner *et al.* (1980).

For practical reasons, social skills training is usually conducted in groups, but, in my opinion, it would be malpractice to completely neglect it in individual therapy sessions. If we consider, for example, the group of younger patients who, as a result of their premorbid situation, have never been given the opportunity to use the skills we all need to live meaningfully in contact with others, it would be disastrous (and unethical) if they were unable (after perhaps years of individual therapeutic contact) to exploit their dearly won insights because they were never trained to cope with various social situations.

In cognitive psychotherapy in particular, and with reference to the assignment of homework as an important component of treatment, it is necessary to ensure that the patient does in fact possess the skills required for the execution of some social tasks in order to avoid the risk of a possible failure. For this reason, a systematic survey of the status of the patient with regard to social proficiency should always be included in the basic assessment package used at intake when judging the suitability of the candidate for psychotherapy.

The training to which I refer does not aim to teach the patient how to fill in a blank check or an employment application form, but rather to recognize and correct possible cognitive distortions that underlie social skills deficits. When rephrased in these terms, it becomes apparent that the training consists of nothing more than the application of the techniques already described to a specific problem area. To be completely meaningful, the training should also include direct learning by the patient of the most basic social communication forms, including how to express dissatisfaction, anger, affection, or approval in an appropriate manner, and how to learn to recognize, and correctly interpret, nonverbal messages.

Two approaches not yet discussed in detail may be particularly useful for identifying possible dysfunctional cognitions that hinder the patient in the performance of various social interactions and for training the most appropriate skills. The first of these is ordinary role playing; the second is the use of cognitive rehearsal. The choice of one or the other of these approaches is mostly a matter of taste, but cognitive rehearsal probably allows a greater number of specific situations to be dealt with, without constraining the patient by the structure of role playing.

Cognitive rehearsal usually implies that patients are encouraged to visualize and to report in detail a situation they regard as trying or a task they find difficult to carry out while simultaneously focusing attention on the thoughts and feelings that these situations and tasks arouse in them.

Irrespective of whether role playing or cognitive rehearsal is used, the primary objects of treatment are not the patterns of behavior themselves but the dysfunctional ideas that are revealed. The exercise is not terminated, however, until the patient has been given the opportunity to train the skills necessary for completing the task in a meaningful way. Obviously, role playing is more appropriate for this part of the training.

When role playing is used, my preference is that it be preceded by cognitive rehearsal. It is even appropriate that patient and therapist shift roles in the execution of the play so that the therapist can act as a model for the patient. It is especially valuable that the exercises mentioned so far include events or situations that may be encountered by the patient in everyday life, so that he or she can test the validity of the newly acquired insights in practice and provide the therapist with feedback, which facilitates the planning of further treatment.

## Training in Problem-Solving

McGuire and Sifneos (1970) have proposed that all psychotherapy is basically a training in problem-solving. This is particularly true of cognitive psychotherapy since focusing on problems rather than on conflicts or symptoms is one of its major characteristics.

Methods of attaining goals differ widely in the various forms of psychotherapy. A problem-solving approach can be used within the framework of individual cognitive psychotherapy although the method is most often and purposefully applied with groups. Since appropriate literature concerning its main characteristics is available (e.g., Kahney, 1986; Priestley, McGuire, Flegg, Hemsley, & Welham, 1978), a more detailed description is not provided here.

Problem-solving enjoys a long history in psychology, although it was largely ignored by behavioral psychologists for an extended period. A possible reason for this lack of interest may be that problem-solving involves cognitive processes that have for a long time been considered beyond the sphere of interest of behaviorism. The so-called cognitive revolution that has become established in psychology during the last decades implies that the importance of paying attention to problem-solving processes has become more widely recognized.

The goals of a problem-solving approach in social work have been characterized by Priestley *et al.* (1978) as follows: to help people to solve their immediate problems; to improve their ability to cope with future problems; and to develop new and increasingly better ways of doing both of these things.

D'Zurilla and coworkers (e.g., D'Zurilla & Goldfried, 1971; D'Zurilla & Nezu, 1982) have shown great interest in problem-solving with regard to disturbances in human relationships; also, important contributions have been made by other researchers, including Gordon and Gordon (1981), Spivak and coworkers (Siegel & Spivak, 1976; Spivak, Platt, & Shure, 1976), and Watzlawick (1978), to name a few.

According to D'Zurilla and Goldfried (1971), problem-solving involves five main steps: problem orientation, problem definition, the search for alternative solutions, the choice and execution of a solution, and a test of its validity. While these different subheadings could be used as the basis for structuring any therapeutic process whatsoever, I wish to underscore that they should not be regarded as completely separate cognitive processes. The fundamental faculties necessary for problem-solving include the ability to think objectively, logically, and causally (i.e., the ability to see the relationship between cause and effect) and the ability to view the problem from a wide perspective that also takes into account the opinions of others. Watzlawick particularly stressed that a common reason for our difficulties in solving different problems is that we are spellbound by established patterns of thought beyond which we cannot go. He illustrated this difficulty by way of a frequently used example; this example entails the linking of nine separate points arranged three by three with four straight lines without lifting the pen or pencil. Those who, after a little thought, solve this problem (by extending the lines beyond the figure) are capable of seeing it from a wide perspective and are not bound by established solutions. Incidentally, this exercise can be used when explaining to a patient who is beginning psychotherapy that one of the therapeutic goals will be to help him or her to learn to see problems and situations from a new, different perspective.

Spivak and coworkers have used a problem-solving approach mainly with children, but they have also reported promising results of its use with chronic patients. Results in chronic patients, however, may be rather modest (Coché & Flick, 1975). Houtz, Ringenbach, and Feldhusen (1973) studied the possible relationship of problem-solving ability to other cognitive variables. They found that problem-solving is separate from measures of school achievement and language abilities but related to logical thinking and conceptual ability. Pishkin and Williams (1977), on the other hand, pointed out that rigidity in information processing was one major contributor to problem-solving difficulties of chronic undifferentiated schizophrenics.

As mentioned earlier, one objective in socializing patients is to help them to regard their difficulties and symptoms as problems that can be solved (distancing); hence, it is clear that an attitude focused on problem-solving is maintained through the whole course of psychotherapy. In practice, this implies that the various problems that have been identified are approached systematically, most often by using the Socratic method, and that patients are encouraged to arrive at solutions whose validity they can later test. The task of the therapist in this connection is, obviously, to help patients to identify solutions other than those they may have already tried without success, without adopting the role of direct advisor.

To give a structure to the training in problem-solving, it is useful to use a schema, adapted from that proposed by Priestley *et al.* (1978); these schema should take into account not only the patient's ability to work through the steps of problem-solving but also his or her ability to identify the feelings and thoughts that occur in connection with each step. The form I use in this connection is shown in Figure 9-2.

## Additional Techniques and a Word of Caution

On several occasions in this book, I have drawn attention to the flexibility of cognitive psychotherapy and illustrated several techniques that might be exploited by the therapist in his or her work. Although different therapists may find it meaningful to use alternative methods, it should be always kept in mind that the main function of techniques is to help the therapist and the patient to identify dysfunctional cognitions by the patient and to facilitate their correction. Thus, the use of different techniques should never be allowed to become a goal in itself. Experiential diaries and Thematic Apperception Test charts (H. Perris, 1985) may be used to help patients to identify their thought disorders and to disrupt the chain of dysfunctional ideas. Also, the empty chair technique used in gestalt therapy (Arnkoff, 1981) may be useful. The interested reader is referred to the handbook published by McMullin (1986), which represents a comprehensive source book of cognitive therapeutic techniques.

Cognitive psychotherapy is not merely an amalgam of different techniques. Similarly, the qualified use of various parameters does not

| STEPS IN PROBLEM SOLVING | PATIENT'S ATTITUDE (WHAT HE/SHE KNOWS) | EMOTION(S) | THOUGHTS |
|---|---|---|---|
| PROBLEM ORIENTATION | | | |
| PROBLEM IDENTIFICATION | | | |
| PROBLEM DEFINITION | | | |
| SEARCH FOR ALTERNATIVE SOLUTIONS | | | |
| CONSIDERATION OF BOTH IMMEDIATE AND FUTURE CONSEQUENCES RELATED TO THE CHOSEN SOLUTION(S) | | | |

FIGURE 9-2. This form, used in formal training in problem-solving, allows the patient to record thoughts and emotions related to each step of the process.

make psychoanalysis with schizophrenic patients a technical form of therapy. There is, nevertheless, a high risk that the importance of technical aids is overestimated, especially by beginners, at the cost of the training that is essential to a good therapist, irrespective of his or her special field. The therapist must always be aware of why he or she wishes to use a particular method at a particular moment; he or she must also be certain that the patient not only has correctly understood a technique's purpose but also is prepared for its use. All mistakes and excesses in the use of methods invariably result in the patient feeling under greater pressure; therefore, the purposeful therapeutic relationship is put at risk. Therapeutic techniques are merely aids with which to maintain a structure and to facilitate the therapeutic process. It is important to remember that their correct, timely application cannot be learned from a handbook but must be learned through individual supervised training.

# 10

# *The Cognitive Psychotherapeutic Process*

This chapter presents a more thorough analysis of the cognitive psychotherapeutic processes discussed throughout this book. This analysis includes a discussion of the usual course of therapy with the average patient (with special emphasis on the different phases), a critical consideration of transference and countertransference reactions, and an attempt to show how the therapeutic process as a whole can be understood. Most of this discussion deals with those aspects of therapy that are relevant to schizophrenic patients; many of the issues, however, are also of concern to the therapeutic work with other types of patients.

## SEQUENTIAL ASPECTS OF THERAPY

This section describes the average sequence of events that characterizes long-term psychotherapy with patients suffering from schizophrenic disorders. Figure 10-1 shows a graphic illustration of this sequence. Although, for didactic reasons, the different phases are described separately, it should be remembered that they are in no way mandatory. Their order, length, and intensity, can, for different reasons (e.g., the actual condition of the patient at the beginning of therapy, the quality of the therapeutic relationship, and the influence of uncontrollable external factors), differ significantly from patient to patient.

The first phase, "the expectant phase," endures from some weeks to several months and includes the establishment of the therapeutic relationship. During this extremely sensitive phase, the patient alternates between trust and suspicion of the therapist and shows a pronounced approaching–withdrawing behavior. This conduct becomes even more apparent if the patient has already experienced different forms of treatment, especially those that, perhaps too optimistically, have been presented as psychotherapeutic (including periodical, supportive contact on an outpatient basis and attempts at training elementary social skills). It appears that, in this phase, the patient expe-

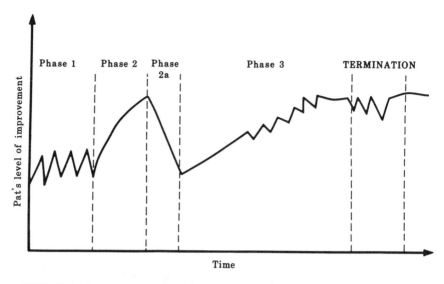

FIGURE 10-1. The successive improvement of the patient's condition during therapy is not a smooth process. This illustrates the (average) succession of phases that can be identified in the therapeutic process. The duration of each phase differs markedly from patient to patient.

riences a hope-fear dilemma similar to that considered by Burnham, Gladstone, and Gibson (1969); on the one hand, the patient wishes to believe in what the therapist says while, on the other, he or she is afraid of disappointment. One of my young patients in a rather confusional state acted out this dilemma quite manifestly. At one moment she approached me to be embraced as a little girl asking for help against her chaotic experiences; at the next moment she withdrew repeating that she could not trust anybody. In terms of behavior, many patients may exhibit an intensification of their symptomatology as if they wish to test the limits of the therapist's tolerance, or they may assert that they are well at present and do not need any help, perhaps to test the therapist's conviction that the new treatment is really worth the effort that will be required.

In this phase, the patient poses a number of delicate questions that demand careful consideration before answers are provided. One persistent question is, "Will I become completely cured if I take part in psychotherapy?" Before answering such a question, I usually take some moments to find out what the patient understands by the term "completely cured." Subsequently, I answer clearly that he or she will probably feel less vulnerable to external stresses, be more aware of potential inner resources, be more independent of other people, and be more satisfied with life than he or she has ever been before. Although no guarantee against possible relapse later in life can ever be given, I firmly believe that the patient can be given hope of withstanding stress in a much more adaptive way than earlier.

Another sensitive question that some patients ask is, "Why have I been given the chance to participate in this type of treatment?" I have found that an answer that is comprehensible to the patient and that includes a therapeutic aspect is provided by saying that I have made an overall assessment of the patient's resources and motivation and have reached the conclusion that he or she would probably benefit from the treatment. (This question is discussed further in the section on countertransference.)

Other common questions during this initial phase concern what will happen if the patient becomes worse or terminates treatment prematurely, whether compulsory measures will be taken, and whether there is a risk that the therapist will lose interest if nothing productive occurs in therapy. I assume that those who plan psychotherapy with this special group of patients are sufficiently qualified and have developed adequate sensitivity to answer these questions meaningfully.

The second phase is called "unrealistic optimism" in order to emphasize that when patients begin to feel secure in their relationship with the therapist, they also believe that all their problems will soon be solved, even without effort on their part. Such a honeymoon phase is well known in all forms of therapy. This is the most suitable time for a more thorough socialization of the patient with the major principles of cognitive psychotherapy and for training some of the more difficult techniques, remembering to apply them on issues that are rather marginal for patients. Success in tasks performed as homework will reinforce patients' hope and favor adherence to therapy.

The third phase, which is the longest, is characterized by "hope and constructive efforts." This phase often commences with a brief relapse when patients discover that they have been all too optimistic and that much work remains before a stable improvement can be achieved. For the most part, this disappointment is transient since a stable therapeutic relationship has probably already been established; in consequence, the therapist encounters no great difficulty in dealing with it. On the other hand, the importance of this short relapse should not be underestimated since it may easily lead to an interruption in therapy.

The occurrence of a relapse in this phase has more serious implications for outpatients than inpatients. Most often, patients who live with their relatives receive pressures to increase their dosage of medication or are exposed to critical comments about the use of continuing a treatment that seems to lead to their deterioration. These problems must be handled carefully. I try, as far as possible, not to resort to additional medication since I interpret this relapse as the beginning of productive work and do not like to have patients cut off from useful collaboration because of medication. Whenever possible, I prefer to resort instead to the help of an assistant therapist who can visit patients at home and speak with their relatives. I also make every effort to meet the patients' closest relatives to explain that the temporary relapse is someting that could be predicted and to mobilize their support for the patients.

As shown in Figure 10-1, the overall course of the third phase is not one of constant improvement but includes several oscillations. The fact that such oscillations are even more pronounced when one treats questions that are extremely sensitive to the patient need not be emphasized. However, it should be recognized that on these occasions the risk of interruption becomes greatest. Oscillations in themselves, however, do not necessarily imply anything negative.

To provide a time frame for the second and third phases is difficult, and I do not attempt to do so. On the other hand, it is important to underscore that the therapist must continuously match the capabilities that he gradually discovers in the patient with the goals of the treatment so that therapy does not become interminable solely because of the therapist's overconfidence in his or her own therapeutic competence. This problem has been little discussed in the literature, from which one receives the impression that therapy is regarded as more meaningful the longer it continues, regardless of the results that are actually achieved. Without doubt, this attitude reflects a newer development in psychoanalysis. However, no unequivocal reason can be found to justify decades-long psychoanalysis; as a matter of fact, at the dawn of psychoanalysis, much shorter analysis was the rule. The duration of treatment is controversial, and I have mentioned earlier the negative reaction that the question of interminable analyses has generated in some analysts.

Among those authors who have raised ethical questions regarding prolonged psychotherapy are Offenkrants and Tobin (1974) who work within a psychoanalytical–psychodynamic model. These authors work in the United States and have, therefore, been forced to consider the economic aspects of their analyses. Economics has not been the focus of their criticism, however, and more emphasis has been placed on the fact that therapy has sometimes been indefensibly long for reasons (including education) that are more important to the therapist than to the patient.

A well-known phenomenon, observed in many forms of therapy, is that when the "terminating phase" is approached, patients may exhibit more pronounced oscillations in their conditions; on occasion, these may resemble a very serious relapse. It may sometimes occur that the therapist feels that nothing at all has been achieved during therapy and that the patient is in exactly the same position as at the start of treatment. In psychoanalysis and in psychodynamic therapy, such a relapse at the end of therapy has often been interpreted as an expression of the patient's resistance to giving up dependence, thus reflecting separation anxiety.

That such a temporary impairment also occurs in connection with cognitive psychotherapy and with the same implications need not be questioned. It is thus of great importance that each termination in therapy is prepared carefully and well in advance. In this respect, however, cognitive psychotherapy shows advantages over other forms of therapy. First, active collaboration that characterizes the therapeutic relationship represents in itself a block against too much dependence; also, follow-up sessions are normally included in the treatment program, so termination is not experienced as quite as decisive by the patient.

With regard to a possible temporary deterioration in the patient's condition at the end of therapy, I emphasize that the possibility of dynamic interpretation should never render the therapist blind to the occurrence of real situations of stress in the environment that the patient assesses quite realistically and that cause the condition.

## TRANSFERENCE AND COUNTERTRANSFERENCE

With a certain degree of simplification, one might say that the core of the therapeutic process in classical psychoanalysis is the development and resolution of the transference neurosis. There are few aspects of psychotherapeutic work with schizophrenic patients that have received more attention in the early literature than the occurrence of transference and countertransference reactions and their treatment. That these issues have generated so much interest is easily understood; the treatment of psychotic patients, when psychotropic drugs were unavailable, placed hitherto unexpected demands on analysts who were primarily trained to treat neurotics in a relatively preestablished setting, with a major emphasis on transference. When later confrontations with psychotics occurred, an initial goal was the establishment of a relationship that would help to withdraw them from their psychotic world rather than passively and neutrally to allow a transference to develop with a freely associating patient reclined on a couch. It was during their pioneering period that a high degree of activity by the therapist and the importance of positive transference were stressed (e.g., Federn, 1943; Fromm-Reichmann, 1939, 1948).

When new hypotheses on the psychopathogenic process in schizophrenic patients were later proposed, and the significance of early object relationships began to prevail, attention was redirected to some extent from transference and countertransference in the traditional sense to the therapeutic relationship itself. Since it is almost unequivocally asserted that the latter should be a relationship characterized by basic trust, with the therapist functioning as a foster parent, it follows that transference in the original analytical meaning has had to be redefined. One current assumption to justify Freud's negative opinion of the schizophrenic patient's capability to develop a "true transference" is that Freud did not focus his attention on very early object relations and was, therefore, unaware of the possible development of a different type of transference, the "object transference."

It is my impression that many therapists who work with schizophrenic patients have accepted Federn's observation (1943) that psychotic patients almost offer their positive transference and the therapists have adopted his recommendation that this transference must be encouraged and cultivated. To a certain extent, this viewpoint is supported in the modern literature by the emphasis that is placed on the "holding" function of the therapist.

This long introduction provides a prologue to my next proposition, which is that every form of psychotherapy leads to the type and degree of transference reaction that it itself tends to generate. Of course, this idea is not new. In 1949, Rioch suggested that the character of transference illusions is determined, to a great extent, by the personality of the analyst. My proposal is, therefore, nothing more than an extension of Rioch's ideas, which I used as a base from which to address the question of transference and countertransference from a cognitive psychotherapeutic perspective.

Of course, transference and countertransference reactions always occur, and they have been seriously considered in cognitive therapy. The difference is that they are not given the same priority in cognitive therapy for understanding the therapeutic process; also, they are not considered to be an expression of constant searching for a source of satisfaction of suppressed needs that were not fulfilled by the parents (particularly the mother) during childhood. Sullivan's ideas (1954) on transference lie closest to those of cognitive psychotherapy. The concept of transference (and everything it implied) was never incorporated in his interpersonal theory, and he preferred to talk about "parataxic distortions" (i.e., a type of cognitive error) in describing the same phenomenon. According to Sullivan, these distortions reflect the patterns of relationships that a person has experienced earlier in life, especially with respect to his or her parents, and, thus, constitute some of the person's habitual characteristics, including the way in which he or she relates to other people. A similar opinion has been expressed by Rioch (1949), who stated that transference reflects all the experiences a person has had in relationships with other people of importance and not only in the relationship with his or her parents.

Horney's viewpoint (1950), which is closer to Sullivan's than Freud's, also has certain points of contact with the cognitive therapeutic interpretation. Like Sullivan, Horney discarded all theories concerning the repetition compulsion and maintained that, when an individual's personality develops in a certain direction, he or she is able to exhibit only specific patterns of behavior in given situations. In cognitive terms, one might say that a person's conduct in relation to others in a particular situation is determined by his or her basic meaning structures. Greenson and Wexler (1969) complained that, according to the Kleinian school of thought, everything emanating from the patient is transference; they believed that, with such a broad definition, the term became deprived of its usefulness. Although this Kleinian opinion is regrettable from a traditional analytic perspective, it is quite consistent with a cognitive therapeutic interpretation of the relationship between patient and therapist.

From a cognitive psychotherapeutic perspective, in fact, transference reactions are regarded as being nothing more than cognitive distortions that are determined partly by an activation of well-established schemata and partly by the distortions in comprehending and processing of information that are committed more or less habitually by each of us. In this connection, it is easy to understand that, in questions concerning a patient's transference patterns, great importance is given to a correct conceptualization of the patient's rules of life and cognitive distortions; at the same time, the therapist is always alert for the various characteristics of himself or herself that can act as cues in activating silent meaning structures.

It should also be clear that in cognitive psychotherapy (as in the cultural psychoanalytical approach of Horney), it is assumed that the dysfunctional schemata that control different types of transference reactions may have developed at times other than very early in life.

Mallinger (1974) discussed transference thoroughly from a cognitive perspective and illustrated, with examples, some of the cognitive mechanisms that promote an understanding of both the occurrence of transference in general in human interactions and the phenomenon known in psychoanalytical terms as "transference resistance." An interesting viewpoint, which Mallinger defended, is that transference is to a great extent the product of our inherent inclination to categorize; it thereby facilitates predictions, which, in the long run, allow us to survive.

Since transference reactions are interpreted in terms of dysfunctional cognitions, it follows that they are treated, as soon as they become evident, with the same techniques and following the same strategies described earlier. The difficulties that may arise in this treatment (e.g., resistance to change) are discussed in more detail in later sections (see "The Path to Insight" and "Resistance to Changing Basic Schemata," below).

Countertransference is also interpreted in the same terms. Thus, it is assumed that the reactions of the therapists are determined by the special schemata activated in them by contact with the patient. Consequently, it is important that therapists continuously observe the fundamental assumptions that affect their conduct and that all questions that are raised in this context be dealt with in the supervision. These questions may include, as indicated earlier, why a certain patient has been accepted for therapy in preference to another, why therapy is discontinued or prolonged, and what are the therapist's motives and expectations. A very high risk of negative countertransference reactions exist when the therapy with a certain patient is intended to satisfy some of the therapist's less conscious needs or wishes. It should be noted, however, that several analysts, including Cohen (1952), Heiman (1950), Little (1957), and Spotnitz (1986), have pointed out that the use of countertransference may become an important tool of the therapist. Such an opinion applies in particular to therapy with the schizophrenic patient.

## CORRECTING COGNITIVE DISTORTIONS

The process that finally leads to a radical restructuring of the patients' understanding of themselves and their relationship (past, present, and future) to the environment must include an alteration or dissolution of prevailing dysfunctional meaning structures and their replacement with others that are more functional or adaptive. In other words, the balance must shift from being prevalently assimilative to becoming (during the therapeutic process) prevalently accommodative. This process can be, for the sake of convenience, divided into two parts, even though these parts are not independent of each other: correction of cognitive distortions and restructuration of the most basic schemata.

Correction of cognitive distortions refers to the change that is gradually produced in the way the patient understands and processes both external and internal stimuli. Emphasis in the therapeutic work is placed on the assistance given to the patient to help him or her to recognize, challenge, and correct the various cognitive distortions that characterize the habitual manner in which he or she deals with information, whether external or internal. In principle, it can be asserted that this component is one of the most important in the therapeutic process; by itself, it is sufficient to lead to a neutralization and, perhaps, a dissolution of more central dysfunctional schemata. The following discussion shows how this process can be conceptualized, based on certain theoretical ideas discussed earlier.

It is generally accepted that our more central schemata (core structures or core constructs), that is, those that concern our self-appraisal or self-image in relation to our surroundings, are maintained by selectively attended, confirmatory feedback information (i.e., self-confirmatory bias). The process by which these structures obtain the information they need to remain intact is influenced markedly by the pervasiveness and intensity of an individual's cognitive distortions with respect to the reception and processing of all the information with which he or she comes into contact.

Some of the more common distortions found in patients with schizophrenic disorders have been described earlier, and a few examples have been illustrated in Figure 3-3. It is certain that the longer patients commit such errors, the more their basic dysfunctional schemata will become established; on the other hand, these errors will decline as patients are trained to correct their distortions. Once again, it can be maintained that, in our patients, assimilative processing prevails.

Therapeutic correction may occur directly or indirectly, by first inducing decentering or by training the patient to utilize various strategies for problem-solving. Whichever of the available techniques is chosen, its primary purpose is always to alter the cognitive distortions that continuously activate and support the more central dysfunctional schemata.

In an attempt to explain how a modification of cognitive distortions can lead to a dissolution of the dysfunctional core schemata, I have—in agreement with Guidano and Liotti (1983)—adopted a metaphorical version of the theory of growth of knowledge presented by Lakatos (1970). Since this analysis is described in detail in one of my earlier books (C. Perris, 1986b) and is also thoroughly treated by Guidano and Liotti, only a short (and extremely simplified) account will be given here.

The terms "dogmatic (or metaphysical) core," "research program," and "protective belt" are central to an understanding of the model proposed by Lakatos. According to the theory, the hard core is composed of metaphysical ideas and may not be affected by research. The core is therefore shielded by a protective belt, which consists of marginal testable hypotheses. The hard core determines various research programs that, in turn, consist of methodological rules; some tell us what paths of research to pursue (positive heuristic) and others what paths to avoid (negative heuristic). If the results of the investigations carried out according to the research programs are negative (i.e., they tend to not support the basic assumption of the dogmatic core), the protective belt is reinforced (and new, *ad hoc*, hypotheses are advanced). If they are positive, the protective belt is enlarged, and the core expands to a certain extent. The hard core is dissolved completely when it is no longer capable of generating new, meaningful hypotheses (i.e., cannot make use of any further positive heuristic results). In terms of the therapeutic process, the dogmatic core of the Lakatos model may be likened to the patient's most fundamental schema, that is, those meaning structures that determine how the patient regards himself or herself in relation to the environment.

"There is no love in this world" is a dysfunctional conviction. Around this core, the individual collects a series of "secondary assumptions" that correspond to the protective belt of Lakatos—for instance, "Nothing is to be gained by trying to make contact with others since no one will ever like me." (To a certain extent, more defined psychopathological symptoms may also be considered as part of the protective belt.) Farther out on the periphery, the research program determined by the secondary assumption reported above, for example, is carried out. Lakatos's positive heuristics might, in this instance, be compared with the particular manner in which the patient comprehends reality in different situations—that is, by means of various self-confirmatory cognitive distortions. The more selectively the cognitive distortions affect the conception of reality, the lesser the role played by the protective belt, and the hard core becomes even more established. Neutralization of the hard core (that is, its dissolution) can be assumed to occur only when it no longer has access to research programs that (pursuing a path of positive heuristic) are able to validate the fundamental conceptions through feedback, that is, when the cognitive distortions committed by the patient are completely corrected and his or her conception of reality becomes completely changed. Figure 10-2 shows a graphic illustration of this process.

Expressed in simpler terms and with reference to my premises, it may be stated that a dissolution of dysfunctional schemata can be expected to occur when these no longer receive the confirmatory (dysfunctional) feedback information on which their continued existence depends, that is, when accommodative processes begin to prevail, at least to a certain extent, over assimilative ones. It is on such an interpretation of the therapeutic process that short-term cognitive psychotherapy is primarily based. In all probability, what takes place is not the complete replacement of dysfunctional schemata with new ones, but rather the deprivation of further nourishment of the former,

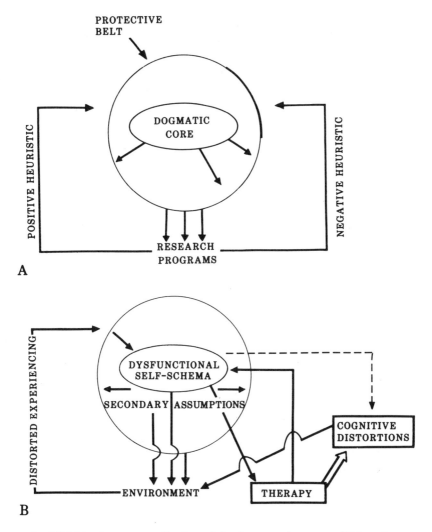

FIGURE 10-2. A conceptualization of the therapeutic process (B) based on an analogy to Lakatos's theory (1970) of research programs (A). Adapted from C. Perris, 1986b.

which remain only slightly modified, along with the development of a new, more functional schema (that is, the process called displacement by Neisser, 1962). During therapy, the patient gains insight into the dysfunctional character of his or her rules of life or working models and learns a series of strategies to counteract their possible continuing negative influence. In psychoanalytically oriented therapy, this type of insight would probably be regarded as a form of intellectualization on the higher level of defense mechanisms proposed by Vaillant (1985). This kind of intellectualization, which belongs to mature mechanisms, refers to the ability of the patient to consciously exploit the insights gained in therapy to restrain the occurrence of new symptoms in situations of stress (e.g., when a patient has learned to recognize and counteract automatic negative thoughts instead of giving way to negative feelings).

## THE PATH TO INSIGHT

The overall goals of cognitive psychotherapy, when the ultimate aim is to produce a radical and permanent reconstruction of the patient's personality, are to assist the patient to identify the dysfunctionality of his or her core misconceptions and to exchange them for new ones that are more realistic and functional. It is thus not sufficient that the dysfunctional schemata become inactivated by the methods described in the previous section. New functional fundamental concepts must also be developed if a thorough cognitive reconstruction is to be achieved; that is, if the process called integration by Neisser (1962) is to occur.

Mahoney (1980) compared this reconstruction with a "personal (cognitive) revolution" and used Kuhn's theories (1962) concerning revolutions in knowledge and the "paradigm shift" to describe it. Since this comparison is pertinent, it is worth considering Kuhn's approach to the question of the growth of knowledge in more detail. This should make clear in what respect "scientific revolution" and "paradigm shift" are relevant concepts in the description of the therapeutic process.

A suitable starting point for this short digression is a clarification of the term "paradigm." Kuhn applied this term to the widely recognized advances in knowledge (i.e., general theories) that, for a period of time, represented models for the formulation and solution of problems within a certain scientific field. In other words, the paradigm provides the scientist with a perspective from which to orient himself or herself in the work. It offers fundamental assumptions concerning the nature of the world as well as theories and techniques with which to approach different problems. In much simpler terms, the paradigm can be regarded as a kind of searchlight that illuminates the path to knowledge.

Kuhn's purpose for the paradigm theory was to provide an explanation of how scientific knowledge evolves and changes. The prevailing idea was that knowledge grows through the addition of facts to a continuously expanding body. According to Kuhn, this cumulative, "normal" change is, however, not the only way in which knowledge grows. He maintained that it is also necessary to take into account the occurrence of scientific revolutions, implying that fundamental scientific conceptions (i.e., the hitherto valid paradigm) are completely replaced. An example is when the belief that the earth was stationary at the center of the universe was discarded in favor of a model in which it orbits around the sun.

A paradigm shift of this kind occurs, according to Kuhn, when the earlier paradigm ceases to function satisfactorily in investigations of that part of reality to which it refers. An important aspect of the change that takes place is that the paradigm shift not only entails the replacement of prevailing theories by others, but it also questions the methods, facts, and criteria concerning what is acceptable knowledge. Another theorist, Feyerabend (1962), maintained that the introduction of a new theory is associated with changes of perspective with regard to both the observable and nonobservable properties of the world. A further aspect of Kuhn's understanding of the paradigm shift is worth emphasizing, namely that different paradigms differ not only in what they deal with, since they are directed not only toward reality, but also toward the knowledge that produced them.

If we now leave the field of knowledge and consider humanity, we quickly discover that the growth of our collective knowledge (including how we regard ourselves in relation to the world in which we live, how we think and feel in various situations, how we approach and solve problems, etc.) and the growth of our intellectual processes follow a pattern very similar to that described by Kuhn. Our basic schemata, working models, or rules of life are paradigms that, as Lundh (1983) pointed out, determine both the way in which we define ourselves and our world and the particular way in which we act in certain situations (e.g., in the selective choice of relevant information and in our acting upon it). It is a point of general agreement that our knowledge increases cumulatively, especially when we are young. Yet again Piaget's conception of assimilation describes how we incorporate new information into our developing cognitive structures. Even for our basic schemata, periods arise when this "normal" growth of knowledge no longer functions, and changes must take place in our basic conceptions themselves—that is, they must be able to accommodate new facts and new knowledge. It is not unreasonable to assert that each major accommodation represents a miniature revolution in the basic schema, entailing a certain shift of perspective in the way in which we regard ourselves and our environment.

On the basis of this assumption, it is not difficult to imagine that the radical alteration in our core schemata that is expected to result from successful psychotherapy is an even more extensive personal revolution. This change thus implies that dysfunctional conceptions must be discarded (i.e., the old personal paradigms must be rejected) and, with them, all the distorted mechanisms that have been used to sustain a feedback of confirmatory information must go. Furthermore, this personal revolution will, in analogy with the consequences of paradigm shifts in science mentioned above, generalize retrospectively to the knowledge that produced the shifts.

## Progress through Fluctuations

Figure 10-1 shows that oscillations in the patient's condition normally occur during the third phase of treatment. Such oscillations are also encountered when one approaches topics that are sensitive for the patient; they are not necessarily negative events. If we stretch the analogy of Kuhn's scientific revolutions a little further, we find that even these fluctuations can be compared with the phenomena that occur when a paradigm begins to lose its explanatory power and a revolutionary discovery is anticipated. Kuhn (1962) expressed this as follows: "Discoveries originate in the awareness of an anomaly, that is, the recognition that nature in some way violates the paradigm-controlled expectations that guide normal science" (p. 52, my translation to English from the Swedish version). Applied to patients during therapy, one might envisage that fluctuations occur at the point where they become conscious (i.e., gain insight) that something is wrong in their basic assumptions (i.e., when a critical anomaly arises). Kuhn pointed out that "although history hardly preserves their names, it is undoubtedly the case that some people have been forced to abandon research because they could not tolerate 'crises'" (p. 71, my translation). On the same basis, we can easily imagine that a patient might drop out of therapy during such a period of unbalance.

An indication that these fluctuations need not be necessarily regarded as negative events can be found in modern physics. Prigogine (1980) proposed, in his theories of dissipative structures, that a loss of equilibrium at a critical level helps to drive open systems toward a reconstruction of their ordering processes ("order through fluctuations," p. 781). Applied to therapy, one might say that disequilibrium or fluctuations occur when radical reconstruction in the patient's working models proceeds and that this unbalance represents a thrust forward. Mahoney (1985), however, drew attention to the fact that, in physics, one has to be aware of the risk that the open system may become locked in a position of unbalance that not only does not lead forward but may also be regressive when its processes for self-organization are limited. Without doubt, the therapeutic process can stagnate in a similar fashion or may even exhibit regression.

## Resistance to Changing Basic Schemata

To achieve a radical reconstruction of basic dysfunctional assumptions in a patient is, if we continue to use the simile of scientific revolution, as difficult as it is for a new paradigm to become accepted by the scientific community. As pointed out in the earlier section concerned with Lakatos' theory, every attack on the dogmatic core is associated with a thickening of the protective belt, that is, a resistance to change.

The term "resistance" occupies an important position in psychoanalytically oriented psychotherapy, where it refers primarily to a defense against the revelation of suppressed impulses and conflictory ideas during therapy. Its occurrence is usually regarded as a suitable starting point for a deeper analysis of the possible relationships between past experiences and present events or for elucidating problems of transference. Since the significance of resistance is quite different in cognitive psychotherapy, it is important to point out where this difference lies.

My remarks are restricted to resistance that represents a specific obstacle to a reconstruction of the patient's basic schemata without taking into account other aspects of this phenomenon that lie at a more superficial level (e.g., resistance that depends on secondary gains or on a misuse of therapeutic techniques). The reader who desires a deeper discussion of the differences in interpretations of the concept of resistance between different schools of therapy are referred to Wachtel (1982), Ellis (1983–1984), and Liotti (1987).

Since the goal of cognitive psychotherapy is an alteration of basic dysfunctional schemata, all resistance against such a change is completely normal. On the basis of the proposal that the schemata referred to are not only cognitive but also include meaning, it is readily concluded (e.g., Fransella, 1985; Liotti, 1987; Mahoney, 1982) that resistance to change tends rather to preserve meaning than to prevent unconscious conflicts from becoming conscious. Mahoney (1985) stressed that the preservation of our basic conceptions can, from an evolutionary viewpoint, be considered to be meaningful for survival; it is not impossible that, through "feedforward," they promote a resistance to change. A similar conception has been maintained, as mentioned earlier, by Liotti *et al.*(1984) and Liotti (1987).

As mentioned earlier, the function of the core meaning structures as a template against which all new information is matched. It has been emphasized how this new information is often selected so that it becomes self-confirmatory. In all probability, it is these self-confirmatory cognitive distortions that Mahoney had in mind when he discussed feedforward mechanisms. Clearly, I do not assert that no change at all ever occurs; changes in our basic schemata are both possible and do take place, even though they arouse a marked affective response.

Two conditions are important though: that the changes do not significantly affect our identities, and that the structure that includes the meaning of important emotional experiences is replaced by a new one that permits the conscious processes of these experiences.

Resistance to changes in self-image has been repeatedly reported in experiments by social psychologists (e.g., Markus & Sentis, 1982), and Mahoney (1985) has stated that attempts to produce alterations are occasionally regarded by the patient to be a threat to his or her identity, even when the change would probably lead to diminished emotional suffering.

The resistance that one meets in cognitive psychotherapy when one approaches the core of the patient's dysfunctional conceptions probably does not differ, phenomenologically, from that described in psychoanalytic psychotherapy. However, the methods used by the therapist to work through it do differ.

In this respect, cognitive psychotherapy shows a certain advantage over psychoanalytical psychotherapy, since the scientific method the patient is trained to use during therapy is felt to be less threatening than a confrontation, through interpretation, with assumed deep-lying conflicts that are indicated by indirect evidence alone. Kelly, Ellis, and Beck, as well as most of the other cognitive therapists, insist that the only route to progress is to allow the patient to examine the validity of his or her convictions by a method that involves the testing of hypotheses. As I have argued earlier at some length, the value of this approach is that hypotheses do not have to be believed, which allows them to be tested without the patient feeling a threat coming from the outside expert.

The disadvantage linked with the use of interpretations by the therapist concerns the contributions these might have to confirming patients' dysfunctional assumption that others are better at ascribing meanings to their experiences than they are themselves. Lakatos has, with poignancy, described this situation as "to receive the grace of proven truth in the course of mystical communication" (1970, p. 99). It is likely that a reconstruction of the patient's fundamental patterns of thought is promoted in a meaningful way if a dissonance is established between his or her basic dysfunctional conceptions and reality in a way that can be tested. It should be observed, however, that I regard progress not so much as proving early assumptions false but as the ability to test the validity of new insights.

## Reconstruction of Earlier Experiences

Many cognitive therapists hold the opinion, as do gestalt therapists, that an examination of the patient's past is of little value in therapy, which should be focused exclusively on the here and now. Such a view should in no way be interpreted to mean that Beck or Perls (both psychoanalysts), for example, were ignorant of the importance of earlier experiences in the development of psychopathological syndromes and even less to mean that cognitive therapists refrain from pointing out to the patient the connection between present problems and events of significance in the past, especially those related to interactions with important others. Beck's cognitive therapy for depression has been introduced primarily as a short-term treatment of moderately severe conditions, and it is a generally accepted procedure in such therapies that only a single problem area is focused on in order to avoid entanglement in an aimless prolonged course of treatment.

Without doubt, the situation is quite different when a radical reconstruction of the patient's basic schemata is planned from the very start and when the therapy is anticipated to take a long time. When approaching severely disturbed schizophrenic patients, it would be almost impossible to avoid a consideration of past memories. At present, a growing group of cognitive therapists who mainly treat severely disturbed patients (including my own group; see also Liotti, 1988) maintain that the self-knowledge one wishes to promote in a patient through long-term cognitive psychotherapy would be incomplete if he or she were not given the opportunity to recognize the historical dimension of life.

Cognitive psychotherapists do not need to use the concept of "screening memories," or to be reminded (Arieti, 1968; Furlan, 1984) that the patient's report of the historical truth is nothing more than a distorted recollection of material events, since such knowledge is the very ground of any schema theory. However, when the patient lacks a well-integrated schema or script for a certain aspect of behavioral response (as might be the case for patients with severe personality disorders), and when the extent of dysfunctionality in the self-image is particularly pervasive, it becomes necessary to help him or her to adopt a more nuanced attitude toward the various events and experiences that may have contributed to the development of the disorder. In this process of reappraisal, it is crucial to avoid the identification of scapegoats in the patient's past, to focus on the way in which dysfunctional convictions have been incorporated in different situations, and to focus on the way in which they have been continuously reconfirmed. Dwelling on traumatic experiences will not help the patient. What is necessary is that he or she is assisted in changing perspective, since it is well known from studies on recollection carried out in other fields of research (e.g., Anderson & Pichert, 1978) that a change of perspective is accompanied by a change in the retrieval process that allows a more differentiated memory of the past to emerge.

An important aspect in this reappraisal process is that the patient is made aware of the capabilities he or she already possesses and has already used to deal with various situations in the past. The value of such connection rests in the fact that the patient is offered a chance to see present or future efforts in terms of personal history.

Another important component in reconstruction, at another level, concerns the experiences that the patient has had in connection with acute psychotic episodes. Regardless of the psychotherapeutic context, one should never leave a past psychotic episode unattended, but should always allow the patient the opportunity to integrate even painful experiences in the continuum of his or her life.

## CONCLUSION

The intent of this book has been to present in some detail an integrative, holistic approach using cognitive psychotherapy, both as a basis for milieu therapy and as an individualized approach to treating severely disturbed patients suffering from schizophrenic syndromes. It has been my aim to stress that cognitive psychotherapy represents a suitable framework to develop a flexible milieu therapeutic program and to give an appropriate structure to effective milieu therapeutic interventions. In the last part of the book, I have described in some detail the individualized use of cognitive psychotherapy. It must be emphasized that cognitive psychotherapy can, when used in an individual format, represent an answer to the search for a nonreductionistic psychotherapeutic approach that takes into account the heterogeneity of the schizophrenic disorders and allows therapists to cope with their complexity.

It is my firm conviction that the assumptions concerning the development and manifestations of dysfunctional cognitions in schizophrenic patients, as well as the implementation of the therapeutic work described, can easily be further elaborated to suit the needs of other categories of severely troubled patients (e.g., those suffering from other psychotic conditions or those presenting with severe personality disorders), which have not been taken into account in this book.

# References

Abramson, L. Y., Seligman, M. E. P., & Teasdale, J. D. (1978). Learned helplessness in humans: Critique and reformulation. *Journal of Abnormal Psychology, 87,* 49-74.

Adams, G. R., & Jones, R. M. (1982). Adolescent egocentrism: Exploration into possible contributions of parent-child relations. *Journal of Youth and Adolescence, 11,* 25-31.

Adams, H. E., Malatesta, V., Brantley, P. J., & Turkat, I. D. (1981). Modification of cognitive processes: A case study of schizophrenia. *Journal of Consulting and Clinical Psychology, 49,* 460-464.

Ainsworth, M. D. S. (1972). Attachment and dependency: A comparison. In J. Gewirtz (Ed.), *Attachment and dependency.* Washington, DC: Winston.

Ainsworth, M. D. S., Blehar, M. C., Waters, E., & Wall, S. (1978). Patterns of attachment: Assessed in the strange situation and at home. Hillsdale, NJ: Lawrence Erlbaum.

Alanen, Y. (1958). The mothers of schizophrenic patients. *Acta Psychiatrica et Neurologica Scandinavica, 33* (Suppl 124).

American Psychiatric Association (1980). *Diagnostic and statistical manual of mental disorders: DSM-III.* Washington, DC: Author.

American Psychiatric Association (1987). *Diagnostic and statistical manual of mental disorders: DSM-III-R.* Washington, DC: Author.

Anastasi, A. (1958). Heredity, environment, and the question "how?" *Psychological Reviews, 65,* 197-208.

Anderson, C. M., Reiss, D. J., & Hogarty, G. E. (1986). *Schizophrenia and the family.* New York, London: Guilford Press.

Anderson, R. C., & Pichert, J. W. (1978). Recall of previously unrecallable information following a shift in perspective. *Journal of Verbal Learning and Verbal Behaviour, 17,* 1-12.

Andreasen, N. C. (1987). The diagnosis of schizophrenia. *Schizophrenia Bulletin, 13,* 9-22.

Angermeyer, M. C. (1982). The association between family atmosphere and hospital care of schizophrenic patients. *British Journal of Psychiatry, 141,* 1-11.

Arendt, H. (1978). *Thinking.* New York: Harcourt Brace Jovanovich.

Arieti, S. (1948). Special logic of schizophrenic and other types of autistic thought. *Psychiatry, 11,* 325-338.

Arieti, S. (1955). *Interpretation of schizophrenia.* New York: Brunner.

Arieti, S. (1957). The two aspects of schizophrenia. *Psychiatric Quarterly, 31,* 403-416.

Arieti, S. (1959). Schizophrenic thought. *American Journal of Psychotherapy, 13,* 537-552.

Arieti, S. (1962a). Psychotherapy of schizophrenia. *Archives of General Psychiatry, 6,* 112-122.

Arieti, S. (1962b). Hallucinations, delusions, and ideas of reference treated with psychotherapy. *American Journal of Psychotherapy, 16,* 56-60.

Arieti, S. (1964). The rise of creativity: From primary to tertiary process. *Contemporary Psychoanalysis, 1,* 51-68.

Arieti, S. (1966). Emphasis on the healthy aspects of the patient in psychoanalysis. *American Journal of Psychoanalysis, 26,* 198-200.

Arieti, S. (1968). The psychodynamics of schizophrenia: A reconsideration. *American Journal of Psychotherapy, 22,* 366-381.

Arieti, S. (1969). The meeting of the inner and the external world: In schizophrenia, everyday life and creativity. *American Journal of Psychoanalysis, 39,* 115-130.

Arieti, S. (1972). Psychodynamic search of common values with the schizophrenic. In D. Rubinstein & Y. O. Alanen (Eds.), *Psychotherapy of schizophrenia* (pp. 94-100). Amsterdam: Excerpta Medica.

Arieti, S. (1974a). Individual psychotherapy of schizophrenia. In S. Arieti (Ed.), *American handbook of psychiatry* (2nd ed., vol. 3, pp. 627-651). New York: Basic Books.

Arieti, S. (1974b). The cognitive-volitional school. In S. Arieti (Ed.), *American handbook of psychiatry* (2nd ed., vol. 1, pp. 877-903). New York: Basic Books.

Arieti, S. (1974c). An overview of schizophrenia from a predominantly psychological approach. *American Journal of Psychiatry, 131,* 241-249.

Arieti, S. (1974d). Schizophrenia: The psychodynamic mechanisms and the psychostructural forms. In S. Arieti (Ed.), *American handbook of psychiatry* (2nd ed., vol. 3, pp. 551-587). New York: Basic Books.

Arieti, S. (1976). The psychotherapeutic approach to schizophrenia. In D. Kemali, G. Bartholini, & D. Richter (Eds.), *Schizophrenia today* (pp. 245-257). Oxford: Pergamon.

Arieti, S. (1981). The family of the schizophrenic and its participation in the therapeutic task. In S. Arieti (Ed.), *American handbook of psychiatry* (2nd ed., vol. 7, pp. 271-284). New York: Basic Books.

Arieti, S., & Lorraine, S. (1972). The therapeutic assistant in treating the psychotic. *International Journal of Psychiatry, 10,* 7-22.

Aristotle (1958). *The pocket Aristotle* (transl., W. D. Ross). New York: Pocket Books.

Arlow, J. A. (1958). Panel: The psychoanalytic theory of thinking. *Journal of the American Psychoanalytical Association, 6,* 143-153.

Armbruster, B., Gross, G., & Huber, G. (1983). Long-term prognosis and course of schizoaffective, schizophreniform and cycloid psychoses. *Psychiatria Clinica, 16,* 156-168.

Arnkoff, D. B. (1981). Flexibility in practicing cognitive therapy. In G. Emery, S. D. Hollon, & R. C. Bedrosian (Eds.), *New directions in cognitive therapy: A casebook* (pp. 203-223). New York: Guilford Press.

Austrin, H. R., & Aubuchon, D. J. (1979). Locus of control and trust in parents: A preliminary study. *Journal of Clinical Psychology, 35,* 304-305.

Azima, H. (1963). Object-relations therapy of schizophrenic states: Technique and theory. In *Psychiatric research reports #17.* Washington, DC: American Psychiatric Association.

Azima, H., Wittkower, E. D., & LaTendresse, J. (1958). Object-relations therapy in schizophrenic states. *American Journal of Psychiatry, 115,* 60-62.

Balint, M. (1937). Early developmental stages of the ego: Primary object love. In M. Balint (Ed.), *Primary love and psychoanalytic technique.* New York: Liveright (1965).

Bandura, A. (1978). The self system in reciprocal determinism. *American Psychologist, 33,* 344-358.

Bannister, D. (1960). Conceptual structure of thought-disordered schizophrenics. *Journal of Mental Science, 108,* 825-842.

Bannister, D. (1977). The logical requirements of research into schizophrenia. *Schizophrenia Bulletin, 4,* 72-77.

Baron, P. (1986). The relation between egocentrism and dysfunctional attitudes in adolescents. *British Journal of Cognitive Psychotherapy, 4,* 71-77.

Bartlett, F. C. (1932). *Remembering: A study in experimental and social psychology.* Cambridge: Cambridge University Press.

Basch, M. F. (1977). Developmental psychology and explanatory theory in psychoanalysis. *Annual of Psychoanalysis, 5,* 229-263.

Bateson, G., Jackson, D. D., Haley, J., & Weakland, J. (1956). Toward a theory of schizophrenia. *Behavioral Science, 1,* 251-264.

Baun, M. M., Bergstrom, N., Langston, N. F., & Thoma, L. (1984). Physiological effects of human/companion animal bonding. *Nursing Research, 33,* 126-129.

Beck, A. M., & Katcher, A. H. (1984). A new look at pet-facilitated therapy. *Journal of the American Veterinary Medicine Association, 184,* 414-421.

Beck, A. T. (1952). Successful outpatient psychotherapy of a chronic schizophrenic with a delusion of borrowed guilt. *Psychiatry, 15,* 305-312.

Beck, A. T. (1963-1964). Thinking and depression. Part I and II. *Archives of General Psychiatry, 9,* 324-333; *10,* 561-571.

Beck, A. T. (1970). Cognitive therapy: Nature and relation to behavior therapy. *Behavior Therapy, 1,* 184-200.

Beck, A. T. (1976). *Cognitive therapy and the emotional disorders.* New York: International Universities Press.

Beck, A. T. (1985). Cognitive therapy, behavior therapy, psycho-analysis, and pharmacotherapy: A cognitive continuum. In M. J. Mahoney & A. Freeman (Eds.), *Cognition and psychopathology* (pp. 325-347). New York: Plenum Press.

Beck, A. T., & Emery, G. (1985). *Anxiety disorders and phobias.* New York: Basic Books.

Beck, A. T., Rush, A. J., Shaw, B. F., & Emery, G. (1979). *Cognitive therapy of depression.* New York: Guilford Press.

Beckwith, L. (1972). Relationships between infants' social behavior and their mothers' behavior. *Child Development, 43,* 397-411.

Bedrosian, R. C. (1981). The application of cognitive therapy techniques with adolescents. In G. Emery, S. D. Hollon, & R. C. Bedrosian (Eds.), *New directions in cognitive therapy: A casebook* (pp. 68-83). New York: Guilford Press.

Bedrosian, R. C., & Beck, A. T. (1980). Principles of cognitive therapy. In M. J. Mahoney (Ed.), *Psychotherapy process* (pp. 127-152). New York: Plenum Press.

Beels, C. C. (1975). Family and social management of schizophrenia. *Schizophrenia Bulletin, 13,* 97-118.

Beitman, B. D., & Klerman, G. L. (1984). *Combining psychotherapy and drug therapy in clinical practice.* New York: Spectrum.

Bell, R. Q. (1975). A congenital contribution to emotional responses in early infancy and the preschool period. In *Parent-infant interaction. CIBA Foundation symposium 33* (pp. 21-212). Amsterdam, New York: Elsevier.

Bell, S. M. (1970). The development of the concept of object as related to infant-mother attachment. *Child Development, 41,* 291-311.

Bellak, A. S., & Hersen, M. (1979). *Research and practice in social skills training.* New York: Plenum Press.

Bemporad, J. R. (1984). From attachment to affiliation. *American Journal of Psychoanalysis, 44,* 79-92.

Benedetti, G. (1972). Psychosynthetic counter-transference in individual psychotherapy of schizophrenia. In D. Rubinstein & Y. O. Alanen (Eds.), *Psychotherapy of schizophrenia* (pp. 85-93). Amsterdam: Excerpta Medica.

Benedetti, G. (1974). What is psychotherapy of psychosis? *Psychotherapy Psychosomatics, 24,* 327-336.

Beres, D., & Arlow, J. (1974). Fantasy and identification in empathy. *Psychoanalytic Quarterly, 43*, 26–50.

Bettelheim, B. (1987). *A good enough parent.* New York: Knopf.

Betz, B. J. (1967). Studies of the therapist's role in the treatment of the schizophrenic patient. *American Journal of Psychiatry, 123*, 963–971.

Bibring, E. (1954). Psychoanalysis and the dynamic psychotherapist. *Journal of the American Psychoanalytical Association, 2*, 745–770.

Biller, H. B. (1974). *Paternal deprivation.* Lexington, MA: Lexington Books.

Billow, R. M. (1977). Metaphor: A review of the psychological literature. *Psychological Bulletin, 84*, 81–92.

Bing, E. (1963). Effect of childrearing practices on development of differential cognitive abilities. *Child Development, 34*, 631–648.

Binswanger, L. (1942). *Grundformen und Erkentnis menschlichen Dasein.* Zurich: Niehans.

Bion, W. R. (1977). *Seven servants.* New York: Jason Aronson.

Birley, J. L. T., & Brown, G. W. (1970). Crises and life changes preceding the onset or relapse of acute schizophrenia: Clinical aspects. *British Journal of Psychiatry, 116*, 327–333.

Blackburn, I. M., & Cottraux, J. (1988). *Thérapie cognitive de la dépression.* Paris: Masson.

Blatt, S. J., & Wild, C. M. (1976). *Schizophrenia: A developmental analysis.* New York. Academic Press.

Bleuler, E. (1908). Die Prognose der Dementia Praecox (Schizophrenie-Gruppe). *Algemeine Zeitschrift für Psychiatrie und Psychiatrische-Gerichtliche Medizine, 65*, 436–464.

Bleuler, E. (1911). *Dementia praecox or the group of schizophrenias* (transl., J. Zinkin). New York: International Universities Press (1966).

Bleuler, M. (1972). *Die schizophrenen Geistesstörungen im Lichte langjähriger Kranken- und Familiengeschichten.* Stuttgart: Thieme.

Bleuler, M. (1974). The offspring of schizophrenics. *Schizophrenia Bulletin, 8*, 93–107.

Bleuler, M. (1979). On schizophrenic psychoses. *American Journal of Psychiatry, 136*, 1403–1409.

Bowen, M., Dysinger, R. H., & Basamania, B. (1959). The role of the father in families with a schizophrenic patient. *American Journal of Psychiatry, 115*, 1017–1020.

Bower, T. G. R. (1971). The object in the world of the infant. *Scientific American, 225*, 30–38.

Bower, T. G. R. (1974). Competent newborns. *New Scientist, 14* (March), 672–675.

Bowers, K. S. (1984). On being unconsciously influenced and informed. In K. S. Bowers & D. Meichenbaum (Eds.), *The unconscious reconsidered.* New York: Wiley.

Bowers, K. S., & Meichenbaum, D. (Eds.). (1984). *The unconscious reconsidered.* New York, Wiley.

Bowlby, J. (1958). The nature of the child's tie to his mother. *International Journal of Psychoanalysis, 39*, 350–373.

Bowlby, J. (1969). *Attachment and loss: Vol. 1. Attachment.* London: Hogarth Press.

Bowlby, J. (1973a). *Attachment and loss: Vol. 2. Separation.* London: Hogarth Press.

Bowlby, J. (1973b). Self-reliance and some conditions that promote it. In J. Bowlby (Ed.), *The making and breaking of affectional bonds* (pp. 103–125). London: Tavistock Publications.

Bowlby, J. (1979). On knowing what you are not supposed to know and feeling what you are not supposed to feel. *Canadian Journal of Psychiatry, 24*, 403–408.

Bowlby, J. (1980). *Attachment and loss: Vol. 3. Loss.* London: Hogarth Press.

Bowlby, J. (1981). Sul possedere nozioni che non si supponeva di possedere e sul provare emozioni che non era permesso provare. In V. F. Guidance & M. A. Reda (Eds.), *Cognitivismo e psicoterapia* (pp. 123-131). Milano: Angeli.

Bowlby, J. (1985). The role of childhood experience in cognitive disturbance. In M. J. Mahoney & A. Freeman (Eds.), *Cognition and psychotherapy* (pp. 181-202). New York, London: Plenum Press.

Boyer, L. B. (1961). Provisional evaluation of psychoanalysis with few parameters employed in the treatment of schizophrenia. *International Journal of Psychoanalysis, 42,* 389-403.

Brady, J. P. (1984). Social skills training for psychiatric patients. I: Concepts, methods, and clinical results. *American Journal of Psychiatry, 141,* 333-340.

Brands, A. B. (1981). *Assessing therapeutic environments for active psychiatric treatment settings.* (DHHS Publication No. (ADM) 81-1109.) Washington DC: US Government Printing Office.

Breemer ter Stege, C., & Gittelman, M. (Eds.). (1987). Trends in mental care in Western Europe in the past 25 years. *International Journal of Mental Health, 16*(1 and 2), 1-243.

Brenner, H. D., Rey, E. R., & Stramke, W. G. (1983). *Empirische Schizophrenieforschung.* Bern, Stuttgart, Wien: Huber.

Brenner, H. D., Stramke, W. G., Mewes, J., Liese, F., & Seeger, G. (1980). Erfahrungen mit einem spezifischen Rehabilitationsprogramm zum Training kognitiver und kommunikativer Fähigkeiten in der Rehabilitation chronisch schizophrener Patienten. *Nervenarzt, 51,* 106-112.

Brenner, H. D., Hodel, B., Kube, G., & Roder, V. (1987). Kognitive Therapie bei Schizophrenen: Problemanalyse und empirische Ergebnisse. *Nervenarzt, 58,* 72-83.

Brickel, C. M., & Brickel, G. K. A. (1980-1981). A review of the role of pet animals on psychotherapy with the elderly. *International Journal of Aging Human Development, 12,* 119-128.

Brockington, I. F., Kendell, R. E., & Leff, J. P. (1978). Definitions of schizophrenia: Concordance and prediction of outcome. *Psychological Medicine, 8,* 387-398.

Brody, E. B. (1976). Societal determinants of schizophrenic behavior. In D. Kemali, G. Bartholini, & D. Richter (Eds.), *Schizophrenia today* (pp. 23-48). Oxford, New York, Toronto, Sidney, Paris, Frankfurt: Pergamon Press.

Brody, E. B. (1981). Can mother-infant interaction produce vulnerability to schizophrenia? *Journal of Nervous and Mental Disease, 169,* 72-81.

Bronfenbrenner, U. (1979a). Contexts of child rearing. *American Psychologist, 34,* 844-850.

Bronfenbrenner, U. (1979b). *The ecology of human development. Experiments by nature and design.* Cambridge, MA: Harvard University Press.

Brown, G. W., & Birley, J. L. T. (1968). Crises and life changes and the onset of schizophrenia. *Journal of Health and Social Behavior, 9,* 203-214.

Brown, G. W., Monck, E. M., Carstairs, G. H., & Wing, J. K. (1962). The influence of family life on the course of schizophrenic illness. *British Journal of Preventive and Social Medicine, 16,* 55-72.

Brown, G. W., Birley, J. L. T., & Wing, J. K. (1972). Influence of family life on the course of schizophrenic disorders. A replication. *British Journal of Psychiatry, 121,* 241-258.

Buber, M. (1954). *Die Schriften über das dialogische Prinzip* (Ital. transl., P. Facchi & U. Schnabel). Milano: Comunità.

Buber, M. (1970). *I and thou.* New York: Scribner.

Burnham, D., Gladstone, A., & Gibson, R. (1969). *Schizophrenia and the need-fear dilemma.* New York: International Universities Press.

Burstein, A. (1959). Primary process in children as a function of age. *Journal of Abnormal and Social Psychology, 59*, 284-286.

Busse, T. V. (1969). Child-rearing antecedents of flexible thinking. *Developmental Psychology, 1*, 585-591.

Cameron, N. (1938). Reasoning, regression and communication in schizophrenia. *Psychology Monographs, 50*, 1-34.

Cancro, R. (1975). Genetic considerations in the etiology and prevention of schizophrenia. In G. Usdin (Ed.), *Schizophrenia: Biological and psychological perspectives.* New York: Brunner/Mazel.

Cancro, R. (1979). The genetic studies of the schizophrenic syndrome. In L. Bellak (Ed.), *Disorders of the schizophrenic syndrome* (pp. 136-151). New York: Basic Books.

Cancro, R. (1982). The schizophrenic disorders. Part II. In L. Grinspoon (Ed.), *Psychiatry 1982: The American Psychiatric Association annual review.* Washington DC: American Psychiatric Press.

Cancro, R., & Angrist, B. (1978). Are drugs more than palliative in the treatment of schizophrenia?—Probably so. In J. P. Brady & H. K. H. Brodie (Eds.), *Controversy in psychiatry* (pp. 199-214). Philadelphia, London, Toronto: W. B. Saunders.

Candland, D. K. (1977). The persistent problems of emotions. In D. K. Candland, J. P. Fell, E. Keen, A. I. Lesow, R. Plutchik, & R. M. Tarpy (Eds.), *Emotion.* Monterey, CA: Brooks/Cole.

Caplan, G. (1964). *Principles of preventive psychiatry.* New York: Basic Books.

Carpenter, W. T. (1984). A perspective on the psychotherapy of schizophrenia project. *Schizophrenia Bulletin, 10*, 599-603.

Carpenter, W. T. (1987). Approaches to knowledge and understanding of schizophrenia. *Schizophrenia Bulletin, 13*, 1-8.

Carpenter, W. T., Strauss, J. S., & Muleh, S. (1973). Are there pathognomic symptoms in schizophrenia? *Archives of General Psychiatry, 28*, 847-852.

Chapman, L. J. (1960). Confusion of figurative and literal usages of words by schizophrenics and brain-damaged patients. *Journal of Abnormal Social Psychology, 60*, 412-416.

Cheek, F. E. (1965). The father of the schizophrenic. *Archives of General Psychiatry, 13*, 336-345.

Ciompi, L. (1980). The natural history of schizophrenia in the long term. *British Journal of Psychiatry, 136*, 413-420.

Ciompi, L. (1985). Aging and the schizophrenic psychosis. *Acta Psychiatrica Scandinavica, 71* (suppl 319), 93-105.

Ciompi, L., & Müller, C. H. (1976). *Lebensweg und Alter der Schizophrenen. Eine katamnestische Langzeitstudie bis ins Senium.* Berlin, Heidelberg, New York: Springer.

Clinton, D. N. (1986). *A critical analysis of Bowlby's theory of attachment.* Reports of the Department of Psychology, University of Stockholm, No. 650.

Coché, E., & Flick, A. (1975). Problem-solving training groups for hospitalized psychiatric patients. *Journal of Clinical Psychology, 91*, 19-29.

Cohen, M. B. (1952). Countertransference and anxiety. *Psychiatry, 15*, 231-243.

Collins, A. (1977). Processes in acquiring knowledge. In R. C. Anderson, R. J. Spiro, W. E. Montague (Eds.), *Schooling and the acquisition of knowledge* (pp. 339-363). Hillsdale, NJ: Lawrence Erlbaum.

Coopersmith, S. (1967). *The antecedents of self-esteem.* San Francisco: Freeman.

Corson, S. A., Corson, E. O., & Gwynn, P. (1977). Pet dogs as nonverbal communication links in hospital psychiatry. *Comprehensive Psychiatry, 18*, 61-72.

Cox, J. L. D. (1986). Long-term psychotherapy of schizophrenia. Personal insights from the experience of long-term psychotherapy of schizophrenia: Crisis and countertransferences. *Psychiatria Fennica, 17*, 111-126.

Crary, W. G. (1966). Reactions to incongruent self-experiences. *Journal of Consulting Psychology, 30*, 246-252.

Crowley, R. M. (1980). Cognitive elements in Sullivan's theory and practice. *Journal of the American Academy of Psychoanalysis, 8*, 115-126.

Crowley, R. M. (1985). Cognition in interpersonal theory and practice. In M. J. Mahoney & A. Freeman (Eds.), *Cognition and psychotherapy* (pp. 291-312). New York, London: Plenum Press.

Dabrowski, K. (1964). *Positive disintegration.* Boston: Little, Brown.

Davis, W. L., & Phares, E. J. (1969). Parental antecedents of internal-external control of reinforcement. *Psychological Reports, 24*, 427-436.

Day, M., & Semrad, E. V. (1978). Schizophrenic reactions. In A. M. Nicholi (Ed.), *The Harvard guide to modern psychiatry* (pp. 199-242). Cambridge, MA: Belknap Press.

Day, R. (1981). Life events and schizophrenia: The "triggering" hypothesis. *Acta Psychiatrica Scandinavica, 64*, 97-122.

Dewald, P. A. (1964). *Psychotherapy. A dynamic approach.* Oxford: Blackwell.

Dillon, J. T. (1980a). Curiosity as nonsequitur of Socratic questioning. *Journal of Educational Thought, 14*, 17-22.

Dillon, J. T. (1980b). Paper chase and the Socratic method of teaching law. *Journal of Legal Education, 30*, 529-535.

Dillon, J. T. (1982). The effect of questions in education and other enterprises. *Journal of Curriculum Studies, 14*, 127-152.

Dow, M. G., & Craighead, W. E. (1984). Cognition and social inadequacy: Relevance in clinical populations. In P. Trower (Ed.), *Radical approaches to social skills training* (pp. 227-259). London, Sidney: Croom Helm.

Dryden, W. (1984). Social skills training from a rational-emotive perspective. In P. Trower (Ed.), *Radical approaches to social skills training* (pp. 314-346). London, Sidney: Croom Helm.

Dryden, W., & Golden, W. (Eds.). (1986). *Cognitive-behavioural approaches to psychotherapy.* London: Harper & Row.

D'Zurilla, T. J., & Goldfried, M. R. (1971). Problem solving and behavior modification. *Journal of Abnormal Psychology, 78*, 107-126.

D'Zurilla, T. J., & Nezu, A. (1982). Social problem solving in adults. In P. C. Kendall (Ed.), *Advances in cognitive-behavioral research and therapy* (vol. 1, pp. 202-275). Orlando, FL: Academic Press.

Easterbrooks, M. A., & Lamb, M. E. (1979). The relationship between quality of infant-mother attachment and infant competence in initial encounters with peers. *Child Development, 50*, 380-387.

Einhorn, H. J., & Hogarth, R. M. (1978). Confidence in judgment: Persistence of the illusion of validity. *Psychological Reviews, 85*, 395-416.

Eisemann, M. (1985). *Psychosocial aspects of depressive disorders.* Umeå University, Medical Dissertations New Series No. 139, Umeå, Sweden.

Eissler, K. (1943). Limitations to the psychotherapy of schizophrenia. *Psychiatry, 6*, 381-391.

Eissler, K. (1953). The effect of the structure of the ego on psychoanalytic technique. *Journal of the American Psychoanalytical Association, 1*, 104-143.

Eldred, S. (1972). Intensive psychotherapy with schizophrenic patients. *Contemporary Psychoanalysis, 8*, 149-164.

Elkind, D. (1970). *Children and adolescents: Interpretive essays on Jean Piaget.* Oxford: Oxford University Press.

Ellis, A. (1962). *Reason and emotion in psychotherapy.* Secaucus, NJ: Lyle Stuart.

Ellis, A. (1973). *Humanistic psychotherapy: The rational-emotive approach.* New York: Crown.

Ellis, A. (1983-1984). Rational-emotive therapy approaches to overcoming resistance. I-III. *British Journal of Cognitive Psychotherapy, 1*(1), 28-38; *1*(2), 1-16; *2*, 11-26.

English, H. B., & English, A. C. (1958). *A comprehensive dictionary of psychological and psychoanalytical terms: A guide to usage.* New York: Longmans, Green.

Enright, R. D., Shukla, D. G., & Lapsley, D. K. (1980). Adolescent egocentrism-sociocentrism and self-consciousness. *Journal of Youth and Adolescence, 9*, 101-116.

Epstein, H. T. (1974a). Phrenoblisis: Special brain and mind growth periods. I. Human brain and skull development. *Developmental Psychobiology, 7*, 207-216.

Epstein, H. T. (1974b). Phrenoblisis: Special brain and growth periods. II. Human mental development. *Developmental Psychobiology, 7*, 217-224.

Epstein, N. (1983). Cognitive therapy with couples. In A. Freeman (Ed.), *Cognitive therapy with couples and groups* (pp. 107-124). New York: Plenum Press.

Epstein, S. (1973). The self-concept revisited. *American Psychologist, 28*, 404-416.

Erikson, H. E. (1953). Growth and crises of the healthy personality. In C. Kluckhohn & H. A. Murray (Eds.), *Personality in nature, society, and culture* (2nd ed., pp. 50-100). New York: Knopf.

Erlenmeyer-Kimling, L. (1979). Advantages of a behavior-genetic approach to investigating stress in the depressive disorders. In R. A. Depue (Ed.), *The psychobiology of the depressive disorders* (pp. 391-408). New York: Academic Press.

Ernst, K. (1956). "Geordnete Familienverhältnisse" späterer Schizophrener im Lichte einer Nachuntersuchung. *Archiv für Psychiatrie, 194*, 355-367.

Evans, A. S., Bullard, D. M., & Solomon, M. D. (1961). The family as a potential resource in the rehabilitation of the chronic schizophrenic patient: A study of 60 patients and their families. *American Journal of Psychiatry, 117*, 1075-1083.

Ewalt, J. R. (1963). Psychotherapy of schizophrenic reactions. In J. H. Masserman (Ed.), *Current psychiatric therapies* (pp. 150-170). New York, London: Grune & Stratton.

Fairbairn, W. R. D. (1944). Endopsychic structure considered in terms of object-relationships. In W. R. D. Fairbairn (Ed.), *Psychoanalytic studies of the personality* (pp. 82-136). London: Routledge & Kegan Paul (1986).

Fairbairn, W. R. D. (1946). Object-relationships and dynamic structure. In W. R. D. Fairbairn (Ed.), *Psychoanalytic studies of the personality* (pp. 137-151). London: Routledge & Kegan Paul (1986).

Falloon, I. R. H., & Liberman, R. P. (1983). Interactions between drug and psychosocial therapy in schizophrenia. *Schizophrenia Bulletin, 9*, 543-554.

Falloon, I. R. H., Boyd, J. L., & McGill, C. W. (1984). *Family care of schizophrenia.* New York, London: Guilford Press.

Farina, A., & Holzberg, J. D. (1967). Attitudes and behaviors of fathers and mothers of male schizophrenic patients. *Journal of Abnormal Psychology, 72*, 381-387.

Federn, P. (1943). *Ego psychology and the psychoses.* New York: Basic Books.

Feffer, M. H. (1959). The cognitive implications of role taking behavior. *Journal of Personality, 27*, 152-168.

Feffer, M. (1967). Symptom expression as a form of primitive decentering. *Psychological Reviews, 74*, 16-28.

Feiring, C. (1983). Behavioral styles in infancy and adulthood: The work of Karen Horney and attachment theorists collaterally considered. *Journal of the American Academy of Child Psychiatry, 22*, 1-7.

Fenton, W. S., Mosher, L. R., & Matthews, S. M. (1981). Diagnosis of schizophrenia: A critical review of current diagnostic systems. *Schizophrenia Bulletin, 7*, 452-476.

Feyerabend, P. (1962). Explanation, reduction and empiricism. In A. Feigl & G. Maxwell (Eds.), *Minnesota studies in the philosophy of science* (vol. 3, pp. 28-97). Minneapolis: University of Minnesota Press.

Field, T. (1985). Attachment as psychobiological attunement: Being on the same wavelength. In M. Reite & T. Field (Eds.), *The psychobiology of attachment and separation* (pp. 415-454). Orlando, FL: Academic Press.

Fischer, A. A. (1972). Therapeutic milieu in the treatment of schizophrenia. Some personal and organizational conditions which determine success or failure. In D. Rubinstein & Y. O. Alanen (Eds.), *Psychotherapy of schizophrenia* (pp. 261-272). Amsterdam: Elsevier.

Fish, B., & Karabenick, S. A. (1971). Relationship between self-esteem and locus of control. *Psychological Reports, 29,* 784.

Flaherty, J. A., & Richman, J. A. (1986). Effects of childhood relationships on the adult's capacity to form social support. *American Journal of Psychiatry, 143,* 851-855.

Fleck, S., Lidz, T., & Cornelison, A. (1963). Comparison of parent–child relationships of male and female schizophrenic patients. *Archives of General Psychiatry, 8,* 1-7.

Fontana, A. F. (1966). Familial etiology of schizophrenia. Is a scientific methodology possible? *Psychological Bulletin, 66,* 214-227.

Forrest, T. (1966). Paternal roots of female character development. *Contemporary Psychoanalysis, 3,* 21-38.

Forrest, T. (1967). The paternal roots of male character development. *Psychoanalytical Reviews, 54,* 81-99.

Fox, N. A. (1985). Behavioral and autonomic antecedents of attachment on high-risk infants. In M. Reite & T. Field (Eds.), *The psychobiology of attachment and separation* (pp. 389-413). Orlando, FL: Academic Press.

Frank, G. H. (1965). The role of the family in the development of psychopathology. *Psychological Bulletin, 64,* 191-205.

Frank, J. (1959). The dynamics of the psychotherapeutic relationship. Determinants and effects of the therapist's influence. *Psychiatry, 22,* 17-39.

Frank, J. (1973). *Persuasion and healing.* Baltimore: Johns Hopkins University Press.

Frank, J. (1985). Therapeutic components shared by all therapies. In M. J. Mahoney & A. Freeman (Eds.), *Cognition and psychotherapy* (pp. 49-80). New York: Plenum Press.

Frank, J., Hoehn-Saric, R., Imber, S. D., Liberman, B. L., & Stone, A. R. (Eds.). (1978). *Effective ingredients of successful psychotherapy.* New York: Brunner/Mazel.

Fransella, F. (1985). Resistance. *British Journal of Cognitive Psychotherapy, 3,* 1-11.

Freedman, D. A. (1972). On the limits of the effectiveness of psychoanalysis: Early ego and somatic disturbances. *International Journal of Psychoanalysis, 53,* 363-370.

Freeman, A. (Ed.). (1983). *Cognitive therapy with couples and groups.* New York: Plenum Press.

Freeman, A. (1986). *General treatment considerations with personality disorders.* Read at the 2nd International Congress of Cognitive Psychotherapy, Umeå, Sweden, September 18-20, 1986.

Freeman, T., & McGhie, A. (1957). The relevance of genetic psychology to the psychopathology of schizophrenia. *British Journal of Medical Psychology, 30,* 176-187.

Freud, A. (1951). *Das Ich und die Abwehrmekanismen.* Stockholm: Natur och Kultur (1983).

Freud, A., & Dann, S. (1951). An experiment in group upbringing. *Psychoanalytic Study of the Child, 6,* 127-168.

Freud, S. (1895). *Project for a scientific psychology.* In J. Strachey (Ed.), *The standard edition of the complete psychological works of Sigmund Freud* (hereafter shortened to *Standard Edition*). London: Hogarth Press (1953).

Freud, S. (1900). *The interpretation of dreams. Standard edition.* London: Hogarth Press.

Freud, S. (1905a). *On psychotherapy. Standard edition.* London: Hogarth Press.

Freud, S. (1905b). *Jokes and their relation to the unconscious. Standard edition.* London: Hogarth Press.

Freud, S. (1911-1914). *Technical papers on psychoanalysis. Standard edition.* London: Hogarth Press.

Freud, S. (1915). *Instincts and their vicissitudes. Standard edition.* London: Hogarth Press.

Freud, S. (1917). *Introductory lectures on psychoanalysis. Part III: Standard edition.* London: Hogarth Press.

Freud, S. (1920). *Drei Abhandlungen der Sexualtheorie. (Ges Werke).* London: Imago.

Freud, S. (1921). *Group psychology and the analysis of the ego* (transl., J. Strachey). New York, Toronto, London: Bantam Books.

Freud, S. (1923). *The ego and the id* (Standard edition). London: Hogarth Press.

Freud, S. (1927). *Humor* (Standard edition). London: Hogarth Press.

Friedman, L. (1978). Piaget and psychotherapy. *Journal of the American Academy of Psychoanalysis, 6,* 175-192.

Fries, M. E. (1946). The child's ego development and the training of adults in his environment. *Psychoanalytic Study of the Child, 2,* 85-112.

Friis, S., Karterud, S., Kleppe, H., Lorentzen, S., Lystrup, S., & Vaglum, P. (1982). Reconsidering some limiting factors of therapeutic communities. In M. Pines & L. Rafaelsen (Eds.), *The individual and the group* (pp. 573-581). New York: Plenum Press.

Frodi, A. (1985). Variations in parental and nonparental response to early infant communication. In M. Reite & T. Field (Eds.), *The psychobiology of attachment and separation* (pp. 351-368). Orlando, FL: Academic Press.

Fromm-Riechmann, F. (1939). Transference problems in schizophrenics. *Psychoanalytic Quarterly, 8,* 412-426.

Fromm-Riechmann, F. (1948). Notes on the development of treatment of schizophrenics by psychoanalytic psychotherapy. *Psychiatry, 11,* 263-273.

Fromm-Reichmann, F. (1954). Psychotherapy of schizophrenia. *American Journal of Psychiatry, 111,* 410-419.

Fromm-Reichmann, F. (1955). Clinical significance of intuitive processes of the analyst. *Journal of the American Psychoanalytical Association, 3,* 82-88.

Füredi, J., & Kun, M. (1972). *Schizophrenic in therapeutic communities.* In D. Rubinstein & Y. O. Alanen (Eds.), *Psychotherapy of schizophrenia* (pp. 292-296). Amsterdam: Elsevier.

Furlan, P. M. (1984). "Recollection" in the individual psychotherapy of schizophrenia. *Psychiatria Fennica, 15,* 107-118.

Fuson, K. C. (1979). The development of self-regulating aspects of speech: A review. In G. Zivin (Ed.), *The development of self-regulation through private speech.* New York: Wiley.

Gaensbauer, T. J., & Sands, K. (1979). Distorted affective communications in abused/neglected infants and their potential impact on caretakers. *Journal of the American Academy of Child Psychiatry, 18,* 236-250.

Gecas, V. (1972). Parental behavior and contextual variations in adolescent self esteem. *Sociometry, 5,* 332-345.

George, L., & Neufeld, R. W. J. (1985). Cognition and symptomatology in schizophrenia. *Schizophrenia Bulletin, 11,* 264-285.

Gjerde, P. F. (1983). Attentional capacity dysfunction and arousal in schizophrenia. *Psychological Bulletin, 93,* 57-72.

Glaser, S. R. (1980). Rhetoric and psychotherapy. In M. J. Mahoney (Ed.), *Psychotherapy process* (pp. 313-323). New York, London: Plenum Press.

Godwin-Rabkin, J. (1980). Stressful life events and schizophrenia: A review of the research literature. *Psychological Bulletin, 87,* 408-425.

Golden, W. L., & Dryden, W. (1986). Cognitive-behavioural therapies: Commonalities, divergences and future developments. In W. Dryden & W. L. Golden (Eds.), *Cognitive-behavioural approaches to psychotherapy* (pp. 356-378). London: Harper & Row.

Goldfried, M. R., & Robins, C. (1983). Self-schema, cognitive bias and the processing of therapeutic experience. In P. C. Kendall (Ed.), *Advances in cognitive-behavioral research and therapy* (vol. 2, pp. 35-81). Orlando, FL: Academic Press.

Goldman, A. E. (1962). A comparative-developmental approach to schizophrenia. *Psychological Bulletin, 59*, 57-69.

Goldstein, M. J., & Rodnick, E. H. (1975). The family's contribution to the etiology of schizophrenia. *Schizophrenia Bulletin*, (14), 48-63.

Goodman, K. D. (1981). Music therapy. In S. Arieti (Ed.), *American handbook of psychiatry* (2nd ed., vol. 7, pp. 564-585). New York: Basic Books.

Gordon, R. E., & Gordon, K. K. (Eds.). (1981). *Systems of treatment for the mentally ill*. New York: Grune & Stratton.

Gottesman, I. I., & Shields, J. (1971). Schizophrenia. Geneticism and environmentalism. *Human Heredity, 21*, 517-522.

Gottesman, L., & Chapman, L. J. (1960). Syllogistic reasoning errors in schizophrenia. *Journal of Consulting Psychology, 24*, 250-255.

Greenson, R. R. (1967). *The technique and practice of psychoanalysis*. New York: International Universities Press.

Greenson, R. R., & Wexler, M. (1969). The non-transference relationship in the psychoanalytic situation. *International Journal of Psychoanalysis, 50*, 27-39.

Greenspan, S., & Lourie. R. S. (1981). Developmental structuralist approach to the classification of adaptive and pathologic personality organizations: Infancy and early childhood. *American Journal of Psychiatry, 138*, 725-735.

Greenwald, A. G. (1980). The totalitarian ego. Fabrication and revision of personal history. *American Psychologist, 35*, 603-618.

Greenwood, V. B. (1983). Cognitive therapy with the young adult chronic patient. In A. Freeman (Ed.), *Cognitive therapy with couples and groups* (pp. 183-198). New York: Plenum Press.

Grojahn, M. (1971). Laughter in group psychotherapy. *International Journal of Group Psychotherapy, 21*, 234-248.

Grünbaum, A. (1984). *The foundations of psychoanalysis. A philosophical critique*. Berkeley: University of California Press.

Guidano, V. F., & Liotti, G. (1983). *Cognitive processes and emotional disorders*. New York: Guilford Press.

Guidano, V. F., & Liotti, G. (1985). A Constructivistic foundation for cognitive therapy. In M. J. Mahoney & A. Freeman (Eds.), *Cognition and psychotherapy* (pp. 101-142). New York: Plenum Press.

Guidano, V. F., & Reda, M. A. (1981). *Cognitivismo e Psicoterapia*. Milano: Angeli.

Gunderson, J. G. (1978a). Patient-therapist matching: A research evaluation. *American Journal of Psychiatry, 135*, 1193-1197.

Gunderson, J. G. (1978b). Defining the therapeutic processes in psychiatric milieus. *Psychiatry, 41*, 327-335.

Gunderson, J. G. (1979). Individual psychotherapy. In L. Bellak (Ed.), *Disorders of the schizophrenic syndrome* (pp. 364-398). New York: Basic Books.

Gunderson, J. G. (1980). A reevaluation of milieu therapy for nonchronic schizophrenic patients. *Schizophrenia Bulletin, 6*, 64-69.

Gunderson, J. G., & Mosher, L. R. (1975). *Psychotherapy of schizophrenia*. New York: Jason Aronson.

Gunderson, J. G., Will, O. A., & Mosher, L. R. (1983). *Principles and practice of milieu therapy*. New York: Jason Aronson.

Gunderson, J. G., Frank, A. F., Katz, H. M., Vannicelli, M. L., Frosch, J. P., & Knapp, P. H. (1984). Effects of psychotherapy in schizophrenia: II. Comparative outcomes of two forms of treatment. *Schizophrenia Bulletin, 10,* 564–598.

Gutheil, T. G. (1985). The therapeutic milieu: Changing themes and theories. *Hospital and Community Psychiatry, 36,* 1279–1285.

Haier, R. J. (1980). The diagosis of schizophrenia: A review of recent developments. *Schizophrenia Bulletin, 6,* 417–428.

Haring, C., & Leickert, K. H. (1968). *Wörterbuch der Psychiatrie und ihrer Grenzgebiete.* Stuttgart, New York: Schattauer.

Harrell, T. H., Beiman, I., & LaPointe, K. A. (1981). Didactic persuasion techniques in cognitive restructuring. *American Journal of Psychotherapy, 35,* 86–92.

Harrow, M., & Ferrante, A. (1969). Locus of control in psychiatric patients. *Journal of Consulting and Clinical Psychology, 33,* 582–589.

Hasher, L., & Zacks, R. (1979). Automatic and effortful processes in memory. *Journal of Experimental Psychology: General, 108,* 356–388.

Haugsgjerd, S. (1983). *Psykoterapi och miliöterapi vid psykoser.* Stockholm: Prisma.

Heilbrun, A. B. (1960). Perception of maternal child rearing attitudes in schizophrenics. *Journal of Consulting Psychology, 24,* 169–173.

Heilbrun, A. B. (1973). *Aversive maternal control.* New York: Wiley.

Heilbrun, A. B., Orr, H. K., & Harrell, S. N. (1966). Patterns of parental childrearing and subsequent vulnerability to cognitive disturbance. *Journal of Consulting Psychology, 30,* 51–59.

Heiman, P. (1950). On countertransference. *International Journal of Psychoanalysis, 31,* 81–84.

Helgason, T. (Ed.). (1985). *The long-term treatment of functional psychoses. Needed areas of research.* Cambridge: Cambridge University Press.

Hetherington, E. M. (1972). Effect of father absence on personality development in adolescent daughters. *Developmental Psychology, 7,* 313–326.

Hess, R. D., & Shipman, V. C. (1965). Early experience and the socialization of cognitive modes in children. *Child Development, 36,* 869–886.

Higgins, J. (1976). Effects of child rearing by schizophrenic mothers: A follow-up. *Journal of Psychiatric Research, 13,* 1–9.

Hilgard, E. R. (1962). Impulsive versus realistic thinking. *Psychological Bulletin, 59,* 477–488.

Hirsch, S. R., & Leff, J. P. (1975). *Abnormalities in parents of schizophrenics.* London: Oxford University Press.

Hoffmann, N. (1978). *Grundlagen kognitiver Therapie.* Bern, Zurich: Huber.

Hogarty, G. E., & Goldberg, S. C. (1973–1974). Drug and sociotherapy in the aftercare of schizophrenic patients. *Archives of General Psychiatry, 28,* 54–64; *31,* 603–608; 609–618.

Hole, R. W., Rush, A. J., & Beck, A. T. (1979). A cognitive investigation of schizophrenic delusions. *Psychiatry, 42,* 312–319.

Hollon, S. D., & Kendall, P. C. (1980). Cognitive self-statements in depression: Development of an automatic thoughts questionnaire. *Cognitive Therapy and Research, 4,* 383–395.

Holt, R. R. (1967). The development of the primary process. In R. R. Holt (Ed.), *Motives and thought.* New York: International Universities Press.

Horney, K. (1937). *The neurotic personality of our time.* New York: Norton.

Horney, K. (1950). *Neurosis and human growth.* New York: Norton.

Houtz, J. C., Ringenbach, S., & Feldhusen, J. F. (1973). Relationship of problem solving to other cognitive variables. *Psychological Reports, 33,* 389–390.

Huber, G., Gross, G., & Schüttler, R. (1975). A long-term follow-up study of schizophrenia: Psychiatric course of illness and prognosis. *Acta Psychiatrica Scandinavica*, *52*, 49–57.

Hymowitz, P., & Spohn, H. (1980). The effects of antipsychotic medication on the linguistic ability of schizophrenics. *Journal of Nervous and Mental Disease, 168*, 287–296.

Ingvar, D. H. (1985). "Memory of the future": An essay on the temporal organization of conscious awareness. *Human Neurobiology, 4*, 127–136.

*International pilot study of schizophrenia*. (1973). Geneva: World Health Organization.

Islam, A., & Turner, D. L. (1982). The therapeutic community: A critical reappraisal. *Hospital and Community Psychiatry, 33*, 651–653.

Isohanni, M. (1986). Humor in the therapeutic community. *Psychiatria Fennica, 17*, 137–144.

Jacobs, L. (1980). A cognitive approach to persistent delusions. *American Journal of Psychotherapy, 34*, 556–563.

Jacobs, L. (1982). Cognitive therapy for schizophrenia in remission. *Current Psychiatric Therapies, 21*, 93–100.

Jacobsson, L., Lindström, H., von Knorring, L., Perris, C., & Perris, H. (1980). Perceived parental behaviour and psychogenic needs. *Archiv für Psychiatrie und Nervenkrankheiten, 228*, 21–30.

James, W. (1890). *The principles of psychology*. New York: Holt.

Jansson, L. (1986). *Handbok i kognitiv terapi vid depression*. Stockholm: Natur och Kultur.

Jaremko, M. E. (1986). Cognitive-behaviour modification: The shaping of rule-governed behaviour. In W. Dryden & W. Golden (Eds.), *Cognitive-behavioural approaches to psychotherapy* (pp. 31–60). London: Harper & Row.

Jaspers, K. (1913). *Allgemeine Psychopathologie*. Heidelberg: Springer.

Joffe, L. S., Vaughn, B. E., Barglow, P., & Benveniste, R. (1985). Biobehavioral antecedents in the development of infant–mother attachment. In M. Reite & T. Field (Eds.), *The psychobiology of attachment and separation* (pp. 323–350). New York: Academic Press.

Jolly, A. (1972). *The evolution of primate behavior*. New York: Macmillan.

Jones, E. (1953). *The life and the work of Sigmund Freud. Vol. 1*. New York: Basic Books.

Jung, C. G. (1928). Two essays on analytical psychology. In C. Jung (Ed.), *Collected works of C. G. Jung* (vol. 7, p. 143). Princeton: Princeton University Press (1966).

Jung, C. G. (1966). Appendix: The realities of practical psychotherapy. In C. Jung (Ed.), *Collected works of C. G. Jung* (vol. 16, 2nd ed., pp. 327–338). Princeton: Princeton University Press.

Jung, C. G. (1972). The psychology of dementia praecox. I. Critical survey of theoretical views on the psychology of dementia praecox. In J. Jung (Ed.), *Collected works of C. G. Jung* (vol. 3, pp. 1–37). Princeton: Princeton University Press.

Kagan, J. (1970). Attention and psychological change in the young child. *Science, 170*, 826–832.

Kagan, J. (1979). The form of early development. Continuity and discontinuity in emergent competences. *Archives of General Psychiatry, 36*, 1047–1054.

Kahneman, D., & Tversky, A. (1973). On the psychology of prediction. *Psychological Reviews, 80*, 237–251.

Kahney, H. (1986). *Problem solving. A cognitive approach*. Philadelphia: Open University Press.

Kant, I. (1791). *Critique of pure reason* (transl., N. Kemp). London: Macmillan (1963).

Kaplan, H. B., & Boyd, I. N. (1965). The social functions of humor in an open psychiatric ward. *Psychiatric Quarterly, 39,* 502-515.

Karasu, T. B. (1982). Psychotherapy and pharmacotherapy: Toward an integrative model. *American Journal of Psychiatry, 139,* 1102-1113.

Karon, B. P. (1963). The resolution of acute schizophrenic reactions: A contribution to the development of non-classical psychotherapeutic techniques. *Psychotherapy: Theory, Research and Practice, 1,* 27-43.

Karon, B. P., & Vandenbos, G. R. (1970). Experience, medication, and the effectiveness of psychotherapy with schizophrenics. *British Journal of Psychiatry, 116,* 427-428.

Kasanin, J. (1933). The acute schizoaffective psychoses. *American Journal of Psychiatry, 13,* 97-126.

Kasl, S. V. (1974). Effects of housing on mental and physical health. *Man-Environment Systems, 4,* 207-226.

Katan, M. (1954). The importance of the non-psychotic part of the personality in schizophrenia. *International Journal of Psychoanalysis, 35,* 119-128.

Kelly, G. (1955). *The psychology of personal constructs.* New York: Norton.

Kelly, G. (1970). A brief introduction to personal construct theory. In D. Bannister (Ed.), *Perspectives in personal construct theory* (pp. 1-29). New York: Academic Press.

Kendell, R. E., Brockington, I. F., & Leff, J. P. (1979). Prognostic implications of six alternative definitions of schizophrenia. *Archives of General Psychiatry, 36,* 25-31.

Kendler, K. S., Glazer, W. M., & Morgenstern, H. (1983). Dimensions of delusional experience. *American Journal of Psychiatry, 140,* 466-469.

Kernberg, O. F. (1982). Self, ego, affects, and drives. *Journal of the American Psychoanalytical Association, 30,* 893-917.

Kety, S. S. (1980). The syndrome of schizophrenia: Unresolved questions and opportunities for research. *British Journal of Psychiatry, 136,* 421-436.

Kilburg, R., & Siegel, A. (1973). Formal operations in reactive and process schizophrenics. *Journal of Consulting and Clinical Psychology, 40,* 371-376.

Klein, G. S. (1970). *Perception, motives, and personality.* New York: Knopf.

Klein. G. S. (1976). *Psychoanalytic theory. An exploration of essentials.* New York: International Universities Press.

Kohut, H. (1959). Introspection, empathy, and psychoanalysis. In P. Ornstein (Ed.), *The search for the self* (pp. 205-232). New York: International Universities Press.

Kohut, H. (1977). *The restoration of the self.* New York: International Universities Press.

Kohut, H., & Levarie, S. (1950). On the enjoyment of listening to music. *Psychoanalytic Quarterly, 19,* 64-87.

Kovacs, M., & Beck, A. T. (1978). Maladaptive cognitive structures in depression. *American Journal of Psychiatry, 135,* 525-533.

Kraepelin, E. (1896). *Dementia praecox and paraphrenia.* Edinburgh: Livingstone (Eng. trans. 1919).

Krause, N., & Stryker, S. (1984). Stress and well-being: The buffering role of locus of control beliefs. *Social Sciences and Medicine, 18,* 783-790.

Kris, E. (1952). *Psychoanalytic explorations in art.* New York: International Universities Press.

Kubie, L. (1971). The destructive potential of humor in psychotherapy. *American Journal of Psychiatry, 127,* 861-873.

Kuhn, T. S. (1962). *The structure of scientific revolutions.* Chicago: University of Chicago Press.

Kuipers, L. (1979). Expressed emotion: A review. *British Journal of Social and Clinical Psychology, 18,* 229-238.

Kuipers, L., & Bebbington, P. (1985). Relatives as a resource in the management of functional illness. *British Journal of Psychiatry, 147,* 465-470.

Lacan, J. (1960). *Subversion du sujet et dialectique du désir dans l'incoscient freudien.* *Écrits, 27.* Paris: Editions du Seuil.

Lakatos, I. (1970). Falsification and the methodology of scientific research programmes. In I. Lakatos & A. Musgrave (Eds.), *Criticism and the growth of knowledge* (pp. 91-195). Cambridge: Cambridge University Press.

Lancet. (1975). Editorial: Family deviance and schizophrenia. *Lancet, 2,* 213-214.

Landau, R., Harth, P., Othnay, N., & Sharfhertz, C. (1972). The influence of psychotic parents on their children's development. *American Journal of Psychiatry, 129,* 38-43.

Larsson, U.-B. (1984). *The creation of pictures as a part of a treatment with a cognitive approach.* Read at the 2nd International Congress of Cognitive Psychotherapy, Umeå, Sweden, September 18-20, 1986.

Lecky, P. (1945). *Self-consistency: A theory of personality.* Long Island, NY: Island Press.

Lefcourt, H. M. (1976). *Locus of control. Current trends in theory and research.* Hillsdale, NJ: Lawrence Erlbaum.

Leff, J. P., & Vaughn, C. (1981). The role of maintenance therapy and relatives expressed emotions in relapse of schizophrenia: A two year follow up. *British Journal of Psychiatry, 139,* 102-104.

Leff, J. P., Kuipers, L., Berkowitz, R., Eberlein Vries, R., & Sturgeon, B. (1982). A controlled trial of social intervention in the families of schizophrenic patients. *British Journal of Psychiatry, 141,* 121-134.

Lehtinen, S. (1981). Developmental stages in primary process manifestations in thought: A follow up study of girls from four to seventeen. *Psychiatria Fennica, 12,* 131-152.

Lehtinen, S. (1983). Consolidation of primary process thought and its integration. Part I: Theoretical aspects. Part II: A longitudinal study of girls from four to seventeen. *Psychiatria Fennica, 14,* 107-118.

Lenrow, P. B. (1966). Use of metaphor in facilitating constructive behavior change. *Psychotherapy: Theory, Research and Practice, 3,* 145-148.

Leon, I. G. (1984). Psychoanalysis, Piaget and attachment: The construction of the human object in the first year of life. *International Review of Psychoanalysis, 11,* 255-277.

Leonhard, K. (1957-1968). *Aufteilung der endogenen Psychosen* (1st-9th ed.). Berlin: Academie.

Leonhard, K. (1975). Gegen die Auffassung einer Einheit Schizophrenie. *Psychiatrie Neurologie und Medizinische Psychologie (Leipzig), 27,* 65-70.

Levenson, H. (1973a). Multidimensional locus of control in psychiatric patients. *Journal of Consulting and Clinical Psychology, 41,* 397-404.

Levenson, H. (1973b). Perceived parental antecedents of internal, powerful others, and chance locus of control orientations. *Developmental Psychology, 9,* 268-274.

Levy, L. H. (1963). *Psychological interpretation.* New York: Holt.

Liberman, R. P., Mueser, K. T., & Wallace, C. J. (1986). Social skills training for schizophrenic individuals at risk for relapse. *American Journal of Psychiatry, 143,* 523-526.

Lichtenberg, J. D. (1963). Untreating—Its necessity in the therapy of certain schizophrenic patients. *British Journal of Medical Psychology, 36,* 311-317.

Lichtenberg, J. D. (1981). Implications for psychoanalytic theory of research on the neonate. *International Review of Psychoanalysis, 8,* 35-52.

Lidz, R., & Lidz, T. (1949). The family environment of schizophrenic patients. *American Journal of Psychiatry, 106,* 332-345.

Lidz, T. (1972). Schizophrenic disorders: The influence of conceptualizations on therapy. In D. Rubinstein & Y. O. Alanen (Eds.), *Psychotherapy of schizophrenia* (pp. 9-24). Amsterdam: Excerpta Medica.

Lidz, T. (1973). *The origins and treatment of schizophrenic disorders.* New York: Basic Books.

Lidz, T. (1974). Schizophrenic thinking. *Journal of Youth and Adolescence, 3,* 95-98.

Lidz, T., Cornelison, A. R., Fleck, S., & Terry, D. (1957). The intrafamilial environment of the schizophrenic patient. I. The father. *Psychiatry, 20,* 329-342.

Liem, J. M. (1980). Family studies of schizophrenia: An update and commentary. *Schizophrenia Bulletin, 6,* 429-455.

Liotti, G. (1986). Structural cognitive therapy. In W. Dryden & W. Golden (Eds.), *Cognitive-behavioural approaches to psychotherapy* (pp. 92-128). London: Harper & Row.

Liotti, G. (1987). The resistance to change of cognitive structures: A counterproposal to psychoanalytic metapsychology. *International Journal of Cognitive Psychotherapy, 1,* 87-104.

Liotti, G. (1988). Attachment and cognition. In C. Perris, I. M. Blackburn, & H. Perris (Eds.), *Cognitive psychotherapy: Theory and practice.* Heidelberg: Springer.

Liotti, G., Onofri, A., Spadafora, R., & Tombolini, L. (1984). Terapia cognitiva, psicologia sperimentale e il problema dell'identità personale. *Ricerche di Psicologia, 8,* 59-80.

Lipsitt, L. (1979). Critical conditions in infancy: A psychological perspective. *American Psychologist, 34,* 973-980.

Litovsky, V. G., & Dusek, J. B. (1985). Perceptions of child rearing and self-concept development during the early adolescent years. *Journal of Youth and Adolescence, 14,* 373-387.

Little, M. (1957). "R"—the analyst's total response to his patient's needs. *International Journal of Psychoanalysis, 38,* 240-254.

Looft, W. (1972). Egocentrism and social interaction across the life span. *Psychological Bulletin, 78,* 73-92.

Luborsky, L., & Spences, D. P. (1971). Quantitative research on psychoanalytic therapy. In A. E. Bergin & S. L. Garfield (Eds.), *Handbook of psychotherapy and behavior change* (pp. 408-437). New York: Wiley.

Lundh, L. G. (1983). *Mind and meaning. Acta Universitatis Upsaliensis, 10.* Uppsala: Sweden.

Lundh, L. G. (1988). Cognitive therapy and the analysis of meaning structures. In C. Perris, I. M. Blackburn, & H. Perris (Eds.), *Cognitive psychotherapy: Theory and practice.* Heidelberg: Springer.

Lungwitz, H. (1980). *Psychobiologie der Neurosen.* Freiburg: Rombach.

Luria, A. R. (1976). *Cognitive development: Its cultural and social foundations.* Cambridge, MA: Harvard University Press.

MacCulloch, M. J., & Waddington, J. L. (1979). Catastrophe theory: A model interaction between neurochemical and environmental influences in the control of schizophrenia. *Neuropsychobiology, 5,* 87-93.

MacDonald, A. P. (1971). Internal–external locus of control: Parental antecedents. *Journal of Consulting and Clinical Psychology, 37,* 141-147.

Magnusson, D. (1983). *Implications of an interactional paradigm for research on human development.* Reports of the Department of Psychology, University of Stockholm, Supplement 59, September, 1983.

Magnusson, D., & Allen, V. L. (1982). *An interactional perspective for human development.* Reports of the Department of Psychology, University of Stockholm, Supplement 56, December, 1982.

Magnusson, D., & af Klinteberg, B. (1987). *Hyperactivity and physiological arousal.* Reports of the Department of Psychology, University of Stockholm, no. 657, June 1987.

Magnusson, D., & Endler, N. S. (Eds.). (1977). *Personality at the crossroads: Current issues in international psychology.* Hillsdale, NJ: Lawrence Erlbaum.

Maher, B. A. (1966). *Principles of psychopathology.* New York: McGraw-Hill.

Mahler, M. S. (1968). *On human symbiosis and the vicissitudes of individuation. Vol. I. Infantile psychosis.* New York: International Universities Press.

Mahler, M. S., Pine, F., & Bergman, A. (1975). *The psychological birth of the human infant.* New York: Basic Books.

Mahoney, M. J. (1980). Psychotherapy and the structure of personal revolutions. In M. J. Mahoney (Ed.), *Psychotherapy process* (pp. 157–180). New York: Plenum Press.

Mahoney, M. J. (1982). Psychotherapy and human change processes. In J. H. Harvey & M. M. Parks (Eds.), *Psychotherapy research and behavior change* (pp. 77–122). Washington, DC: American Psychological Association.

Mahoney, M. J. (1985). Psychotherapy and human change processes. In M. J. Mahoney & A. Freeman (Eds.), *Cognition and psychotherapy* (pp. 3–48). New York: Plenum Press.

Mahoney, M. J., & A. Freeman (1985). *Cognition and psychotherapy.* New York: Plenum Press.

Mallinger, A. (1974). Transference: A cognitive approach. *American Journal of Psychoanalysis, 34,* 51–62.

Mandler, G. (1982). The structure of value: Accounting for taste. In M. Sydnor Clark & S. T. Fiske (Eds.), *Affect and cognition* (pp. 3–36). Hillsdale, NJ: Lawrence Erlbaum.

Mandler, G. (1984). *Mind and body. Psychology of emotion and stress.* New York: Norton.

Markus, H. (1977). Self-schemata and processing information about the self. *Personality and Social Psychology, 35,* 63–78.

Markus, H., & Sentis, K. (1982). The self in social information processing. In J. H. Harvey & M. M. Parks (Eds.), *Psychological perspectives on the self* (vol. 1). London: Lawrence Erlbaum.

Marneros, A. (1984a). Frequency of occurrence of Schneider's first rank symptoms in schizophrenia. *European Archives of Psychiatry and Neurological Sciences, 234,* 78–82.

Marneros, A. (1984b). Sichern die Symptome ersten Ranges die Diagnose Schizophrenie? *Nervenarzt, 55,* 365–370.

Marsella, A. J. (1987). *Cross-cultural aspects of severe psychiatric disorders: Issues and research findings.* Read at the XI Berzelius Symposium on Transcultural Psychiatry, Stockholm, Sweden, April 8–10, 1987.

Marzillier, J. S. (1978). Outcome studies of skills training: A review. In P. Trower, B. M. Bryant, & M. Argyle (Eds.), *Social skills and mental health.* London: Methuen.

Marzillier, J. S. (1980). Cognitive therapy and behavioural practice. *Behaviour Research and Therapy, 18,* 249–258.

Massie, H. N., & Beels, C. C. (1972). The outcome of the family treatment of schizophrenia. *Schizophrenia Bulletin* (6), 24–37.

Matas, L., Arend, R. A., & Sroufe, L. A. (1978). Continuity of adaptation in the second year: The relationship between quality of attachment and later competence. *Child Development, 49,* 547–556.

Matte-Blanco, I. (1954). *Lo psiquico y la naturaleza humana.* Santiago, Chile: Editorial Universitaria.

Matte-Blanco, I. (1959). Expression in symbolic logic of the characteristics of the system Ucs or the logic of the system Ucs. *International Journal of Psychoanalysis, 40,* 1–5.

Matte-Blanco, I. (1965). A study of schizophrenic thinking: Its expression in terms of symbolic logic and its representation in terms of multidimensional space. *International Journal of Psychiatry, 1,* 91–95.

Matte-Blanco, I. (1976). Basic logico-mathematical structures in schizophrenia. In D. Kemali, G. Bartholini, & D. Richter (Eds.), *Schizophrenia today* (pp. 211-233). Oxford: Pergamon Press.

Matussek, P. (1976). *Psychotherapie schizophrener Psychosen*. Hamburg: Hoffman und Campe.

Matussek, P. (1981). The situation of the schizophrenic: The starting point of psychotherapy. *Hexagon (Roche), 2,* 18-24.

Matussek, P., & Triebel, A. (1974). Die Wirksamheit der Psychotherapie bei 44 Schizophrenen. *Nervenarzt, 45,* 569-575.

McCreadie, R. G., Crorie, J., Barron, E. T., & Winslow, G. S. (1982). The Nithsdale schizophrenia survey: III. Handedness and tardive dyskinesia. *British Journal of Psychiatry, 140,* 591-594.

McFarlane, W. R. (1983). *Family therapy in schizophrenia*. New York: Guilford Press.

McGlashan, T. H. (1984). Testing four diagnostic systems for schizophrenia. *Archives of General Psychiatry, 41,* 141-144.

McGuire, M. T., & Sifneos, P. E. (1970). Problem-solving in psychotherapy. *Psychiatric Quarterly, 44,* 667-674.

McKinney, W. T. (1985). Separation and depression: Biological markers. In M. Reite & T. Field (Eds.), *The psychobiology of attachment and separation* (pp. 201-222). Orlando, FL: Academic Press

McLaughlin, J. T. (1982). Issues stimulated by the 32nd Congress. *International Journal of Psychoanalysis, 63,* 229-240.

McMullin, R. E. (1986). *Handbook of cognitive therapy techniques*. New York: Norton.

McNeil, T. F., & Kaij, L. (1976). *Obstetric factors in the development of schizophrenia*. Read at the 2nd Rochester International Conference on Schizophrenia, May 2-5, 1976.

Mednick, S. A., Mura, E., Schulsinger, F., & Mednick, B. (1982). Perinatal conditions and infant development in children with schizophrenic parents. *Social Biology, 29,* 264-275.

Meichenbaum, D. (1977). *Cognitive-behavior modification*. New York: Plenum Press.

Meichenbaum, D., & Cameron, R. (1973). Training schizophrenics to talk to themselves: A means of developing attentional controls. *Behavior Therapy, 4,* 515-534.

Meltzer, H. Y., & Liberman, R. P. (1982). What is schizophrenia? *Schizophrenia Bulletin, 8,* 433-437.

Meyer, A. (1958). *Psychobiology: A science of man*. Springfield, IL: Charles C Thomas.

Meyers, A., Mercatoris, M., & Sirota, A. (1976). Use of covert self-instruction for the elimination of psychotic speech. *Journal of Consulting and Clinical Psychology, 44,* 480-483.

Meyersburg, H. A., & Post, R. M. (1979). An holistic developmental view of neural and psychological processes: A neurobiologic:psychoanalytic integration. *British Journal of Psychiatry, 135,* 139-155.

Milani Comparetti, A. (1982). Protagonismo e identità dell'essere umano nel processo ontogenetico. In A. Trasimeni (Ed.), *Giornate Italoamericane di ultrasonografia*. Bologna: Moduzzi.

Miller, A. (1981). *Du sollst nicht merken*. Frankfurt: Suhrkamp.

Milton, F., Patwa, V. K., & Hafner, R. J. (1978). Confrontation vs. belief modification in persistently deluded patients. *British Journal of Medical Psychology, 51,* 127-130.

Modell, A. H. (1963). Primitive object relationships and predisposition to schizophrenia. *International Journal of Psychoanalysis, 44,* 282-292.

Mosher, L. R., & Keith, S. J. (1979). Research on the psychosocial treatment of schizophrenia: A summary report. *American Journal of Psychiatry, 136,* 623-631.

Mosher, L. R., & Keith, S. J. (1980). Psychosocial treatment: Individual, group, family, and community support approaches. *Schizophrenia Bulletin, 6,* 10–41.

Mosher, L. R., & Menn, A. Z. (1978). Community residential treatment for schizophrenia: A two-year follow-up. *Hospital and Community Psychiatry, 29,* 715–723.

Moss, H. (1967). Sex, age, and state as determinants of mother-infant reaction. *Merrill-Palmer Quarterly of Behavior and Development, 13,* 19–36.

Neisser, U. (1962). *Cognitive psychology.* New York: Meredith.

Nicholi, A. M. (1978). The therapist-patient relationship. In A. M. Nicholi (Ed.), *The Harvard guide to modern psychiatry* (pp. 3–22). Cambridge, MA: Belknap Press.

Nowicki, S., & Segal, W. (1974). Perceived parental characteristics, locus of control orientation, and behavioral correlates of locus of control. *Developmental Psychology, 1,* 33–37.

Noy, P. (1969). A revision of the psychoanalytic theory of the primary process. *International Journal of Psychoanalysis, 50,* 155–178.

Noy, P. (1979). The psychoanalytic theory of cognitive development. *Psychoanalytic Study of the Child, 34,* 169–216.

Nuechterlein, K. H., & Dawson, M. E. (1984a). A heuristic vulnerability/stress model of schizophrenic episodes. *Schizophrenia Bulletin, 10,* 300–312.

Nuechterlein, K. H., & Dawson, M. E. (1984b). Information processing and attentional functioning in the developmental course of schizophrenic disorders. *Schizophrenia Bulletin, 10,* 160–203.

Offenkrants, W., & Tobin, A. (1974). Psychoanalytic psychotherapy. *Archives of General Psychiatry, 30,* 593–606.

Ollinen, K. (1986). *Dysfunktionella tankemönster och upplevelse av uppfostran i en normalgrupp.* Institute of Applied Psychology, Umeå University, Umeå, Sweden (mimeographed).

O'Neil, P., & Robins, L. N. (1958). Childhood patterns predictive of adult schizophrenia: A 30 year follow-up study. *American Journal of Psychiatry, 115,* 385–391.

O'Reilly, J. (1977). The interplay between mothers and their children: A construct theory viewpoint. In D. Bannister (Ed.), *Perspectives in personal construct theory* (pp. 195–219). New York: Academic Press.

Ortony, A. (1975). Why metaphors are necessary and not just nice. *Educational Theory, 25,* 45–53.

Orzack, M. H., Kornetsky, C., & Freeman, H. (1967). The effects of daily administration of carphenazine on attention in schizophrenic patients. *Psychopharmacologia, 11,* 31–38.

Padesky, C. (1986). *Cognitive therapy of avoidant personality.* Read at the 2nd International Conference on Cognitive Psychotherapy, Umeå, Sweden, September 18–20, 1986.

Pao, P.-N. (1975). On the diagnostic term "schizophrenia." *Annuals of Psychoanalysis,* 221–238.

Parker, G. (1983). *Parental overprotection.* Orlando, FL: Grune & Stratton.

Pastor, D. L. (1981). The quality of mother–infant attachment and its relationship to toddlers' initial sociability with peers. *Developmental Psychology, 17,* 326–335.

Paul, G. L. (1969). Chronic mental patient: Current status—Future directions. *Psychological Bulletin, 71,* 81–94.

Paul, G. L., & Lentz, R. J. (1977). *Psychosocial treatment of chronic mental patients: Milieu vs social-learning programs.* Cambridge, MA: Harvard University Press.

Paul, H. A. (1984). Horneyan developmental psychoanalytic theory and its application to the treatment of the young. *American Journal of Psychoanalysis, 44,* 59–71.

Perls, F. S. (1973). *The gestalt approach and eye witness to therapy.* Palo Alto, CA: Science and Behavior Books.

Perris, C. (1963). Reflektioner kring verksamheten vid ett "therapeutic community." *Nordisk Psykiatrisk Tidskrift, 18*, 386-396.

Perris, C. (1966). A study of bipolar (manic depressive) and unipolar recurrent depressive psychoses. *Acta Psychiatrica Scandinavica* (suppl 194).

Perris, C. (1974). A study of cycloid psychoses. *Acta Psychiatrica Scandinavica* (suppl 253).

Perris, C. (1981a). Course of schizophrenia and some organic psychoses. In H. M. van Praag, M. H. Lader, O. J. Rafaelsen, & E. J. Sachar (Eds.), *Handbook of biological psychiatry* (part IV, pp. 82-157). New York: Dekker.

Perris, C. (1981b). Recent developments and current issues in the study of depression. *Ideggyógyászati Szemle, 34*, 481-490.

Perris, C. (1983). Depression: Pointers to a hereditary factor in its etiology. In J. Korf & L. Pepplinkhuizen (Eds.), *Depression. Molecular and psychologically based therapies* (pp. 73-82). Drachten, Netherlands: TGO Foundation.

Perris, C. (Ed.). (1984). *International symposium on "Alternatives to institutional psychiatric care—Issues of evaluation." Umeå (Sweden), March 15-17, 1982.* Stockholm: Swedish Planning and Rationalization Institute of the Health and Social Services (SPRI).

Perris, C. (1985a). *An integrative, interactionistic approach to the study of depression.* Read at the WPA Symposium on Affective Disorders, Athens, Greece, October 13-17, 1985.

Perris, C. (1985b). *Milieu-therapeutic processes and cognitive therapy.* Read at the XIII International Congress of Psychotherapy, Opatija, Yugoslavia, October 6-12, 1985.

Perris, C. (1985c). Alternatives to hospitals: A field of promises and of not-yet answered questions. In T. Helgason (Ed.), *The long-term treatment of functional psychoses* (pp. 25-37). Cambridge: Cambridge University Press.

Perris, C. (1986a). The case for the independence of cycloid psychotic disorder from the schizoaffective disorders. In A. Marneros & M. T. Tsuang (Eds.), *Schizoaffective psychoses* (pp. 272-308). Berlin, New York: Springer.

Perris, C. (1986b). *Kognitiv terapi i teori och i praktik.* Stockholm: Natur och Kultur.

Perris, C. (1986c). *Psykiatri i omvandling: Umeå modellen.* Stockholm: Swedish Planning and Rationalization Institute of the Health and Social Services (SPRI).

Perris, C. (1986d). Kognitiv terapi vid behandling av psykotiska och postpsykotiska tillstånd: En översikt. *Läkartidningen, 83*, 1488-1491.

Perris, C. (1987a). *Cognitive psychotherapy with patients suffering from schizophrenic syndromes.* Read at the 2nd Congress of the Hungarian Psychiatric Association. *Ideggyógyászati Szemle, 40*, 398-408.

Perris, C. (1987b). Development of psychiatry in Sweden with particular reference to one of the Northern counties. *International Journal of Mental Health, 16*, 198-224.

Perris, C. (1987c). *A theoretical framework for linking the experience of dysfunctional parental rearing attitudes with manifest psychopathology.* Read at the XI. Berzelius symposium on "Transcultural psychiatry," Stockholm, April 8-10, 1987.

Perris, C. (1988a). The concept of cycloid psychotic disorder. *Psychiatric Developments 1*, 37-56.

Perris, C. (1988b). *Individualized cognitive psychotherapy with patients suffering from schizophrenic syndromes.* Read at the International Conference on New Trends in Schizophrenia, Bologna, Italy, April 15-17, 1988.

Perris, C. (1988c). The foundations of cognitive psychotherapy and its standing in relation to other psychotherapies. In C. Perris, I. M. Blackburn, & H. Perris (Eds.), *Cognitive psychotherapy: Theory and practice.* Heidelberg: Springer.

Perris, C. (1988d). *Psykoterapi, personliga revolutioner och kunskapstillväxt. Det kognitiva terapeutiska perspektivet.* Läkartidningen (in press).

Perris, C. (1988e). Intensive cognitive-behavioural psychotherapy with patients suffering from schizophrenic syndromes. In C. Perris, I. M. Blackburn, & H. Perris (Eds.), *Cognitive psychotherapy: Theory and practice.* Heidelberg: Springer.

Perris, C. (1988f). A cognitive psychotherapeutic orientation and the milieutherapeutic processes in psychiatric in-patients units. *International Journal of Cognitive Psychotherapy, 2,* 35–50.

Perris, C., Arrindell, W. A., Perris, H., Eisemann, M., van der Ende, J., & von Knorring, L. (1986). Perceived depriving parental rearing and depression. *British Journal of Psychiatry, 148,* 170–175.

Perris, C., Carlsson, M., & Fröberg, G. (1966). Efterundersökning av schizofrena patienter med hänsyn till social återanpassning. *Nordisk Psykiatrisk Tidskrift, 20,* 3–12.

Perris, C., Eisemann, M., Ericsson, U., von Knorring, L., & Perris, H. (1983). Parental rearing behaviour and personality characteristics of depressed patients. *Archiv für Psychiatrie und Nervenkrankheiten, 233,* 77–88.

Perris, C., Jacobsson, L., von Knorring, L., Oreland, L., Perris, H., & Ross, S. B. (1980). Enzymes related to biogenic amine metabolism and personality characteristics in depressed patients. *Acta Psychiatrica Scandinavica, 61,* 265–272.

Perris, C., & Kemali, D. (1985). Focus on the Italian psychiatric reform. *Acta Psychiatrica Scandinavica, 71* (suppl 316).

Perris, C., Maj, M., Perris, H., & Eisemann, M. (1985). Perceived parental rearing behaviour in unipolar and bipolar depressed patients. *Acta Psychiatrica Scandinavica, 72,* 172–175.

Perris, C., & Perris, H. (1985). A biological, psychological and social approach to the study of depression and its implications for treatment. *Neurologia Psichiatria Scienze Umane, 5* (suppl, 67–93).

Perris, C., Perris, H., & Eisemann, M. (1987). Perceived parental rearing practices, parental affective disorders, and age at onset in depressed patients. *International Journal of Family Psychiatry, 8,* 183–200.

Perris, C., Perris, H., Ericsson, U., & von Knorring, L. (1982). The genetics of depression. *Archiv für Psychiatrie und Nervenkrankheiten, 232,* 137–155.

Perris, C., Rodhe, K., Palm, A., Hällgren, S., Lilja, C., & Söderman, H. (1985). Fully integrated in- and out-patient services in a psychiatric sector. *Social Psychiatry, 20,* 60–69.

Perris, H. (1982a). *A multifactorial study of life events in depressed patients.* Umeå University Medical Dissertations, New Series no. 78. Umeå, Sweden.

Perris, H. (1982b). Biological correlates of personality in depressed patients. In *Intern symposium: Theoretical problems of modern psychiatry, Moscow, May 11–12, 1982* (pp. 45–49). Basel: Sandoz.

Perris, H. (1984). Life events and personality characteristics in depression. *Acta Psychiatrica Scandinavica, 69,* 350–358.

Perris, H. (1985). *Use of experiential diaries in the cognitive therapy of uncommunicative patients.* Read at the XIII International Congress of Psychotherapy, Opatija, Yugoslavia, October 6–12, 1985.

Perris, H. (1986). *Presentation of a cognitive-behavioural treatment centre for partially hospitalized severe neurotics.* Read at the 2nd International Congress of Cognitive Psychotherapy, Umeå, Sweden, September 18–20, 1986.

Perris, H., von Knorring, L., Oreland, L., & Perris, C. (1984). Life events and biological vulnerability: A study of life events and platelet MAO activity in depressed patients. *Psychiatry Research, 12,* 111–120.

Perris, R. (1987). *Cell-matrix interactions in neural crest development.* Acta Universitatis Upsaliensis. Comprehensive Summaries of Uppsala Dissertations from the Faculty of Science, 94. Uppsala, Sweden.

Peterfreund, E. (1971). *Information, systems, and psychoanalysis.* New York: Academic Press.

Peterfreund, E. (1976). How does the analyst listen? On models and strategies in the psychoanalytic process. *Psychoanalysis and Contemporary Science, 4,* 59-101.

Peterfreund, E. (1978). Some critical comments on psychoanalytic conceptualizations of infancy. *International Journal of Psychoanalysis, 59,* 427-441.

Peterfreund, E. (1983). *The process of psychoanalytic therapy.* New York: Academic Press.

Peterfreund, E., & Franceschini, E. (1973). On information, motivation, and meaning. In B. B. Rubinstein (Ed.), *Psychoanalysis and contemporary science* (vol. 2, pp. 220-262). New York: International Universities Press.

Piaget, J. (1923). *The language and thought of the child.* London: Routledge & Kegan Paul (1932).

Piaget, J. (1932). *The moral judgement of the child.* Glencoe, IL: Free Press (1948).

Piaget, J. (1936). *The origins of intelligence in children* (2nd ed.). New York: International Universities Press.

Piaget, J. (1962). *Play, dreams, and imitation in childhood.* New York: Norton.

Piaget, J. (1971). *Biology and knowledge.* Chicago: University of Chicago Press.

Piaget, J. (1973). The affective unconscious and the cognitive unconscious. *Journal of the American Psychoanalytical Association, 21,* 249-261.

Piaget, J. (1978). *The development of thought. Equilibration of cognitive structures.* Oxford: Blackwell.

Piaget, J., & Inhelder, B. (1969). *The psychology of the child.* London: Routledge & Kegan Paul.

Piety, K. R. (1967). Patterns of parent perceptions among neuropsychiatric patients and normal controls. *Journal of Clinical Psychology, 23,* 428-433.

Pishkin, V., & Williams, W. V. (1977). Cognitive rigidity in information processing of chronic undifferentiated schizophrenics. *Journal of Clinical Psychology, 33,* 625-630.

Polanyi, M. (1966). *The tacit dimension.* Garden City, NY: Doubleday.

Prechtl, H. F. (1963). The mother-child interaction in babies with minimal brain damage. In B. M. Foss (Ed.), *Determinants of infant behavior* (pp. 53-66). New York: Wiley.

Priestley, P., McGuire, J., Flegg, D., Hemsley, V., & Welham, D. (1978). *Social skills and personal problem solving. A handbook of methods.* London: Tavistock Publications.

Prigogine, I. (1980). Time, structure, and fluctuations. *Science, 201,* 777-785.

Rabin, A. I., Doneson, S. L., & Jentons, R. L. (1979). Studies of psychological functions in schizophrenia. In L. Bellak (Ed.), *Disorders of the schizophrenic syndrome* (pp. 181-231). New York: Basic Books.

Rapaport, D. (1960). Motivation of thinking. In M. R. Jones (Ed.), *Nebraska symposium on motivation.* Lincoln: University of Nebraska Press.

Rapaport, D. (1967). Psychoanalysis as a developmental psychology. In *Collected papers of D. Rapaport.* New York: Basic Books.

Rapoport, R. N. (1960). *Community as a doctor.* London: Tavistock.

Reda, M. A. (1986). *Sistemi cognitivi complessi e psicoterapia.* Roma: La Nuova Italia Scientifica.

Refsnes-Kniazzeh, C. (1981). Art therapy. In S. Arieti (Ed.), *American handbook of psychiatry* (2nd ed., vol. 7, pp. 526-552). New York: Basic Books.

Reichhard, S., & Tillman, C. (1950). Patterns of parent–child relationship in schizophrenia. *Psychiatry, 13*, 247–257.

Reiss, D. (1967). Individual thinking and family interaction. *Archives of General Psychiatry, 16*, 80–93.

Reiss, D. (1971). Varieties of consensual experience. I. A theory for relating family interaction to individual thinking. *Family Process, 10*, 1–28.

Reiss, D. (1975). Families and the etiology of schizophrenia: Fishing without a net. *Schizophrenia Bulletin*, (14), 8–11.

Reite, M., & Capitanio, J. P. (1985). On the nature of social separation and social attachment. In M. Reite & T. Field (Eds.), *The psychobiology of attachment and separation* (pp. 389–413). Orlando, FL: Academic Press.

Reite, M., & Field, T. (1985). *The psychobiology of attachment and separation.* Orlando, FL: Academic Press.

Rendon, M. (1985). Cognition and psychoanalysis: A Horneyan perspective. In M. J. Mahoney & A. Freeman (Eds.), *Cognition and psychotherapy* (pp. 277–290). New York: Plenum Press.

Riley, T., Adams, G. R., & Nielsen, E. (1984). Adolescent egocentrism: The association among imaginary audience behavior, cognitive development, and parental support and rejection. *Journal of Youth and Adolescence, 13*, 401–417.

Rioch, J. M. (1949). The transference phenomenon in psychoanalytic therapy. In P. Mullay (Ed.), *A study of interpersonal relations* (pp. 80–87). New York: Hermitage Press.

Roeder, H. (1986). Mothers of schizophrenic patients. In P. Matussek (Ed.), *Symposium on schizophrenia.* Ringberg Castle, West Germany (in press).

Rohner, E. C., Chaille, C., & Rohner, R. R. (1980). Perceived parental acceptance-rejection and the development of children's locus of control. *Journal of Psychology, 104*, 83–86.

Rosch, E. (1975). Cognitive representations of semantic categories. *Journal of Experimental Psychology: General, 104*, 192–233.

Rosch, E., Mervis, C. B., Gray, W. D., Johnson, D. M., & Boyes-Braem, P. (1976). Basic objects in natural categories. *Cognitive Psychology, 8*, 382–439.

Rose, G. J. (1969). King Lear and the use of humor in treatment. *Journal of the American Psychoanalytic Association, 17*, 927–940.

Rosen, J. N. (1947). The treatment of schizophrenic psychosis by direct analytic therapy. *Psychiatric Quarterly, 21*, 3–17, 117–119.

Rosen, J. N. (1962). *Direct psychoanalytic psychiatry.* New York: Grune & Stratton.

Rosenfeld, H. (1965). *Psychotic states.* London: Hogarth Press.

Rosenheim, E. (1974). Humor in psychotherapy: An interactive experience. *American Journal of Psychotherapy, 28*, 584–591.

Rosenthal, D., Wender, P. H., Kety, S. S., Schulsinger, F., Welner, J., & Rieder, R. O. (1975). Parent–child relationships and psychopathological disorder in the child. *Archives of General Psychiatry, 32*, 466–476.

Rothstein, A. (1982). The implications of early psychopathology for the analysability of narcissistic personality disorders. *International Journal of Psychoanalysis, 63*, 177–188.

Rotter, J. (1966). Generalized expectancies for internal versus external control of reinforcement. *Psychological Monographs 80* (609).

Rubins, J. L. (1969). A holistic (Horney) approach to the psychoses: The schizophrenias. *American Journal of Psychoanalysis, 29*, 131–146.

Rubins, J. L. (1972). A holistic (Horney) approach to the schizophrenias. III. The therapeutic process. *American Journal of Psycohanalysis, 32*, 16–44.

Rubins, J. L. (1976). Five-years results of psychoanalytic therapy and day care for acute schizophrenic patients. *American Journal of Psychoanalysis, 36,* 3–26.

Rubins, J. L., & Rucker, M. S. (1974). On evaluating the effectiveness of psychoanalytic therapy for the acute schizophrenias. American Journal of Psychoanalysis, *34,* 241–256.

Rumelhart, D. E., & Ortony, A. (1977). The representation of knowledge in memory. In R. C. Anderson, R. J. Spiro, & W. E. Montague (Eds.), *Schooling and the acquisition of knowledge* (pp. 99–135). Hillsdale, NJ: Lawrence Erlbaum.

Rumke, H. C. (1967). *Eine blühende Psychiatrie in Gefahr.* Berlin: Springer.

Rund, B. R., & Blakar, R. M. (1986). Schizophrenic patients and their parents. *Acta Psychiatrica Scandinavica, 74,* 396–408.

Rutter, M. (1979). Maternal deprivation, 1972–1978; New findings, new concepts, new approaches. *Child Development, 50,* 283–305.

Rutter, M. (1985). Resilience on the face of adversity. Protective factors and resistance to psychiatric disorder. *British Journal of Psychiatry, 147,* 598–611.

Ryle, A. (1978). A common language for the psychotherapies? *British Journal of Psychiatry, 132,* 585–594.

Salmon, P. (1970). A psychology of personal growth. In D. Bannister (Ed.), *Perspectives in personal constructs theory* (pp. 197–221). New York: Academic Press.

Salokangas, R. K. R. (1986). Psychosocial outcome in schizophrenia and psychotherapeutic orientation. *Acta Psychiatrica Scandinavica, 74,* 497–506.

Sameroff, A. J. (1975). Transactional models in early social relations. *Human Development, 18,* 65–79.

Sameroff, A. J., & Zax, M. (1973). Perinatal characteristics of the offspring of schizophrenic women. *Journal of Nervous and Mental Disease, 157,* 191–199.

Sass, L. A., Gunderson, J. G., Thaler-Singer, M., & Wynne, L. C. (1984). Parental communication deviance and forms of thinking in male schizophrenic offspring. *Journal of Nervous and Mental Disease, 172,* 513–520.

Schafer, R. (1959). *Generative empathy in the treatment situation. Psychoanalytic Quarterly, 28,* 342–373.

Schalling, D., Åsberg, M., Edman, G., & Oreland, L. (1987). Markers for vulnerability to psychopathology: Temperament traits associated with platelet MAO activity. *Acta Psychiatrica Scandinavica, 76,* 172–182.

Schmideberg, M. (1970). Psychotherapy with failures of psychoanalysis. *British Journal of Psychiatry, 116,* 195–200.

Schneider, K. (1959). *Klinische psychopathologie.* Stuttgart: Thieme.

Schulsinger, H. (1976). A ten-year follow-up of children of schizophrenic mothers. Clinical assessment. *Acta Psychiatrica Scandinavica, 53,* 371–386.

Schulz, C. G. (1975). An individualized psychotherapeutic approach with the schizophrenic patient. *Schizophrenia Bulletin* (13), 46–69.

Schwartz, D. P. (1975). Processes of psychotherapy of schizophrenia. In G. J. Gunderson & L. R. Mosher (Eds.), *Psychotherapy of schizophrenia* (pp. 24–41). New York: Jason Aronson.

Seiler, T. B. (1984). Developmental cognitive theory, personality, and therapy. In N. Hoffman (Ed.), *Foundations of cognitive therapy* (pp. 13–50). New York, London: Plenum Press.

Searles, H. (1958a). The schizophrenic vulnerability to the therapist's unconscious processes. *Journal of Nervous and Mental Disease, 127,* 247–262.

Searles, H. (1958b). Positive feelings in the relationship between the schizophrenic and his mother. *International Journal of Psychoanalysis, 39,* 569–586.

Searles, H. (1959). The effort to drive the other person crazy. An element in the aetiology and psychotherapy of schizophrenia. *British Journal of Medical Psychology, 32,* 1–18.

Searles, H. (1962). The differentiation between concrete and metaphorical thinking in the recovering schizophrenic patient. *Journal of the American Psychoanalytical Association, 10,* 22-49.

Searles, H. (1965). *Collected papers on schizophrenia and related subjects.* New York: International Universities Press.

Segal, S. P., & Aviram, V. (1978). *The mentally ill in community based sheltered care.* New York: Wiley.

Serafica, F. C. (1978). The development of attachment behaviors: An organismic-developmental perspective. *Human Development, 21,* 119-140.

Shepherd, G. (1984). Assessment of cognitions in social skills training. In P. Trower (Ed.), *Radical approaches to social skills training* (pp. 261-283). London: Croom Helm.

Shevrin, H., & Dickman, S. (1980). The psychological unconscious. A necessary assumption for all psychological theory? *American Psychologist, 35,* 421-434.

Shotter, J. (1970). Men, the man-makers: George Kelly and the psychology of personal constructs. In D. Bannister (Ed.), *Perspectives in personal constructs theory* (pp. 223-253). New York: Academic Press.

Shulman, B. H. (1968). *Essays in schizophrenia.* Baltimore: Williams & Wilkins.

Shulman, B. H. (1985). Cognitive therapy and the individual psychology of Alfred Adler. In M. J. Mahoney & A. Freeman (Eds.), *Cognition and psychotherapy* (pp. 243-258). New York: Plenum Press.

Siegel, J. M., & Spivak, G. (1976). A new therapy program for chronic patients. *Behavior Therapy, 7,* 129-130.

Simon, K. (1986). *Treatment of borderline disorders.* Read at the 2nd International Congress of Cognitive Psychotherapy, Umeå, Sweden, September 18-20, 1986.

Singer, W. (1986). The brain as a self-organizing system. *European Archives of Psychiatry and Neurological Sciences, 236,* 4-9.

Sloane, R. B., Cristol, A. H., Peppernick, M. C., & Staples, F. R. (1970). Role preparation and expectation of improvement in psychotherapy. *Journal of Nervous and Mental Disease, 150,* 18-26.

Sollod, R. N., & Wachtel, P. L. (1980). A structural and transactional approach to cognitions in clinical problems. In M. J. Mahoney (Ed.), *Psychotherapy process* (pp. 1-27). New York: Plenum Press.

Snyder, S. H., Kety, S. S., & Goldstein, M. J. (1982). What is schizophrenia? *Schizophrenia Bulletin, 8,* 595-602.

Sontag, L. W. (1966). Implications of fetal behavior and environment for adult personalities. *Annals of the New York Academy of Science, 34,* 782-786.

Spitzer, R. L., Andreasen, N. C., & Endicott, J. (1978). Schizophrenia and other psychotic disorders in DSM-III. *Schizophrenia Bulletin, 4,* 489-509.

Spivak, G., Platt, J. J., & Shure, M. B. (1976). *The problem-solving approach to adjustment.* San Francisco: Jossey-Bass.

Spohn, H. E., Lacoursiere, R. B., Thompson, K., & Coyne, L. (1978). The effects of antipsychotic drug treatment on attention and information processing in chronic schizophrenics. In L. C. Wynne, R. Cromwell, & S. Matthysse (Eds.), *The nature of schizophrenia.* New York: Wiley.

Spotnitz, H. (1986). *Modern psychoanalysis of the schizophrenic patient* (2nd ed.). New York: Human Sciences Press.

Sroufe, L. A., & Waters, E. (1977). Attachment as an organizational construct. *Child Development, 48,* 1184-1199.

Stanton, A. H., & Schwartz, M. S. (1954). *The mental hospital.* New York: Basic Books.

Stein, L. I., & Test, M. A. (1978). *Alternatives to mental hospital treatment.* New York: Plenum Press.

Stevens, A. L., & Collins, A. (1977). *The goal structure of a Socratic tutor.* Cambridge, MA: Bolt Beranek and Newman.

Stewart, I. (1975). The seven elementary catastrophes. *New Scientist, 68,* 447–454.

Strachan, A. M. (1986). Family intervention for the rehabilitation of schizophrenia: Toward protection and coping. *Schizophrenia Bulletin, 12,* 678–697.

Sullivan, H. S. (1931a). The modified psychoanalytic treatment of schizophrenia. *American Journal of Psychiatry, 11,* 519–536.

Sullivan, H. S. (1931b). Socio-psychiatric research: Its implications for the schizophrenia problem and for mental hygiene. *American Journal of Psychiatry, 10,* 977–991.

Sullivan, H. S. (1953). *The interpersonal theory of psychiatry.* New York: Norton.

Sullivan, H. S. (1954). *The psychiatric interview.* New York: Norton.

Swann, W. B., & Hill, C. A. (1982). When our identities are mistaken: Reaffirming self-conceptions through social interaction. *Journal of Personality and Social Psychology, 43,* 59–66.

Swann, W. B., & Read, S. J. (1981). Self-verification processes: How we sustain our self-conceptions. *Journal of Experimental Social Psychology, 17,* 351–372.

Szalita-Pemow, A. (1951). Remarks on pathogenesis and treatment of schizophrenia. *Psychiatry, 14,* 295–300.

Szalita-Pemow, A. (1955). The "intuitive process" and its relation to work with schizophrenics. *Journal of the American Psychoanalytic Association, 3,* 7–18.

Tähkä, V. (1984). Psychoanalytic treatment as a developmental continuum of disturbed structuralisation and its phase-specific encounter. *Scandinavian Psychoanalytic Review, 7,* 133–159.

Test, M. A., & Stein, L. I. (1975). The clinical rationale for community treatment: A review of the literature. In L. I. Stein & M. A. Test (Eds.), *Alternatives to mental hospital treatment* (pp. 3–22). New York: Plenum Press (1978).

Thom, R. (1975). *Structural stability and morphogenesis.* London: Addison-Wesley.

Thomas, A., Chess, S., & Birch, H. G. (1970). The origin of personality. *Scientific American, 223,* 102–109.

Tienari, P. (1986). Psychotherapy research on schizophrenia. *Psychiatria Fennica, 17,* 127–136.

Tronick, E., Als, H., Adamson, L., Wise, S., & Brazelton, T. B. (1978). The infant's response to entrapment between contradictory messages in face-to-face interaction. *Journal of Child Psychiatry, 17,* 1–13.

Trower, P. (1984). *Radical approaches to social skills training.* London, Sidney: Croom Helm.

Tulving, E. (1972). Episodic and semantic memory. In E. Tulving & W. Donaldson (Eds.), *Organization of memory.* New York: Academic Press.

Tversky, A., & Kahneman, D. (1971). Belief in the law of small numbers. *Psychological Bulletin, 76,* 105–110.

Vaglum, P., Friis, S., & Karterud, S. (1985). Why are the results of milieu therapy for schizophrenic patients contradictory? An analysis based on four empirical studies. *Yale Journal of Biology and Medicine, 58,* 349–361.

Vaillant, G. E. (1985). An empirically derived hierarchy of adaptive mechanisms and its usefulness as a potential diagnostic axis. *Acta Psychiatrica Scandinavica, 71* (suppl 319), 171–180.

van Praag, H. M. (1976). About the impossible concept of schizophrenia. *Comprehensive Psychiatry, 17,* 481–497.

Vaughn, C., & Leff, J. (1976). The measurement of expressed emotion in the families of psychiatric patients. *British Journal of Social and Clinical Psychology, 15,* 157–165.

Verkozen, J. (1975). Egocentrism: Stage or state? *Psychoanalytic Review, 62,* 305–308.

Von Domarus, E. (1944). The specific laws of logic in schizophrenia. In J. S. Kasanin (Ed.), *Language and thought in schizophrenia* (pp. 104-114). Berkeley: University of California Press.

von Knorring, L., Jacobsson, L., Perris, C., & Perris, H. (1980). Reactivity to incoming stimuli and the experience of life-events. *Neuropsychobiology, 6,* 297-303.

von Knorring, L., Oreland, L., & Winblad, B. (1984). Personality traits related to monoamine oxidase (MAO) activity in platelets. *Psychiatry Research, 12,* 11-26.

Vygotsky, L. S. (1934). *Storia dello sviluppo delle funzioni psichiche superiori.* Bari: Giunti-Barbera (1974).

Vygotsky, L. S. (1980). *Il Processo Cognitivo.* Torino: Boringhieri.

Wachtel, P. (1977). Interaction cycles, unconscious processes, and the person situation-issue. In D. Magnusson & N. Endler (Eds.), *Personality at the crossroads: Towards an interactional psychology.* Hillsdale, NJ: Lawrence Erlbaum.

Wachtel, P. L. (Ed.). (1982). *Resistance: Psychodynamic and behavioral approaches.* New York: Plenum Press.

Waldrop, M. F., Bell, R. Q., McLaughlin, B., & Halverson, C. F. (1978). Newborn minor physical anomalies predict short attention span, peer aggression, and impulsivity at age 3. *Science, 199,* 563-565.

Walker, L. S., & Greene, J. W. (1986). The social context of adolescent self-esteem. *Journal of Youth and Adolescence, 15,* 315-322.

Wallace, C. J. (1984). Community and interpersonal functioning in the course of schizophrenic disorders. *Schizophrenia Bulletin, 10,* 233-257.

Ward, P. B., Catts, S. V., Norman, T. R., Burrows, G. D., & McConaghy, N. (1987). Low platelet monamine oxidase and sensation seeking in males: An established relationship? *Acta Psychiatrica Scandinavica, 75,* 86-90.

Waring, E. M. (1981). Cognitive family therapy in the treatment of schizophrenia. *Psychiatric Journal of the University of Ottawa, 6,* 229-233.

Washburn, S., & Conrad, M. (1979). Organization of the therapeutic milieu in the partial hosptial. In R. F. Luber (Ed.), *Partial hospitalization* (pp. 47-70). New York: Plenum Press.

Waters, E., Wippman, J., & Sroufe, L. A. (1979). Attachment, positive affect, and competence in the peer group: Two studies in construct validation. *Child Development, 50,* 821-829.

Watson, G. (1957). Some personality differences in children related to strict or permissive parental discipline. *Journal of Psychology, 44,* 227-249.

Watt, D. C., Katz, K., & Shepherd, M. (1983). The natural history of schizophrenia: A 5-year prospective follow-up of a representative sample of schizophrenics by means of a standardized clinical and social assessment. *Psychological Medicine, 13,* 663-670.

Watt, N. F. (1978). Patterns of childhood social development in adult schizophrenics. *Archives of General Psychiatry, 35,* 160-165.

Watzlawick, P. (1978). *The language of change.* New York: Basic Books.

Waxler, N. E. (1975). The normality of deviance: An alternate explanation of schizophrenia. *Schizophrenia Bulletin* (14), 38-47.

Weathers, L., Bedell, J. R., Marlowe, H., Gordon, R. E., Adams, J., Reed, V., Palmer, J., & Gordon, K. K. (1981). Using psychotherapeutic games to train patients' skills. In R. E. Gordon & K. K. Gordon (Eds.), *Systems of treatment for the mentally ill* (pp. 109-124). New York: Grune & Stratton.

Weinberger, D. R. (1987). Implications of normal brain development for the pathogenesis of schizophrenia. *Archives of General Psychiatry, 44,* 660-669.

Werner, H. (1948). *Comparative psychology of mental development.* Chicago: Follett.

Wessler, R. L. (1986). Conceptualizing cognitions in the cognitive-behavioural therapies. In W. Dryden & W. Golden (Eds.), *Cognitive-behavioural approaches to psychotherapy* (pp. 1-30). London: Harper & Row.

Wessler, R. A., & Wessler, R. L. (1980). *The principles and practice of rational-emotive therapy.* San Francisco: Jossey-Bass.

Wexler, M. (1951). The structural problem in schizophrenia: Therapeutic implications. *International Journal of Psychoanalysis, 32,* 157-166.

Will, O. A. (1968). Proposal for a psychotherapeutic center. *International Journal of Psychiatry, 6,* 442-448.

Will, O. A. (1975). Schizophrenia. Psychosocial treatment. In A. M. Freedman, H. I. Kaplan, & B. J. Sadock (Eds.), *Comprehensive textbook of psychiatry* (2nd ed., vol. 1, pp. 939-955). Baltimore: Williams & Wilkins.

Willenson, D. (1960). Relationship of adult personality characteristics to perceived parental behavior. *Dissertations Abstracts, 20,* 3393-3394.

Wilmer, H. A. (1981). Defining and understanding the therapeutic community. *Hospital and Community Psychiatry, 32,* 95-99.

Wilson, C. C. (1987). Physiological responses of college students to a pet. *Journal of Nervous and Mental Disease, 175,* 606-612.

Wing, J. K. (1974). Principles of evaluation. In J. K. Wing & A. M. Hailey (Eds.), *Evaluating a community psychiatric service* (pp. 11-39). London: Oxford University Press.

Wing, J. K. (1978). The social context of schizophrenia. *American Journal of Psychiatry, 135,* 1333-1339.

Winnicott, D. W. (1965). *The maturational process and the facilitating environment.* New York: International Universities Press.

Wolff, P. H. (1960). *The developmental psychologies of Jean Piaget and psychoanalysis. Psychological issues 2: Monograph 5.* New York: International Universities Press.

Wynne, L. C. (1981). Current concepts about schizophrenics and family relationships. *Journal of Nervous and Mental Disease, 169,* 82-89.

Wynne, L. C., Toohey, M. C., & Doane, J. (1979). Family studies. In L. Bellak (Ed.). *Disorders of the schizophrenic syndrome* (pp. 264-290). New York: Basic Books.

Yakovlev, P. I., & Lecours, A. R. (1967). The myelogenetic cycles of regional maturation of the brain. In A. Minkowski (Ed.), *Regional development of the brain in early life.* Philadelphia: Davis.

Yalom, I. D. (1980). *Existential psychotherapy.* New York: Basic Books.

Young, J. E. (1982). Loneliness, depression and cognitive therapy, theory and application. In L. A. Peplau & D. Perlman (Eds.), *Loneliness* (pp. 379-406). New York: Wiley.

Young, J. E. (1986). *Treatment of personality disorders.* Read at the 2nd International Congress of Cognitive Psychotherapy, Umeå, Sweden, September 18-20, 1986.

Young, M. A., Tanner, M. A., & Meltzer, H. Y. (1982). Operational definitions of schizophrenia. What do they identify? *Journal of Nervous and Mental Disease, 170,* 443-447.

Zeeman, E. C. (1976). Catastrophe theory. *Scientific American, 234,* 65-83.

Zimmerman, D. (1982). Analysability in relation to early psychopathology. *International Journal of Psychoanalysis, 63,* 189-200.

Zubin, J., & Spring, B. (1977). Vulnerability—A new view of schizophrenia. *Journal of Abnormal Psychology, 86,* 103-126.

# Index